AIDA Europe Research Series on Insurance Law and Regulation
Volume 16

Pierpaolo Marano
Editor

Emerging Legal Frontiers in Insurance

Digital Transformation, Cross-Border Challenges, and Market Innovation

Springer

Editor
Pierpaolo Marano
Department of Insurance and Risk Management
University of Malta
Malta

ISSN 2662-1770 ISSN 2662-1789 (electronic)
AIDA Europe Research Series on Insurance Law and Regulation
ISBN 978-3-032-09715-6 ISBN 978-3-032-09716-3 (eBook)
https://doi.org/10.1007/978-3-032-09716-3

This Springer imprint is published by the registered company Springer Nature Switzerland AG.
The registered company address is: Gewerbestrasse 11, 6330 Cham, Switzerland.

Preface

The insurance industry is undergoing a significant transformation, driven by the convergence of digital innovation, shifting market structures, and evolving regulatory developments. As new technologies reshape how insurance is created, distributed, and regulated, legal frameworks are increasingly expected not just to adapt but to lead. 'Emerging Legal Frontiers in Insurance: Digital Transformation, Cross-Border Challenges, and Market Innovation' gathers a distinguished group of scholars and practitioners who critically analyze these changes and their impact on the current and future landscape of insurance regulation.

The volume is divided into two interconnected sections. The first, "Digital Realities and Technological Disruptions in Insurance Law," discusses how emerging technologies are transforming the conceptual and regulatory foundations of insurance markets. Professor Tadao Koezuka begins the discussion with an innovative analysis of transactions in the metaverse, questioning how insurance law can address intangible risks in a virtual yet experience-rich environment. Dr. Shu Li then examines the rise of robo-advisers in insurance distribution, providing a comprehensive legal analysis of accountability frameworks under the EU Artificial Intelligence Act and product liability regulations. Meanwhile, Dr. Can Luo investigates how blockchain technology is utilized in Chinese insurance markets, focusing on its impact on the traditional duty of representation and the shifting evidentiary and contractual balance between policyholders and insurers. Professor Aleksandra Nowak-Gruca examines the intersection of copyright and insurance law, employing economic analysis to assess whether the monopolistic aspects of copyright may hinder the effective distribution of digital insurance products.

The second section, "Jurisdictional Perspectives and Cross-Border Insurance Market Dynamics," examines the structural and normative tensions arising from the trans nationalization of insurance markets. Dr. Stephan Stolz re-examines the promise of the European single market concerning life insurance, highlighting the ongoing and often overlooked legal barriers that still hinder cross-border offerings despite many decades of harmonization efforts. Prof. Mariusz Fras provides a detailed chapter on group insurance, approached from a comparative perspective, offering valuable insights into the historical and legal development of this contract in France and Germany, and raising important questions about consumer protection and regulatory imbalance. Professors Michał Ziemiak and Marcin Kawinski present a considered account of co-opetition among insurance brokers in Poland, demonstrating how legal uncertainty and regulatory gaps influence the cooperative behavior of intermediaries in competitive markets. Finally, Professor Monika Szaraniec provides an in-depth analysis of the growing influence of EU soft law in Polish insurance distribution, assessing the legal effectiveness and supervisory role of EIOPA guidelines and recommendations, which could serve as a model for other EU jurisdictions.

Each of these contributions reflects a shared concern about the challenges that digitalization, cross-border complexities, and regulatory fragmentation pose to the coherence and legitimacy of insurance law. As an editor, I want to emphasize the broader importance of these themes. The regulation of insurance – traditionally based on principles of prudence, good faith, and territorial supervision – is increasingly vulnerable to forces that challenge its assumptions. Technologies such as AI and blockchain introduce new actors, asymmetries, and risks that are not easily reconcilable with existing legal categories. Similarly, the cross-border provision of insurance remains hindered by incompatible national regulations and persistent regulatory inertia, despite formal commitments to market integration.

In this context, the volume calls for a more comprehensive examination of the future direction of insurance regulation. How can we ensure that innovation does not undermine customer protection? What types of supervision are most appropriate for distributed and digital environments? How should legal systems balance flexibility with certainty when addressing new kinds of risk? Most importantly, how can the regulatory framework for insurance remain resilient, adapting to change while staying true to its core principles of fairness, solidarity, and public trust?

This book does not provide definitive answers to these questions, but it outlines the landscape where they must be addressed. I sincerely thank all the contributors for their intellectual generosity and thorough analysis. I would also like to congratulate AIDA Europe and my colleagues who peer-review and make this collective effort possible. I hope the volume serves not only as a scholarly reference but also as a platform for further discussion – across jurisdictions and disciplines – on how insurance law and regulation can meet the challenges of a rapidly evolving digital society.

Malta, July 2025 Pierpaolo Marano

Contents

Part I
Digital Realities and Technological Disruptions in Insurance Law

The Legal Challenges Surrounding Transactions in the Metaverse: The Case of Insurance

Tadao Koezuka

1 Introduction

In the Metaverse-World,[1] various entities that appear visually existent, such as avatars, parks, trees, skies, and buildings, differ from tangible objects in the Real-World as they lack a material substance. Nevertheless, when a user wears a VR Headset[2] (or VR Goggles, Head Mount Display), enters the Metaverse-World, and rides a roller coaster in a virtual amusement park, their heartbeat will accelerate, experiencing sensations akin to those in a Real-World roller coaster ride. As the Metaverse-World becomes socially implemented and widely utilized across different countries, discussions on the necessity of legal regulations governing the Metaverse-World will inevitably arise.

At present, there are neither Metaverse courts with jurisdiction over disputes unique to the Metaverse-World nor Metaverse Parliament or Executive Branch. Furthermore, many countries have yet to establish sufficient legal regulations concerning legal

[1] Metaverse is a place for communication, but it is unique in that the method of communication is carried out by the "person inside" the avatar. Even today, communication a take place in a real space, either in person to person, via telephone, fax, Zoom, or other communication devices, or via e-mail, letters (including video letters), etc. In contrast, communication in the metaverse is carried out by expressing oneself in a free avatar that is free from realistic appearance and appearance, just as the "person inside" the avatar wears a costume, so to speak. Therefore, it is technically possible for an avatar to express itself as an animal, an inorganic bottle, a pebble, or whatever it wants to be, regardless of the physically defined gender, age, race, height, or physique of the "person inside the avatar" in real space, and regardless of whether it has a disability.

[2] Unlike the real world, the Metaverse-World requires users to wear VR Headset when checking the world with the naked eye. Of course, the user can check the appearance of the Metaverse-World from a PC screen or smartphone screen, but the space that develops on the PC screen or smartphone screen that the user sees is not sufficiently separated from the real world. This is because the

T. Koezuka
School of Law, Waseda University, Shinju-ku, Japan
email: koezuka@aoni.waseda.jp

P. Marano (ed.), *Emerging Legal Frontiers in Insurance*,
AIDA Europe Research Series on Insurance Law and Regulation,
https://doi.org/10.1007/978-3-032-09716-3_1

acts or torts occurring within the Metaverse-World. Issues arise regarding consumer protection for users, especially the safeguarding of minors who may become overly engrossed in gaming. Additionally, the anonymity of avatars complicates the relief of victims suffering mental harm due to harassment.[3] Moving forward, new risks will likely emerge in the Metaverse-World, raising questions about the type of insurance required and whether it should align with the Real-World insurance frameworks.

This chapter[4] focuses on Transactions in the Metaverse-World. First, I will discuss the legal epistemology of the metaverse. Second, I will confirm the definition of the metaverse and what it is. Third, it explores the legal relationship of whether the Metaverse-World should be regarded as an extension of the Real-World or as an independent, separate entity. Fourth, I will examine the legal issues surrounding transactions in the metaverse. Finally, it presents a concluding discussion.

2 The Metaverse-World and Legal Epistemology

2.1 Legal Epistemology

Human beings understand and perceive the world from the perspective of meaning. We cannot recognize an existence to which we cannot assign meaning, even if it is right in front of us. That is, if we cannot find meaning in something, we are unable to perceive its existence.

Based on accumulated experiences, our brains assign meaning to what is in front of us and recognize it as an image. This epistemology of experience is said to originate from John Locke's "An Essay Concerning Human Understanding." However, when confronted with advanced scientific technology that we have never experienced before, we are unable to comprehend its nature due to our lack of prior experience. In other words, we cannot recognize something unless we integrate it into our own world.

user operates the PC screen or smartphone screen visually while perceiving the real world with the five senses. In this paper, the virtual space in which the user wears VR goggles and feels a sense of immersion is called the Metaverse-World. Such a the Metaverse-World stands in front of the user as a space in another dimension that is separate from the real world with its physical constraints.

[3] It has been argued that the protection of users from harassment and similar misconduct is not aimed at safeguarding consumers per se, but rather at maximizing shareholder value for metaverse platform operators. *See*, Lee, Yang & Hui (2024), p. 280.

[4] In Koezuka (2024a), pp. 1–30, the author directed attention to the law-generating function inherent in the metaverse world, and undertook an analysis of the theoretical possibility that, contingent upon the manner in which the terms of use – constituting the substance of the user agreement – are formulated, legal personality may be conferred upon avatars. The author further considered that, through the normative effect of such terms, it is also feasible to prescribe insurance contracts pertaining to the metaverse world with freely determined content. Moreover, in Koezuka (2025), pp.320–340, the author examined the proposition that, under the Civil Code, the concept of "death" denotes the extinction of legal capacity, and therefore applies exclusively to "natural persons" endowed with such capacity. Nevertheless, invoking the law-generating function of the metaverse world, the author explored the potential for the concept of an avatar's "death" to be

Consequently, in every society of every nation, unknown entities are always given names and integrated into that society. Even unidentified flying objects have been incorporated into society by being named "UFOs." If this process is not possible, unknown entities are relegated to the realm outside society as mere unknown objects, ghosts, illusions, or conspiracy theories. Recently, they have been treated as non-existent and as having no impact on the current social order. Conversely, this implies that human beings and our societies are vulnerable and susceptible to the unknown.

In the Metaverse-World, various visually perceived entities, such as avatars, parks, trees, skies, and buildings, lack material substance but can be visually recognized in the same way as tangible objects in the Real-World. From the perspective of visual recognition, the Metaverse-World allows recognition of buildings, land, cars, drones, forests, people, and other elements just as they are perceived in the Real-World. If this is the case, the Metaverse-World, where people gather and purchase land and items, could be seen as a legal domain like the Real-World.

Conversely, if the Metaverse-World were merely a part of a private space within a house and did not constitute a space comparable to the Real-World, then there would be no need to discuss it from a legal perspective.

2.2 *The Metaverse-World and Movies*

The people, cars, and buildings depicted on a movie screen may appear real to the eye, but they do not exist in the Real-World. However, when watching a movie, one may experience emotions such as being moved, crying, laughing, or feeling tense, creating an illusion as if the events unfolding on screen are occurring in the Real-World. The information gained from watching a movie is transmitted to the brain through visual and auditory senses, and is understood in the same way as images unfolding in the Real-World. However, the images in a movie are not of the Real-World.

In the metaverse, avatars, cars, and buildings visible through sight are sent to the brain through visual stimuli in the same way as images in a movie and are understood as images unfolding in the Real-World. However, movie images are reproductions of real people, cars, and buildings filmed in the Real-World, and therefore, for example, people do not move freely. In contrast, in the metaverse, people and cars can move freely, and the images unfold as if in the Real-World. People, cars, and buildings are data entities, and they do not take the same form as those in the Real-World. They only appear to have shape.

On the other hand, in the Real-World, objects like the human body or cars, which are perceived to have shape, are actually full of holes at the level of subatomic particles, and the appearance of shape is a result of the brain's functioning. In both the metaverse and the Real-World, the recognition of the existence of shape through sight is ultimately a function of the brain, and the human body or cars in the Real-World may, in a sense, be similar to the entities seen in the metaverse.

legally constructed – provided that the terms of use so stipulate – and concluded that, if the defined criteria are met, the "death" of an avatar may be contemplated as a legal notion.

2.3 *Ethical, Legal, and Social Issues*

Even in the Real-World, rights, obligations, and rules are not visible to the naked eye, nor can they be physically grasped and confirmed. Instead, in common law jurisdictions, they are recognized through case law, while in civil law jurisdictions, they are acknowledged through statutes. In other words, we empirically perceive and understand the factual premises upon which these rights, obligations, and rules are established, even though they are not visually recognizable.

However, advances in modern cutting-edge science and technology often produce effects that appear as "magic" or "illusions" to the general public in their daily lives, astonishing them. Simply put, when ordinary people witness the wonders of advanced technology, they are unable to predict, based on their prior experience, how the introduction of such technology into society will alter their stable lives. This uncertainty frequently leads to vague anxiety or fear among the public, triggering ethical, legal, and social concerns, as well as resistance or rejection. Therefore, for advanced technological innovations to be successfully integrated into society, it has been pointed out that it is necessary to address the Ethical, Legal, and Social issues (ELSI)[5] that the public perceives.

3 What Is the Metaverse?: The Definition of Metaverse

The term "Meta" in Metaverse generally signifies something that transcends or is of a higher level (such as a step in a ladder), while "verse" is said to represent a part of "Universe," meaning a domain or realm. Therefore, "Metaverse"[6] is a coined word

[5] Regarding the relationship between the social implementation of advanced scientific technology and ELSI, the overarching concept should be the social acceptability of advanced scientific technology. Under this, the resolution of ELSI, and in addition, resolution through Risk Management should be considered subordinate concepts. This perspective seems to align with the reality of integrating advanced scientific technology into society. if the social acceptance of advanced science and technology is not increased, it will be extremely difficult to implement advanced science and technology in society. In order for advanced science and technology to be implemented in society, it is necessary not only to solve ethical and legal issues, but also to provide insurance and public funds for the risks that may arise from the implementation of advanced science and technology in society. In other words, this relationship can be expressed as: Social Acceptability > Ethical Issues, Legal Issues, and Risk Management.

[6] For the definition of the metaverse in Japan, *see* AMT Metaverse Legal Research Group (2022), p. 16; Okajima (2022), p. 1. According to the Center for Research and Development Strategy (CRDS), Japan Sicence and Technology Agency (2025), p. 6, the metaverse is defined as "a new sphere of activity in which interaction, mediated through one's avatar and transcending constraints of physical location and the human body, is possible, and where the real and the virtual are continuously integrated" (https://www.jst.go.jp/crds/pdf/2023/RR/CRDS-FY2023-RR-04.pdf). The Cabinet Office's Public-Private Partnership Meeting on Response to New Legal Issues Concerning Content, etc. on the Metaverse (2023), p. 2, considers the metaverse to be "a virtual space accessible through a network and capable of communication between users, particularly those with characteristics such as self-projection, immersion, real-time nature, and openness (accessibility to anyone), or similar". The Virtual City Consortium (2023), p. 6, presents a common understanding

combining "Meta" and "Universe." The Metaverse-World is a world constructed in a form that is either similar to or transcends the Real-World.[7,8] On the other hand, an avatar, like a costume, serves as a symbol through which the "person inside"[9] expresses themselves. However, there are avatars that do not have an actual "person inside." In the Metaverse-World, avatars provide a space where various experiences can be had and communication with other avatars can occur, surpassing physical constraints.

The essence of the Metaverse lies in being a space in a different dimension, liberated from the physical constraints of the Real-World. To experience this essence, it is necessary for the Metaverse user to wear VR goggles and immerse themselves in the Metaverse-World. The Metaverse-World experienced on a smartphone or PC without wearing VR goggles cannot provide the essence of the Metaverse, as when the user changes their viewpoint, the Real-World environment comes into view, interrupting the experience. Therefore, in this chapter, the term "The Metaverse-World"

---

of the metaverse as "a three-dimensional virtual space on the Internet accessed via avatars and Internet services using that virtual space." Justin (2023), pp.326–327. The Virtual Consortium is an organization formed by the following four entities: KDDI Corporation, Shibuya Mirai Design (a General Incorporated Association), Tokyu Corporation, and Mizuho Research & Technologies, Ltd. Its purpose is to conduct open discussions and research on the development of the Japan-originated metaverse, including the deployment of models similar to "Virtual Shibuya," an officially endorsed distribution platform of Shibuya City, in other cities, as well as the promotion of new business and technological development, and to formulate guidelines and disseminate information. https://news.kddi.com/kddi/corporate/newsrelease/2021/11/09/5522.html.

[7] A concept similar to, but distinct from, the Metaverse-World is the concept of the Digital Twin. The Digital Twin is a space created for conducting simulations, as real-world simulations are economically expensive. Instead of performing experiments in the real world, a Digital Twin is built to carry out simulations in a more accessible and efficient manner. Therefore, the Digital Twin is defined by the real world and is designed to reflect the real world as closely as possible, which limits its degree of freedom. In contrast, within the Metaverse-World, there are currently no international treaties or legal regulations regarding the construction of Metaverse spaces. Those attempting to build a Metaverse are free to create any space they desire, liberated from the constraints of the real world. Here, we can recognize the "law creation function" of the Metaverse-World.

[8] In Japan, the Cabinet Office has set ten Moonshot goals, aiming to achieve them by 2050. One of these goals is to 'overcome the limitations of physical bodies and space'. The societal implementation of the metaverse would be beneficial to the achievement of these Moonshot goals. https://www8.cao.go.jp/cstp/english/moonshot/top.html

[9] While the operator behind an avatar – the so-called *"person inside"* – is an individual, in real-world interpersonal relationships, we are required to engage with others on a continuous basis. Hirano (2012), p.62, p.68. Accordingly, a single individual may be divided into multiple *"dividuals"* – distinct versions of the self that correspond to particular social relationships – and the aggregation of these *dividuals* constitutes the self (*watakushi*). Hirano (2012), p.86, p.89. If such a conceptual framework is accepted, it follows that an avatar in the metaverse world can also be regarded as a form of *dividual*. Under this view, an avatar is no longer merely a superficial "costume" or external shell. Furthermore, Satō asserts that one's real-world personality is largely shaped and constrained by one's physical body, and that, when liberated from the body, even the person themselves cannot fully know what kind of personality their *self* (*watakushi*) may assume Satō (2022), p. 222. This suggests that, in the metaverse world, the nature of the avatar one adopts may lead the same *self* to manifest as a different *dividual*, thereby enabling individuals to shift or differentiate their personality depending on the specific environment of the metaverse. Satō (2022), p. 220, p.224.

refers to the virtual space or virtual world[10] in which the user feels immersed by wearing VR goggles. This chapter excludes virtual spaces or virtual world used on PCs or smartphones without wearing VR goggles.

4 The Legal Relationship Between the Metaverse-World and the Real-World

4.1 Extension Theory vs. Independence Theory

When considering legal issues in the metaverse, understanding the legal relationship between the metaverse and the Real-World is of paramount importance.[11] I have always believed that this question serves as the starting point for analyzing legal issues in the metaverse.[12] As previously mentioned, human beings experience anxiety and fear not only toward advanced scientific technologies but also toward new entities they possess or encounter for the first time. Based on their existing worldview, shaped by prior experiences and understanding, they attempt to position and accept these new entities. Until they successfully integrate new entities into their worldview, they often exhibit hesitation and confusion. Similarly, even when experiencing the metaverse, human beings attempt to understand and accept it by positioning it within the context of their existing world and worldview.

[10] In Japan, the term *"virtual"*, as used in expressions such as "virtual space" or "virtual world," is generally interpreted – both in legal discourse and by the public – as meaning "not real" or "inauthentic." However, such an interpretation is misguided. Rather, the term *"virtual"* ought to be understood as signifying something that is, in substance or effect, equivalent to its real-world counterpart. Katō (2022), p.172.

[11] In the real world, at the macro level, borders are established between countries, and at the micro level, ownership rights are set for physical assets such as land and buildings (real estate), as well as movable assets like vehicles, precious metals, and other personal property. In contrast, in the metaverse, reality is entirely represented as data in cyberspace, so there are no borders, and ownership rights for physical real estate or movable property do not exist.

[12] In Japan, as well as in other countries, there is no legal framework regarding the rights and obligations of avatars in the metaverse, nor are there any regulations concerning land use within such spaces. At most, regulations are limited to the protection of personal data, regulations related to NFTs or cryptocurrencies, or regulations under general consumer protection frameworks. In the event of a legal dispute occurring in the metaverse, the resolution will likely rely primarily on the existing legal frameworks in the real world. However, it is theoretically important to consider how to understand the legal relationship between the real world and the metaverse. Koezuka (2024a), pp.17–18.

Consequently, people generally perceive the metaverse as an extension of the Real-World or as possessing attributes of the Real-World. This is likely how the public understands it, and viewing the metaverse as an extension of the Real-World provides a practical foundation for comprehension. This perspective, which considers the metaverse as an extension of the Real-World, is referred to as the "extension theory." According to this theory, the Real-World legal regulations naturally extend to the metaverse. However, careful consideration is required to determine whether Real-World legal regulations, which govern a world composed of physical and tangible objects, can be directly applied to the metaverse, which exists purely as digital data.

In contrast to this perspective, an alternative view sees the metaverse as a separate dimension freed from the physical constraints of the Real-World. Under this view, the metaverse is understood as an independent space distinct from the Real-World. In reality, the metaverse is composed of data and does not operate under the same principles of causality as the Real-World. In the Real-World, visible "people" and "objects" inevitably decay and disappear. However, in the metaverse, data does not degrade, allowing entities to exist perpetually. Consequently, avatars, unlike humans, do not have physical bodies, meaning they do not experience death or physical deterioration. Strictly speaking, understanding the metaverse as a separate, independent space aligns more closely with its nature. This perspective, which treats the metaverse as an independent domain, is referred to as the "independence theory." According to this theory, legal regulations in the metaverse should not automatically follow the Real-World laws but should instead be developed separately based on the unique characteristics of the metaverse.

The legal interpretation of the relationship between the metaverse and the Real-World is reflected in the legal relationship between avatars and their human operators. According to the extension theory, an avatar is considered an extension of its human operator. In other words, the avatar is perceived as an extension of the physical body of the natural person controlling it. This theory, however, encounters significant challenges in explaining AI-driven avatars that operate without a human operator (hereinafter referred to as "AI avatars"[13,14]).

---

[13] Shimpo (2024), pp.25–28, p.29. Currently, a singing and dancing vocaloid called "Hatsune Miku" is performing live in the Metaverse-World. "Hatsune Miku" is a singing voice synthesizer featuring a female persona with a turquoise twin tail hairstyle who uses Yamaha Corporation's Vocaloid 2, Vocaloid 3, and Vocaloid 4 singing synthesizing technologies. In a near-future society where the 6th generation mobile communication system (6G) is implemented in society, it is anticipated that many avatars without a "person inside" will appear, such as deceased people and historical figures being revived in the Metaverse-World in the form of realistic 3D avatars and acting by AI. For avatars of the deceased, *see* Nakagawa (2023), pp.9–13.

[14] There is a high possibility that deceased individuals may be brought back to life through AI avatars. The legal issues arising in such cases are discussed by Matsuo (2024), p. 241. *See also*,

Conversely, under the independence theory, AI avatars are understood as independent entities separate from human operators.[15] For example, when people travel abroad, they find themselves in a completely different environment from before their journey. As they build new relationships and accumulate experiences in this foreign setting, their identity evolves. Similarly, when individuals enter the metaverse, they become a different version of themselves, much like how a traveler's identity shifts in a foreign country. Under the independence theory, the existence of AI avatars in the metaverse, despite their absence in the Real-World, becomes easier to explain.

4.2 *Legal Creation Function by Law in the Metaverse-World*

In the metaverse, the space is not filled with tangible objects, so designers of the metaverse can freely create using data and imagination without being bound by the physical constraints of the Real-World. For example, humans can become elderly, young boys or girls, change from male to female, transform into animals like dogs or cats, or even become inorganic objects such as a soda can or a pebble. Designers can create worlds inspired by films like "*Jurassic Park*" or even the surface of Mars. In universities, it is possible to construct metaverse classrooms where avatars of various forms – fried eggs, hot dogs, pandas, cats, tigers, cans, bottles, and human-shaped figures – can be created and used for teaching.[16]

In the Real-World, except during times of war, murder is considered illegal under criminal law, but in the metaverse, games in which individuals kill each other are permitted. For example, in the game "*Fortnite*", murder is commonplace. Since the avatars in the game are not human, it is generally believed that Real-World murder charges do not apply. Although this may seem obvious, at least in the case of "*Fortnite*", the metaverse is not considered an extension or expansion of the Real-World.

Moreover, in the metaverse, even sexual abuse of avatars representing minors is not subject to the Real-World legal regulations if the participants consent, because

[15] One of the problems with AI avatars is that, based on the independence theory regarding the legal relationship between the avatar and the "person behind it," the AI avatar may continue to exist and operate in the metaverse world even after the death of the "person behind it." It is important how Metaverse Operators incorporate provisions and clauses in their terms of service to address this issue. Matsuo (2024), p. 241. Moreover, it should also be noted that, in the event legal personality is conferred upon AI avatars, concerns have been raised that recognizing such legal personhood may enable malicious natural persons to exploit the system to carry out immoral or unlawful acts. Cheong (2022), p.481.

[16] At the Faculty of Law, Waseda University, a donor-funded course titled 'Metaverse and Law' (taught by Professor Tadao KOEZUKA) was offered in the fall semester of 2024, with a donation from Aioi Nissay Dowa Insurance Co., Ltd. In this course, both the professor and all the students wore VR goggles and took on various avatars, conducting classes within a metaverse classroom.

the avatar's appearance does not necessarily reflect the age of the person controlling it.

Under this understanding, in the metaverse, clusters of avatars with shared hobbies, ideologies, or interests might engage in activities that would be considered illegal in the Real-World, with an implicit agreement that such actions are permissible. If a consensus is formed or rules are established, actions that are illegal in the Real-World could become illegal in the metaverse as well. This phenomenon is referred to as the legal creation function based on customs in the metaverse. This function is derived when the legal relationship between the metaverse and the Real-World is understood according to the theory of independence. Under the theory of extension, the Metaverse-World would be defined by the Real-World, making it difficult to freely create it as an independent space.

The key issue is determining the legal basis for the metaverse's legal creation function.[17]

One approach is to derive it from the user agreement between the metaverse provider and the users. The terms and conditions of the user agreement are defined by the terms of service.[18] Therefore, by defining the Metaverse-World that the provider offers to the users in terms of service, i.e., by defining the Metaverse-World – the effects of the user agreement will extend to the Metaverse-World, and it will be defined as such a space.

In other words, the legal creation function of the Metaverse-World is based on the user agreement derived from the terms of service.

Another approach is when, as mentioned above, the terms of service do not define the metaverse space. In this case, the avatars gather to define a specific area or the entire space of the metaverse. The condition for avatars to make such a decision is that the terms of service do not specify that avatars lack the authority to decide what kind of space they will create within a specific area or the entire metaverse.

5 Transactions in the Metaverse-World

5.1 Transaction in the Metaverse-World and the Real-World

In developed countries where capitalism is highly advanced, leading a self-sufficient lifestyle – such as cultivating crops in fields, fishing in the sea or rivers, weaving clothes, and constructing homes – is extremely difficult.

Most people live as consumers, purchasing goods from retail stores as part of their daily lives in the Real-World. This consumer lifestyle remains fundamentally

[17] Narihara (2022), p.26. Associate Professor Narihara makes a similar claim in this chapter.

[18] For the terms of service established by Metaverse Operators, *see* Mori, A. & Tomotsune Law Firm ed. (2024), pp. 174–175.

unchanged in the Metaverse-World. However, since avatars in the Metaverse do not require food, clothing, or shelter, they do not engage in daily consumption activities such as purchasing mineral water or bread at a supermarket, ordering coffee at a café, or eating spaghetti at a restaurant, as consumers do in the Real-World.

Sometimes avatars in the Metaverse may still purchase and wear branded shoes made as NFTs, enjoying fashion and distinguishing themselves from others. Furthermore, when live performances featuring popular figures singing and dancing are held in the Metaverse, many fans participate as avatars.

The subject matter of a transaction can be categorized into two types: (1) those that exist in the Metaverse-World and (2) those that exist in the Real-World. Similarly, the parties involved in a transaction can be categorized into (1) those that exist in the Metaverse-World and (2) those that exist in the Real-World. As a result, transactions can be classified into a total of four types.[19]

Type 1 transactions refer to cases where a "person" in the Real-World enters into a sales contract for a "product" that also exists in the Real-World. Type 2 involves a "Real-World" person selling a "product" in the Metaverse-World. A typical example is when a promoter who plans and operates the Real-World concerts plans a live performance in the Metaverse-World and sells tickets for it in the Metaverse-World.

Type 3 is when an avatar in the Metaverse-World sells a product in the Metaverse-World. A typical example is when a salesclerk avatar at a department store that has a branch in the Metaverse-World sells NFT-made brand shoes for avatars in the Metaverse-World. Type 4 is when an avatar in the Metaverse-World sells a Real-World product. In Type 4, we can envision a case where a person inside the avatar in the Metaverse-World sells their own the Real-World items, such as a bicycle or a PC. In this Type 4, if the person inside the metaverse avatar does not have ownership of the Real-World product, the legal structure will differ depending on whether the focus is placed on the avatar or the person inside.

Thus, it is Types 2 and 4 where a conflicting relationship arises between the Metaverse-World and the Real-World. In this case, the question becomes which world should be the basis for legal structuring.

5.2 *Contradictory Relationship Between the Metaverse-World and the Real-World, and Transaction Protection*

5.2.1 Issues Arising from Types 2 and 3

In the case of type 2,[20] when the Metaverse-World concert tickets are sold in the Real-World, the Metaverse-World ticket sales rules may conflict with the

[19] Koezuka (2024a), p.14. *See,* Yoshizawa (2023), p.50,. Yoshizawa (2024), p.111.

[20] In addition, there may be intermediate forms of transactions between Type 1 and Type 2. This is where the policyholder, insurer, insured, or insurance benefit recipient all exist in the real world,

Real-World ticket sales rules. In particular, the pricing of tickets for the Metaverse-World concerts, where many participants can be recruited by increasing the server capacity, may differ from the pricing of tickets in the Real-World, where there are physical limitations in the first place. There may also be differences in cancellation policies when the promoter cancels the concert, and differences in rules regarding resale. In this case, the question arises as to which rules, the Real-World or the Metaverse-World, take precedence. In the case of type 3, perhaps the most problematic case is when a minor in the Real-World, disguised as an adult avatar, purchases a high-priced item. The question arises whether the minor should be protected by the Real-World rules, or whether the seller should be protected based on the adult avatar's appearance in the Metaverse-World. Thus, in types 2 and 3, the issue is how to view the legal relationship between the Metaverse-World and the Real-World.

5.2.2 Issues Arising from Type 4

In Type 4 scenarios, both contracting parties and the subject of transaction exist entirely within the Metaverse-World.[21] This refers to cases where, in the Metaverse-World, Avatar A (with 'person inside' a) purchases NFT-based shoes from Avatar B (with 'person inside' b).

According to the extension theory regarding the legal relationship between the Metaverse-World and the Real-World, even in Type 4 cases, while the purchaser is the adult avatar A, the 'person inside' a may be a minor. How this contradiction should be resolved is one issue. Specifically, in the case of the extension theory, the question arises as to whether the Real-World or the Metaverse-World should take precedence when a conflict arises between them. Since the extension theory considers the Metaverse-World as an extension of the Real-World, it should be interpreted that the Real-World takes precedence.[22]

but the effect of this insurance contract occurs in the Metaverse-World, and the insurance benefit recipient in the real space enjoys that effect. Specifically, this is an insurance contract where the deceased or deceased pets are resurrected in the Metaverse-World.This legal structure is complex. If structured as a life insurance contract, after the insured's death, the deceased would be resurrected in the Metaverse-World as a benefit in kind. The recipient of the benefit of the deceased's resurrection would be the legal representative. There is a question of whether benefits in kind are recognized in life insurance contracts. In this case, the resurrection of a deceased pet is not possible.Another possible structure is a damage insurance contract. If the insured dies, parents, spouse, or children who have a personal relationship with that person (these individuals become the insurance benefit recipients) receive a benefit in kind as compensation for the emotional distress they have suffered. In the case of a deceased pet, if the policyholder, who is the insured, suffers emotional distress due to the pet's death, they would receive a benefit in kind in the form of the pet's resurrection.

[21] *See,* Mori, A. & Tomotsune Law Firm ed. (2024), pp.173–177.

[22] Professor Kozuka believes that the principles of the real world should take precedence in the event of a conflict between the Metaverse-World and the real world. Kozuka (2022), p.76, p.82, p.84, p.86, p.87.

Under the independence theory, when the purchaser is the adult avatar A while the 'person inside' a is a minor, the basic principle is to process the matter based on the adult avatar A.

However, in reality, it is not possible to explain everything solely from the perspective of either the extension theory or the independence theory. This is because various types of Metaverse spaces can exist in practice. Specifically, as mentioned earlier, Metaverse Operators conclude user agreements with users and provide safe and secure Metaverse Services. Therefore, by strictly verifying user identity at the time of contract conclusion and taking measures such as excluding use by minors alone or obtaining parental consent, legal risks are prevented in advance. This is precisely the responsibility of Metaverse Operators as Metaverse Platformers.

In contrast, according to the independent theory, the nature of the Metaverse-World is determined by the content of the Metaverse Operator's "Space Definition." If the Metaverse insurance contract provides a meaningful "space definition," there are essentially two possibilities: ① when items in the Metaverse-World are the subject of the insurance, and ② when the avatar is the insured party.

In the case of ①, at the very least, among the parties involved in the insurance contract, the avatar who holds the digital ownership of items other than the avatar itself within the Metaverse-World is the one to whom the risk is attributed. Therefore, the avatar becomes the insured party. The conclusion of such an insurance contract is made by other parties within the Metaverse-World.[23]

In the case of ②, depending on the content of the "space definition," when an AI avatar is granted legal personality and defined events such as death, injury, or illness occur, the cost to "repair" the avatar would be considered a loss, leading to the need for a type of accident and health insurance contract in which the AI avatar is the insured party.

5.3 *Risk Management and Liability for Risks*

5.3.1 Liability of Metaverse Platform Operators

Considering this, it can be seen that in the independence theory, how the Metaverse-World is defined as a "space" in the terms of use has a very important meaning. It can also be seen that it has a very important meaning in that the terms of use will resolve any contradictions or conflicts between the Metaverse-World

[23] As for the copyright of items owned by the copyright holders of the items, it will likely need to be stipulated in the terms of use to realize and maintain the "space definition."

and the Real-World. This means that the Metaverse Operator also plays the role of a risk manager who reduces the risk of disputes in the Metaverse-World in advance.

If such a Metaverse Operator is a risk manager, it also means that the Metaverse Operator is in a position to be responsible as a Metaverse Platformer.[24,25] In other words, of the total number of users of the Metaverse-World, many are individual users and consumers who use the Metaverse Services provided by the Metaverse Operator. Metaverse Operators can exercise law-creating functions by defining the "space definition" of what kind of space the Metaverse-World is in the terms of use. In other words, whether to make it a space for gaming that involves killing many enemies, a space for enjoying communication, or a space for enjoying dancing depends on the "space definition" of the Metaverse Operator. Depending on what kind of "space definition" is made, there are naturally points where rules are set. In other words, Metaverse Operators can also establish behavioral norms according to the "space definition." Conversely, if a Metaverse Operator establishes rules that contradict the "space definition," and legal disputes arise between avatars as a result,

[24] When a Metaverse-World is constructed, there exists an operator responsible for its creation. This operator can leverage the metaverse by allowing users to utilize it, hosting events within the Metaverse-World, and generating revenue by enabling advertisers to place advertisements within the virtual space. If the Metaverse-World is sold to another Metaverse Operator, the purchasing entity then assumes the role of the Metaverse Operator. Of course, an existing Metaverse Operator may also commission a Metaverse Development Company to construct a Metaverse-World on its behalf. Such a metaverse world serves as a platform, similar to how Amazon, an e-commerce company, provides a marketplace where various sellers can offer their products. This type of platform is referred to as a Metaverse Platform. A Metaverse Platform consists of various virtual spaces, each defined in the terms of use under a "Space Definition." Some spaces function as shopping malls, where different sellers can establish virtual shops and sell their products. In most cases, the Metaverse Operator also acts as the Metaverse Platform Provider, or the Metaverse Platformer.

[25] In a case involving a victim of fraud (Plaintiff X) who brought a lawsuit against the platform operator (Defendant Y) of an online auction service, the Nagoya District Court, in its judgment of March 28, 2008 (Hanrei Jiho No. 2045, p.152), held that: "Under the duty of good faith in the contract of use, Y is obligated to provide the service through a system free from defects for the benefit of users, including X." Accordingly, the court recognized Y's liability. This implies that a metaverse platform operator is under a duty to enforce its terms of service and to take protective measures for users against those who violate them. Matsuo (2024), p.20, Mori, A. & Tomotsune Law Firm ed. (2024), pp.99–102 and p.103–104. In Japan, transactions conducted by consumers on digital platforms are categorized as mail-order sales transactions. To protect consumers from malicious vendors, the *Act on the Protection of Consumers Who Use Digital Platforms for Shopping* (Act No. 32 of 2021) was enacted. Additionally, the *Act on the Limitation of Liability for Damages of Specified Telecommunications Service Providers and the Right to Demand Disclosure of Identification Information of the Senders* (Act No. 137 of 2001) was amended and renamed the *Information Distribution Platform Act (IDPA)* in order to facilitate the prompt removal of defamatory or rights-infringing posts on social networking services (SNS).

the Metaverse Operator will be responsible for compensating for the "damages"[26] suffered by the injured avatar.[27]

5.3.2 Insurance Contract and Metaverse Platformers

According to the independence theory regarding the legal relationship between the Metaverse-World and the Real-World, Metaverse Operators are granted the authority to freely "define the space" of the Metaverse-World under the "freedom of business" recognized by liberal states. However, while Metaverse Operators conclude usage contracts with consumers who use the Metaverse-World, since the content of the usage contract pertaining to each the Metaverse-World is to provide safe and secure Metaverse Services to consumers, Metaverse Operators have the authority to "define the space," but also have the obligation to provide safe and secure Metaverse Services to users. This is also a responsibility as a Metaverse Platformer. For example, if a Metaverse Operator defines a space that deals with spiritual phenomena that are not supposed to exist in this world, they will have an obligation to give prior notice to consumers using this space that it deals with spiritual phenomena. If a consumer suffers mental "damage" in a case where the Metaverse Operator has not fulfilled their obligation to ensure that safe and secure Metaverse Services are available, the Metaverse Operator will be liable for damages. In this case, even under the independence theory, since it is the "real person" who suffers the mental "damage," the terms of use must be established consistently so that the pursuit of the Metaverse Operator's responsibility can be properly carried out. Regarding the content of the terms of use, it is highly likely that approval by the supervisory authorities of each country will be required.

Metaverse Operators bear responsibility as Metaverse Platformers in this way, but the question becomes how to legally deal with this liability risk. Since Metaverse Operators will be liable for damages, if Metaverse Operator liability insurance is developed with non-life insurance companies in the Real-World,

[26] The question arises as to what constitutes "damage" in the Metaverse-World. Is it the same as the concept of "damage" in the real world? In Japan, under the influence of Germany, it has been traditionally understood that "damage" is the difference (difference theory) between the state of profit that should have existed if there had been no cause of harm and the current state of profit in which harm has been caused. Oho (1972), p. 135.

[27] For example, in the event that all or part of the Metaverse-World is annihilated or rendered inoperable due to a "digital disaster" triggered by phenomena such as solar flares generating electromagnetic pulse (EMP) waves or large-scale, unpreventable cyberattacks, a proposal has been advanced advocating the establishment of a private right of action to provide individual redress (Kennedy (2023), pp.348–349). However, considering the potential for such events to produce catastrophic, transnational harm, it would be legally and institutionally appropriate to implement a comprehensive public response. This should include the creation of a public insurance scheme and the strategic allocation of public funds, with the objective of facilitating expedited disaster recovery and ensuring adequate remedial relief for affected parties. Koezuka (2024b), p.447 et seq.

they will conclude this liability insurance contract. The contractual parties of this liability insurance in this case are those who exist in the Real-World. That is, the policyholder is the Metaverse Operator, the insurer is the non-life insurance company, and the insured is the Metaverse Operator. The victim is also the "real person" in the Real-World.

In other words, liability insurance that covers damages resulting from a Metaverse Operator's failure to fulfill its obligation to ensure safe and secure use for users – leading to legal liability for damages – ultimately has the same fundamental contract structure as liability insurance in the Real-World.

Next, even if a Metaverse Operator does not bear legal liability for damages related to the "space" it has defined, other risks may still arise within the Metaverse-World. The following sections will sequentially examine the main risks in Type 2, Type 3, and Type 4 scenarios and explore the corresponding metaverse insurance solutions.

5.4 Risks That May Arise in Type 2 or Type 3 and Corresponding Metaverse Insurance

5.4.1 The Cases of Type 2

Since an insurance contract is also a form of insurance transaction, it is included as one of the transactions in Type 2. Insurance transactions classified as Type 2 involve cases where the insurer, policyholder, insured, or beneficiary (hereinafter referred to as "insurance benefit recipient") exists either wholly or partially in the Real-World, while the insurance object (in the case of property insurance) or the insured (in the case of life insurance, accident insurance, or health insurance) exists in the Metaverse-World.

When the insurance object or insured exists in the Metaverse-World, if the risks arising therein are attributed to an avatar within the Metaverse-World through the insured or the insurance object, the insurance contract addressing these risks is referred to as a "Metaverse insurance contract."

In Type 2 insurance transactions, according to the extension theory, which considers the Metaverse-World as an extension of the Real-World, if the insurance object or insured exists in the Metaverse-World, the risk ultimately belongs to a specific individual in the Real-World. Therefore, under this theory, a "Metaverse insurance contract" does not exist.

On the other hand, under the independence theory, in the case of property insurance contracts, if the digital owner of the insurance object in the Metaverse-World is an avatar existing in the Metaverse-World, the risk is attributed to that avatar. In the case of life insurance contracts, when a "death" event occurs within the "space definition" of the Metaverse set by the Metaverse Operator, the risk is attributed to the avatar insurance benefit recipient. Thus, under the independence theory, insurance transactions in Type 2 can be regarded as Metaverse insurance contracts.

However, it is important to note that within the "space definition" set by the Metaverse Operator, it must be determined whether avatars are granted legal personhood, whether they are recognized as "persons," and what constitutes "death" for avatars.

Meanwhile, there are cases where an insurance contract may be designed to provide insurance benefits within the Metaverse-World. Such insurance contracts, strictly speaking, should be considered insurance contracts in the Real-World, as the risk ultimately belongs to a specific person in the Real-World, and therefore do not qualify as "Metaverse insurance contracts." However, these insurance contracts are new types of contracts that did not exist in traditional insurance frameworks and are close to Type 2 insurance contracts.

A typical example of such a new insurance contract, which may become a reality and gain business traction in the future, is the "Resurrection of the Deceased" insurance contract. In this type of insurance, the insured is a "person" in the Real-World, and upon the insured's death, the insurer in the Real-World provides an insurance benefit in the Metaverse by creating an avatar that closely resembles the deceased, effectively bringing them back to life.[28]

Such insurance can be structured either as a life insurance contract or a property insurance contract.[29] If structured as a life insurance contract, whereas traditional life insurance pays a fixed amount to the beneficiary upon the insured's death, in this case, the insurance benefit recipient (who is often a legal heir) would receive the "resurrection of the deceased" as an in-kind benefit. Depending on the specifics of the life insurance contract, which reflects the cost-benefit relationship of the insurance premium, the deceased's 3D avatar could be created using photos, videos, or voice recordings, bringing them back to life in the Metaverse-World. Furthermore, AI technology could recreate the deceased's personality, enabling interactive conversations.

[28] In China, technology has been developed to meet the needs of those who, in their grief and search for healing after losing a loved one, wish to preserve, create videos of, and even interact with the deceased. However, it has not yet reached a fully completed state. Avatars still appear somewhat awkward and robotic. Nevertheless, this technology has entered a stage of maturity, with at least six companies currently offering such services, and thousands of users already paying for them. Throughout history, Chinese people have found comfort in expressing their innermost feelings to the deceased. In China, the cost of "resurrection" services, also known as "digital immortality," has significantly decreased, making this technology increasingly accessible to the public. Yang (2024). https://www.technologyreview.com/2024/05/07/1092116/deepfakes-dead-chinese-business-grief/

[29] Under Japanese Insurance Act, if benefits provided by an insurer under life insurance policies or fixed-amount accident and health insurance policies after the occurrence of an insured event are made in kind rather than in cash, such life insurance policies or fixed-amount accident and health insurance policies are not deemed invalid under Japanese Insurance Act. However, since neither of these contracts falls under the definition of an "insurance contract" as prescribed by §2(1) of Japanese Insurance Act, they do not qualify as life insurance policies or fixed-amount accident and health insurance policies under Japanese Insurance Act. Therefore, such contracts are treated as ordinary contracts under the Japanese Civil Code.

If structured as a property insurance contract, the death of the insured typically causes emotional distress to their legal heirs. To compensate for this mental anguish, a 3D avatar of the deceased would be created to bring them back to life in the Metaverse-World.

Regardless of whether it is a life insurance contract or a property insurance contract, when such a scenario becomes a reality, legal issues related to the deceased's personality rights may arise. For example, if the deceased had an irritable personality in life but their avatar is created with a kinder personality to match the preferences of the surviving relatives, it could lead to a violation of the deceased's personality rights.[30]

5.4.2 The Cases of Type 3

Since an insurance contract is also a form of insurance transaction, it falls within the scope of transactions classified as Type 3. Insurance transactions belonging to Type 3 involve cases where the insurer, policyholder, insured, or beneficiary (hereinafter referred to as the "insurance benefit recipient") exists entirely or partially within the Metaverse-World, while, on the other hand, the insured object (in the case of property insurance), the insured person (in the case of life insurance, accident insurance, or health insurance), or the insurance benefit itself exists within the Real-World.

Type 3 insurance contracts are the inverse of Type 2 insurance contracts. Even if the insured object or the insured person exists in the Real-World or if the insurance benefit is provided in the Real-World, an insurance contract in which the contractual parties (excluding the insured person in some cases) exist and conclude the contract within the Metaverse-World may also be classified as a "Metaverse Insurance Contract."

[30] In Sato & Ichikawa & Aruga (2023), p.28, p.30, p.44, a detailed explanation of "Death-Tech" – technology related to death – is provided. The paper introduces criticisms that emphasize the inviolability of the deceased, arguing that bringing back the dead and allowing the living to "use" them constitutes a denial of the dignity of the deceased. In my opinion, the deceased are not subjects of rights and, therefore, are not entitled to fundamental human rights. However, with the rapid advancements in cutting-edge technology, if data related to the deceased – such as images, voice recordings, and videos (hereinafter referred to as "data of the deceased") – is available, it is possible to recreate an avatar that is indistinguishable in appearance from the deceased within a metaverse world. If that is the case, given that the deceased lack legal subjectivity, does it mean that anyone is free to resurrect them using their data? The deceased themselves do not hold any rights over their own data. Typically, their legal heirs would be considered the rightful holders of such rights. In this context, if someone other than the legal heirs, who are the rightful holders, were to revive the deceased without permission, it could constitute an infringement of their rights, potentially leading to liability for damages under tort law. Furthermore, complex legal questions arise, such as whether legal heirs or other rights holders are permitted to alter the personality of the deceased – e.g., changing a deceased father's personality from short-tempered to kind-hearted using his data. This raises fundamental issues regarding the nature of a deceased person's personality and whether they possess any posthumous personality rights.

However, a Metaverse Insurance Contract should primarily be understood as an insurance contract in which, when a risk materializes, the resulting consequences affect an avatar in the Metaverse (who is designated as the insured or the insurance benefit recipient under the contract).[31]

Therefore, under the extension theory – which views the Metaverse-World as an extension of the Real-World – the risk in a property insurance contract ultimately belongs to a specific person in the Real-World (typically the insured), and in a life insurance contract, the insurance proceeds generally belong to the insurance benefit recipient. Since the risk ultimately belongs to a specific person in the Real-World, the extension theory would not classify Type 3 as a Metaverse Insurance Contract .

In contrast, under the independence theory, the classification of Type 3 as a Metaverse Insurance Contract depends on the "space definition" established by the Metaverse Operator. Specifically, in a property insurance contract, if the materialization of the insured risk results in consequences affecting the insured avatar, or in a life insurance contract, if the avatar is considered "deceased" under the space definition and the resulting insurance benefit is provided to the insurance benefit recipient, then the contract can be recognized as a "Metaverse Insurance Contract."

5.5 Risks That May Arise in Type 4 and Corresponding Metaverse Insurance

In the case of Type 4 transaction types, according to the extension theory, which posits that the Metaverse-World is an extension of the Real-World, even if insurance parties conduct transactions in the Metaverse-World or if the insurance object or the insured avatar exists in the Metaverse-World, ultimately, the risks arising from these transactions would be attributed to the insured party or the insurance benefit recipient in the Real-World. This situation combines the characteristics of Type 2 and Type 3 transaction types. In other words, in a property insurance contract, if the insurance object exists in the Metaverse-World, the risks associated with that object would be attributed to the owner of the insurance object, who would be the insured party in the Real-World. In the case of a life insurance contract, the "person behind" the insured avatar becomes the insured party. Therefore, even though it might appear that a life insurance contract involves the insured avatar as the insured party within the Metaverse-World, in essence, the insured avatar is the insurance object, and the "person behind" holds the insurable interest over the insured avatar, making it a property insurance contract in the Real-World.

[31] Yoshizawa (2023), p.51.

6 Conclusions

With this, I conclude my examination of "The Legal Challenges Surrounding Transactions in the Metaverse: The Case of Insurance".

The findings of this chapter can be summarized as follows: When the Metaverse-World is defined as a separate space from the physical constraints of the Real-World, experienced with a sense of immersion by wearing VR goggles, the legal relationship between the Metaverse-World and the Real-World becomes an issue. There are two possible theories: the extension theory, which considers the Metaverse-World as an extension of the Real-World, and the independent theory, which considers the Metaverse-World as a separate dimension independent from the Real-World. According to the extension theory, avatars are basically regarded as extensions of the "person behind them," and it is easy to apply the laws and rules of the Real-World to the Metaverse-World. On the other hand, according to the independent theory, avatars and the "person behind them" are considered separate entities, and it is difficult to directly apply the laws and rules of the Real-World to the Metaverse-World. These theories are theoretical concepts, and in practice, there will be differences in degree. However, in the case of the independent theory, Metaverse Operators can stipulate the "space definition" in the terms of use regarding what kind of space it should be. On the other hand, Metaverse Operators bear the responsibility of defining it as a safe and secure metaverse space, which also serves as the basis for the responsibility of Metaverse Platformers.

In the world, there exists both the Metaverse-World and the Real-World. When conducting transactions, the parties involved and the objects (goods) being transacted exist either in the Metaverse-World, the Real-World, or both. This results in four possible combinations. When there is a contradiction between the world where the transaction takes place and the world where the object exists, legal explanations become difficult. Specifically, this issue arises when the object is in the Metaverse-World but the transaction occurs in the Real-World (Type 2) or when the object is in the Real-World but the transaction occurs in the Metaverse-World (Type 3). Furthermore, when both the object and the transaction take place within the Metaverse-World (Type 4), unique legal challenges specific to the Metaverse-World emerge.

The legal issues in such transactions are theoretically linked to how the legal relationship between the Metaverse-World and the Real-World is understood and ultimately lead to the question of the Metaverse Operator's responsibility as a Metaverse Platformer. Therefore, in order to cover the Metaverse Operator's liability as a Metaverse Platformer, it is necessary to establish Metaverse Operator liability insurance contracts. This Metaverse Operator liability insurance is a Real-World insurance contract.

Even if a Metaverse Operator does not bear responsibility as a Metaverse Platformer, risks may still arise in transactions of Type 2 through Type 4. Therefore, for each transaction type from Type 2 to Type 4, corresponding insurance transactions can be considered to mitigate their respective risks. In other words, insurance contracts addressing the risks associated with transactions from Type 2 to Type 4 can be developed.

Although the Metaverse-World and the Real-World can be theoretically distinguished, in reality, they influence each other. Furthermore, as these interactions occur, risks may arise within each transaction type. Therefore, in the future, it will be necessary for each country to establish legal frameworks for the Metaverse-World while also developing insurance products tailored to the risks associated with each type of transaction, taking into account the mutual influence between the Metaverse-World and the Real-World.

References

AMT Metaverse Legal Research Group. (2022). "*(1st) General Remarks - Metaverse and Law*," *NBL* 1223.

Cabinet Office's Public-Private Partnership Meeting on Response to New Legal Issues Concerning Content, etc. on the Metaverse (2023). "Summary of Points of Discussion on New Legal Issues, etc. Concerning Content, etc. on the Metaverse".

Cheong, B. C. (2022). *"Avatars in the metaverse: Potential legal issues and remedies"*, *Int. Cybersecur. Law Rev.* 3, 467–494.

Hirano, K. (2012). What Am I? — From the Individual to the "Dividual" (Kōdansha Gendai Shinsho No. 2171).

Katō, N. (2022). *The Metaverse: Farewell to the Age of Atoms* (Shueisha).

Kennedy, J. (2023). *"Metaverse Property: Advocating for the Regulation of Metaverse Land and Property through a Real Estate Legal Regime*", 17 *Ohio St. Bus. L.J.* 2.

Koezuka, T. (2024a).*"The Legal Status of Avatars and Legal Creation in the Metaverse-World: A Study on the legal possibilities of insurance contacts"*, *Journal of Insurance Science* 667.

Koezuka, T. (2024b). *"Legal Frameworks for Digital Risk and Disaster Relief in Society 5.0"*, in Tadashi Otsuka & Shigeto Yonemura eds., *Legal Responses to Diverse Risks and Civil Liability*, 447–473, (Yuhikaku).

Koezuka, T. (2025). *"Can Avatars Die in the Metaverse World? — Exploring the Legal Possibilities of Insurance Contracts in the Metaverse"*, in *The New Trends in Contemporary Corporate Law: Essays in Honor of Professor Tadahiko Fukuhara on His 70th Birthday* (Editorial Comm. For the Festschrift ed., Bunsendo 2025).

Kozuka, S. (2022). *"Basic Perspectives on Legal Issues in Cyberspace – A 'Conflict of Laws'Approach to the Real World"*, 6 *Journal of Information and Communications Policy*.1.

Lee, J.-A., Yang, L., & Hui, P. (2024). *"Legal Implications of Self-presence in the Metaverse"*, 25 *Media & Arts Law Review* 4.

Matsuo, T. (2024). *Legal Issues of Cybernetic Avatars – Toward a Safe and Secure Virtual Space in the Vtuber Era*, (Kobunsha).

Ministry of Economy, Trade and Industry of Japan (2021). *"Report: FY2020 Content Overseas Expansion Promotion Project (Survey and Analysis Project on the Future Potential and Challenges of Virtual Space)"*.

Mori, A. & Tomotsune Law Firm ed. (2024). Metaverse and Law, (Financial and Fiscal Affairs Research Association).

Nakagawa, H. (2023). *Avatar after the Death of the Master Person*, .41 *Journal of the Robotics Society of Japan* 1.

Narihara, S. (2022). *"The Architecture and Law of the Metaverse: A World-Creating Platform and its Governance"*, *Nextcom* 44.

Oho, F. (1972). *General Theory of Obligations* [New Edition], (Yuhikaku).

Okajima, H. (2022). *"What is the Metaverse?"*, *National Life* 121.

Satō, K. (2022). *World 2.0: How to Navigate and Build the Metaverse* (Gentosha).

Sato, K., Ichikawa, G., &Aruga, F. (2023). "*Technology to Meet the Dead Again Digitally: Considerations on Artificial Intelligence of the Dead and its Problems*", Annual of the Institute for Life and Death Studeis Toyo Eiwa University ed., 19 Annual of the institute of thanatology.
Shimpo, F. (2024). "*Authentication of Cybernetic Avatars and Legal System Challenges; With a View to the Trial Concept of New Dimensional Challenges; With a View to the Trial Concept of New Dimensional Domain Jurisprudence (AI, Robot, and Avatar Law) Domain Jurisprudence (AI, Robot, and Avatar Law)*", *Japanese Society and Culture*: Vol. 6, Article 3.
Virtual City Consortium (2023). "Virtual City Guidelines ver 2.0.0".
Yang, Z. (2024). "Deepfakes of your dead loved ones are a booming Chinese business", *MIT Technology Review*: https://www.technologyreview.com/2024/05/07/1092116/deepfakes-dead-chinese-business-grief/. Accessed on 4 Dec 2025.
Yoshizawa, T. (2023). "*Legal Issues Related to Insurance for the Metaverse (Virtual Space) in the Real World*", 85 *Research on No-Life Insurance* 3.
Yoshizawa, T. (2024). "*Legal Issues Concerning Applicable Law of Metaverse Insurance*", *Journal of Insurance Science* 667.

Bringing Trustworthy Robo-Advisers into the Insurance Distribution Process: An Accountability Perspective

Shu Li

1 Introduction

Digitalization is transforming the landscape of insurance distribution. In recent years, emerging digital innovations, such as comparison websites and peer-to-peer insurance, have significantly empowered insurance distributors.[1] These advancements enable them to better tailor their services, meet customer demands more effectively, and achieve their strategic goals. Beyond these digital applications, robo-advisers have also emerged as a key development in insurance distribution. Traditionally, providing professional insurance advice has been the responsibility of human advisors, who undergo rigorous training and obtain the necessary certifications before practicing. These professionals are expected to exercise diligence in recommending suitable insurance products based on their clients' profiles.[2] Failure to comply with these standards may result in penalties. Additionally, from an *ex post* perspective, if adverse consequences arise due to an advisor's fault, issues of professional liability may also come into play.

In general, robo-advisers are developed to assist and even replace insurance professionals to handle a variety of different tasks. For customers, robo-advisers rather than human advisers will be their first contact point. Robo-advisers, especially those rule-based, are able to automate the underwriting processing on the

[1] See e.g. Marano (2019).

[2] Coombs and Redman (2018), p. 1–2.

S. Li
Erasmus School of Law, Erasmus University Rotterdam, Rotterdam, The Netherlands
email: li@law.eur.nl
ORCID: https://orcid.org/0000-0002-5889-5359

P. Marano (ed.), *Emerging Legal Frontiers in Insurance*,
AIDA Europe Research Series on Insurance Law and Regulation,
https://doi.org/10.1007/978-3-032-09716-3_2

basis of the input information from customers. More advanced robo-advisers leverage technologies such as machine learning and big data analytics to ensure that the insurance products offered to customers are always optimized to meet their needs.[3] Robo-advisers are able to respond the demand from customers quickly, which enhances customers experiences and improve the overall efficiency along the insurance value chain. Robo-advisors are also considered a promising application to facilitate precise insurance distribution, as they are expected to overcome certain shortcomings resulting from human professionals, such as the lack of capability to adapt insurance product to the dynamic changes and the potential of bias and errors when advising their customers.[4] From the viewpoint of suppliers, according to a report from European Insurance and Occupational Pensions Authority (EIOPA), around 40 percent of surveyed insurance companies have already adopted or are ready to deploy robo-advisers in support of their business.[5]

Despite the benefits of developing and deploying robo-advisers for the purpose of insurance distribution, their potential challenges shall not be underestimated. Robo-advisers may result in biased outcome by processing sensitive information (e.g., race, gender, disability, etc.) and assessing the risk based on these factors.[6] In this regard, people with vulnerable attributes will be further disadvantaged when accessing insurance products.[7] In addition, the decision-making process of a robo-adviser may not be transparent, so that impacted persons can hardly explain the advice given to them and find a way to contest it.[8] Robo-advisers may also manipulate customers in the course of communication. As a result, customers may be directed to make decisions that they would not have made given that they are well informed.[9]

The increasing delegation of various tasks to robo-advisers indicates the importance of accountability issue. To enhance the level of trust, law shall make clear which party is accountable for what throughout the lifetime of a robo-adviser. This chapter aims to delve into the accountability issues relating to robo-advisers that are used for insurance distribution. The structure of this chapter is as follows. After introduction, Section 2 provides a theoretical framework for accountability. Section 3 and Section 4 analyze the mechanisms to implement accountability, respectively from the perspective of the recently published *ex ante* AI Act and *ex post* liability regimes, such as the revised product liability directive and emerging debated on AI liability. Section 5 concludes.

---

[3] RapidValue Solutions (2017).

[4] Infosys BPM (2018).

[5] EIOPA (2024), p. 10.

[6] Van Bekkum, Borgesius and Heskes (2025).

[7] Marano and Li (2023), p. 9.

[8] Baker and Dellaert (2017), p. 735.

[9] Marano and Li (2023), p. 12.

2 Mapping Out the Concept of Accountability in the Digital Age

The concept of accountability is difficult to generalize as it can be split into multiple dimensions. In general, it refers to 'an obligation to inform about, and justify one's conduct to an authority'.[10] In the era of digitalization, the concept of AI becomes even more complex, considering the delegation relationship between digital technologies like AI and humans. The multiple dimensions of accountability in the context of AI can be perceived from the Ethical Guidelines drafted by the High-Level Expert Group (HLEG). According to the HLEG Ethical Guidelines, accountability is defined as a term that that can necessitate 'mechanisms be put in place to ensure responsibility and accountability for AI systems and their outcomes, both before and after their development, deployment and use'.[11] Later, HLEG in the Assessment List for Trustworthy AI (ALTAI) defines accountability as 'one is responsible for their action – and as a corollary their consequences – and must be able to explain their aims, motivations, and reasons'.[12]

Based on the up to date discussion about accountability, we may further unpack its meaning from four facets: dimension, accountable person, stage and mechanism. The following parts of this section provide an extensive explanation of each of these components.

2.1 Dimension

First of all, accountability can be roughly split into three dimensions: *ex ante*, *ex post* and *procedural* dimension.

From the *ex ante* perspective, accountability means that the law must explicitly clarify the responsibility and duty of relevant parties. The *ex ante* dimension of accountability provides certainty to all relevant parties that the measures that they must comply with. In other words, they are informed of the possible consequences if they fail to do so. These predefined rules serve with a deterrence function, incentivizing all relevant parties to behave properly.

From the *ex post* perspective, accountability means that the law must clearly determine which party shall bear the liability when harmful consequences occurred. The *ex post* dimension of accountability discloses the specific parties that shall undertake the accident costs of harmful consequences. In addition, the *ex post* dimension of accountability is crucial for compensation, making sure that victims could recover their loss fully and effectively.

[10] Novelli, Taddeo and Floridi (2024).

[11] HLEG (2019), p. 19.

[12] HLEG (2020), p. 23.

In practice, whether or not a person is accountable is not self-evident. The claimant needs to take measures to recognize the accountable persons and prove that they are accountable by meeting other essential requirements, such as fault, defect, causal link, damage, etc. Therefore, there is a third perspective when conceptualizing accountability, which is the *procedural* one. The procedural dimension of accountability aims to provide the necessary degree of transparency in support of the first two dimensions. The meaning of transparency composes multiple facets, including traceability, answerability, explainability, etc. Therefore, the procedural dimension of accountability is important to facilitate trustworthy AI, since it addresses crucial practical issues, such as who to which extent contributed to damage.[13]

2.2 Accountable Person

Accountable person is an indispensable angle when decoupling the concept of accountability, as it is the target of relevant mechanisms. Accountability must be assigned to specific persons beforehand. In the context of AI, in principle, all parties including natural persons and legal persons along the supply chain may be accountable under certain conditions.

Manufacturers determine the technical specifications of an AI system. Accountability shall cover manufacturers, so that they will be properly incentivized when designing and manufacturing AI systems.[14] They will also be obliged to take necessary conformity assessment to ensure that the product has meet all legal requirements before being placed on the market.

After an AI system is put into circulation, importers and various distributors take the role in making the AI system available on the market and spreading the AI system to a broader range of regions. Although their activity does not directly determine the function or performance of an AI system, they can facilitate the process of distribution, which thereby indirectly influences the scale of accidents. In this digital age, online platforms take a crucial role in facilitating the distribution of AI-enabled applications in various manners, such as cloud services and software as a service (SaaS). Therefore, it is necessary to hold online platforms accountable as well.[15]

After circulation, the next stop for an AI system is to be deployed in a certain context. In reality, depending on the concrete application of an AI system, the typical deployers may include educational institutes, healthcare organization, public authorities and many others. It is noteworthy that although the whole operation and monitoring of an AI system is normally under the umbrella of deployers, they need

[13] Larsson and Heintz (2020), p. 3.

[14] Li and Schütte (2023).

[15] Ulfbeck and Verbruggen (2022).

to assign specific natural persons (i.e., user) to operate the AI system. In practice, users can be teachers, doctors and civil servants, who take the concrete control over an AI system. To ensure that AI systems are deployed for intended purposes and operated as expected, deployers including the assigned users shall also be considered as accountable persons.

Users are indeed not the end point in the spectrum of accountable persons. The use of AI can influence a variety of parties (e.g., consumers, students and patients). In principle, these parties are often not considered as accountable parties, since they are impacted persons.[16] However, in a bilateral accident, where the activity of impacted persons can also influence the likelihood and severity of damage, impacted persons shall also be motivated to behave properly.[17] From the accountability perspective, this normally means that impacted persons shall also take necessary care and their fault may reduce or even disallow the liability of others.

2.3 Stage

Accountability must be secured throughout the lifecycle of an AI system. As the HLEG Ethical Guidelines points out, accountability shall cover the stages 'both before and after their development, deployment and use'. From this perspective, four facets are distinguished when designing mechanisms for accountability.

The first stage is 'before development', which covers the stage from design to manufacturing. This is the stage that sets up the architecture and technical specification of an AI system.

The next stage covers the activities between development and deployment. In this stage, an AI system is ready to be or has already been placed on the market. By the end of this stage, the AI system is physically under the control of a deployer, even if the manufacturers may still maintain some control (e.g., through software updates).[18] In this regard, accountability should cover both manufacturers as well as deployers.

The third stage spans from deployment to use. Normally, this refers to the assignment of human oversight to the appropriate people within the deployer's organization. This person shall in principle be technically and knowledgably competent in terms of operating the AI system under the instructions of use provided by the manufacturer.

The last stage starts from the moment when an AI system is put into use. It specifically refers to the interaction between impacted persons and the AI system. This process also includes the necessary updates provided by the upstream parties.

[16] Shavell (2004), p. 193.

[17] Li and Faure (2024).

[18] Wendehorst (2020), p. 175–176.

To summarize, the lifetime of an AI system can be split into four concrete stages. The discussion in this paragraph explains that varying activities featured in each stage. This also indicates the necessity of developing diverse mechanisms for different stages, which is the central topic of the next part.

2.4 Mechanism

The last, but not the least, dimension of understanding accountable AI lies in the mechanisms that are adopted for the purpose of implementing accountability. Traditionally, a variety of mechanisms have been introduced prior to the appearance of AI systems. Risk regulation provides the requirement that a product must meet before they are allowed to be placed on the market. It also lays down the obligations that parties must comply with. Besides risk regulation, liability is also a crucial mechanism in terms of allocation liability and compensation.

In recent years, new mechanisms are developed in order to catch up the challenges posed by new technologies. For example, meta-regulation (e.g., self-regulation, impact assessment and standardization) provides the essential flexibility to strike accountability and other social goals, such innovation.[19] In addition, the law starts to require manufacturers to embed ethical values (e.g., accountability and transparency) into the designing and manufacturing process of a product. This 'by design' insight is considered an important approach toward accountability issue.[20] Education, e.g., digital literacy, is another arising mechanism that is important for properly materializing accountability.[21] In the era of AI, literacy means that accountable persons (e.g., users) shall be sufficiently educated to the extent that they understand how to properly comply with the obligations.

3 Accountability for Robo-Advisers: The Example of the EU AI Act

Having distinguished the different dimensions of accountability in Section 2, the following two sections analyze how accountability issues concerning robo-advisers are addressed in recent EU legislation and proposals. In specific, Section 3 discusses the accountability for robo-advisers under the framework of the recently adopted

[19] Dong and Chen (2024).

[20] Almada (2023).

[21] Long and Magerko (2020).

EU AI Act. Further, in Section 4, the accountability for robo-advisers will be analyzed in the sphere of liability.

3.1 *The Background of Regulating Robo-Advisers: IDD and/or AI Act?*

In the EU, sector-specific regulations are the main mechanisms to address the risk occurred in particular activities. In the sphere of insurance distribution, Insurance Distribution Directive (IDD)[22] provides harmonized requirements that Member States must transform when regulating the activities of insurance distribution. As insurance technologies (e.g., robo-advisers) are constantly introduced to insurance distribution, the questions arise are (1) whether such innovative applications fall under the regulatory framework of the IDD, and (2) whether the IDD is the right mechanism to regulate the risk of these insurance technologies.

For the first question, as literature explained, the application of robo-advisers will fall under the IDD without any doubt, since the provision of insurance advice regardless its form (by humans or by machines) is clearly a sort of insurance distribution.[23] Nevertheless, the regulatory framework provided by the IDD is largely principle-based, meaning that concrete regulatory rules specifically designed to address the challenges caused by robo-advisers are missing.

Then it comes to the second question, i.e., whether the IDD is the right mechanism to introduce new rules for robo-advisers. Regarding this issue, authorities at the EU level (e.g., EIOPA) contends that the regulation for AI-related applications (including robo-advisers) in the insurance sector shall still be sector-specific.[24] This indicates the confidence of insurance authorities to rely on existing insurance regulations to resolve the challenges raised by emerging technological challenges. Nevertheless, the EU ultimately determined to introduce a horizontal approach to regulate the risk of all AI applications.

Therefore, in the aftermath of the AI Act, robo-advisers should comply with the IDD as well as the horizontal AI Act. They are complementary each other, which has significant implications for insurance distributors, as they need to not only respect the obligations as deployers of AI system laid down in the AI Act but also follow the obligations within the IDD as insurance distributors.

---

[22] Directive (EU) 2016/97 of the European Parliament and of the Council of 20 January 2016 on insurance distribution (recast), OJ L 26, 2.2.2016, p. 19–59.

[23] Marano (2019), p. 310.

[24] EIOPA (2022).

3.2 *An Overview of the EU AI Act and Its Implication for Accountability*

In April 2021, the European Commission introduced its proposal for a comprehensive regulatory framework specifically for AI applications.[25] After three years discussion, the final version of the EU AI Act came into force as of 1 August 2024.[26] The EU AI Act followed a so-called risk-based approach that has been widely adopted in product safety regulations.[27] Depending on the risk-profiles of their applications, all AI systems are distinguished into the four groups which are subject to different regulatory requirements.

First of all, some AI applications that result in serious fundamental rights concerns are considered with unacceptable risks. They are banned according to the AI Act.[28] What is more, a wide range of AI systems are categorized as high-risk AI applications, as they may pose substantial risks to safety and fundamental rights. High-risk AI systems are in principle allowed for circulation, but they must firstly meet specific mandatory safety requirements (laid down by the AI Act as well as other sector-specific regulations, if there is any) and have them verified through necessary conformity assessment procedures.[29] In addition, the AI Act laid down obligations for the operators of high-risk AI systems.[30] Moreover, the AI Act set up transparency obligations for the providers or deployers of certain AI applications.[31] The objective is requiring their operators to take proper transparency measures to ensure that the impacted persons can make an informed decision. Last but not least, for all other AI applications, the AI Act does not provide any additional requirements or obligations for them or their operators. They can be placed directly on the market, once they meet the mandatory requirements from relevant sector-specific regulations. Besides the regulatory measures toward various AI systems, the AI Act also extends to regulating General Purpose AI models by obliging their operators to respect certain obligations.[32]

To summarize, the AI Act provides a comprehensive regulatory framework for all kinds of AI applications. Insurance technologies, such as robo-advisers, are thereby not isolated from this framework.

---

[25] European Commission. (2021).

[26] Regulation (EU) 2024/1689 of the European Parliament and of the Council of 13 June 2024 laying down harmonised rules on artificial intelligence and amending Regulations (EC) No 300/2008, (EU) No 167/2013, (EU) No 168/2013, (EU) 2018/858, (EU) 2018/1139 and (EU) 2019/2144 and Directives 2014/90/EU, (EU) 2016/797 and (EU) 2020/1828 (Artificial Intelligence Act). OJ L, 2024/1689, 12.7.2024.

[27] Ebers (2024). See also Almada and Petit (2025).

[28] Article 5, AI Act.

[29] Section 2 of Chapter III, AI Act.

[30] Section 3 of Chapter III, AI Act.

[31] Article 50, AI Act.

[32] Chapter V, AI Act.

3.3 Locating Robo-Advisers in the Risk-Based Matrix in the EU AI Act

As analyzed, robo-advisers are in nature developed to take a role as professional insurance advisers. They may engage in a variety of tasks, including communication, risk-differentiation and advice provision. Therefore, robo-advisers may fall under different risk profiles depending on their concrete practices.[33]

First and foremost, robo-advisers may generate unacceptable risks, if they are designed with subliminal and deceptive techniques and has the potential to result in harmful consequences. For robo-advisers that are used for supporting insurance distribution, it is highly likely that they more or less employ manipulative techniques in its design for the purpose of persuading customers to make decisions that ultimately benefit insurance distributors. Manipulative techniques, as the AI Act interprets, will only be prohibited if they (are likely to) cause significant harms.[34] The concept of significant harm under the AI Act is complementary to unfair commercial practices, meaning that any commercial practices, irrespective of AI-driven or not, shall be prohibited under all circumstances, as long as it generates economic or financial harms to consumers. Therefore, the standard of 'significant harm' is very low, which is mostly linked to the disadvantage of the economic benefits of consumers. Robo-advisers have the potential to lead consumers to make wrong decisions and caused economic losses by purchasing a coverage that they do not need. If this falls under the scope of significant harm defined by the AI Act, then the application of rob-advisers would be substantially limited in terms of recommending insurance products to customers. In the aftermath of the AI Act, two clarifications are important: firstly, the distinction between manipulative techniques and others should be explicitly interpreted; secondly, the meaning of significant harm should be clarified, especially in the context of financial sectors.

Secondly, robo-advisers with a function of using biometric information to infer *certain protected attributes*, may be prohibited as well. For instance, if a robo-adviser embeds facial recognition technology (FRT), uses the data collected from FRT to infer the race of their customers and then categorizes the risk-level of customers based on race, such a robo-adviser will be prohibited.[35] According to the AI Act, the 'certain protected attributes' that are prohibited for inference are limited to race, political opinions, trade union membership, religious or philosophical beliefs, sex life and sexual orientation. Therefore, if a robo-advisers uses biometric data to infer protected attributes other than the aforementioned ones, they will not be prohibited. Instead, they may fall under the scope of high-risk AI applications and be subject to a different framework of accountability.

---

[33] Marano and Li (2023).

[34] Recital (29), AI Act.

[35] Article 5(1)(g), AI Act.

Thirdly, robo-advisers for insurance distribution may be categorized as a high-risk AI application. To begin with, biometric-based robo-advisers may be defined with a high risk. In particular, in the case that a robo-adviser is used to categorize the risk of insureds based on their biometric information or it is able to infer their emotional status, it will be considered as a high-risk application.[36] In addition, robo-advisors that are used for *assessing and pricing the risk of natural persons in the case of life and health insurance* are also defined as with a high-risk.[37] Accordingly, from an accountability perspective, additional regulatory requirements and obligations shall be fulfilled before a high-risk robo-adviser is allowed for circulation.

Fourthly, if robo-advisers are developed to facilitate the communication between insurance distributors and customers (e.g., chatbots), the AI Act will also apply to them by exerting a specific transparency obligation onto their providers. In this regard, providers should make sure that robo-advisers are developed in a manner that impacted natural persons are sufficiently informed that they are interacting with AI rather than a human.[38]

To summarize, the discussion in this part is intended to clarify the multiple facets of robo-advisers. Depending on the concrete techniques that they employ and the purposes that they intend to apply for, robo-advisers may fall under different risk categories outlined by the AI Act. As a result, they themselves and their operators shall also be subject to particular requirements and obligations. In essence, the risk-based approach laid down by the AI Act is a pertinent reflection of the different components of accountability: different mechanisms (e.g., regulatory requirement and obligation) shall be developed to relevant accountable persons (e.g., providers and deployers) throughout the lifetime of robo-advisers depending on their risk profiles.

3.4 A Further Look into the Accountability for High-Risk Robo-Advisers

Having mapped out robo-advisers under the risk-based approach introduced by the AI Act, it is clear that high-risk applications are the main target under the new regulatory framework. As aforementioned, robo-advisers that are used for insurance distribution purposes are considered with a high-risk in several scenarios, if, e.g., they employ biometric systems as well as they are used for assessing and pricing the risk of natural persons in the case of life or health insurance. From the accountability perspective, this means that the operators of robo-advisers are subject to new obligations beyond the existing insurance regulations (e.g., the IDD). Therefore, it

[36] Point 1 of Annex III, AI Act.

[37] Point 5(c) of Annex III, AI Act.

[38] Article 50(1), AI Act.

is of great importance to unveil the specific regulatory requirements and obligations for high-risk robo-advisers.

The AI Act established new essential legal requirements for high-risk AI systems. According to Section 2 of Chapter III, the requirements that a high-risk AI system must meet include risk management system, data and data governance, technical documentation, record-keeping, transparency and provision of information to deployers, human oversight and accuracy. In practice, the proof of meeting such legal requirements must be supported on the technical side. This requires providers of high-risk AI systems to use reliable technical specifications (e.g., standards) to explain how their products have complied with the legal requirements.[39] Furthermore, they need to follow the necessary conformity assessment procedures to verify their compliance.

The demonstration of compliance in line with harmonized standards can significantly reduce the effort of verifying conformity, because it will lead to a presumption of meeting relevant legal requirements. Nevertheless, as harmonized standards are instruments that the Commission requires European standardization organizations to draft, in reality it may take a long time before they are established. This is also the challenge for standardizing AI products.[40] At the moment, the European standardization organizations are busy with developing harmonized standards regarding all legal requirements set out in the AI Act.[41] It, however, is unknown whether such standards match the expectation within the insurance sector.

The AI Act also sets up obligations respectively for providers and deployers of high-risk AI systems. Noticeably, the obligations for deployers will have significant impact on insurance distributors from the accountability perspective. According to Article 26, insurance companies that adopt robo-advisers with high risks shall respect a wide range of obligations. First of all, insurance companies shall assign human oversight to competent natural persons within the organization to operate and supervise robo-advisers. Such persons must also be provided with necessary training in support of their supervision. What is more, to the extent that the input data of a high-risk robo-adviser is under the control of insurance companies, they must ensure that the data is representative for the purpose that high-risk robo-adviser is intended to use. Moreover, insurance company is the ultimate party to monitor the proper operation of robo-advisers. Their operation shall follow the instructions of use and they shall notify providers and competent authorities in the cases where robo-advisers present risk to safety and fundamental risks and where a serious accident resulted. Last but not least, insurance companies must make sure the logs are automatically kept when logs are under their control.

[39] Article 40-44, AI Act.

[40] Laux, Wachter and Mittelstadt (2024).

[41] Commission implementing decision on a standardization request to the European Committee for Standardisation and the European Committee for Electrotechnical Standardisation in support of Union policy on artificial intelligence, C(2023)3215.

The obligations for the insurance companies are *de facto* the duties that they must respect. From an accountability perspective, setting up obligations for deployers like insurance companies will incentivize them to take due care. In the cases that they fail to respect the obligations, it would be an important signal to indicate and establish the fault of them in a liability claim.

Besides the aforementioned obligations for deployers, the AI Act also obliges in Article 27 certain deployers of high-risk AI systems to conduct a so-called fundamental rights impact assessment (FRIA).[42] It is noteworthy that the FRIA does not apply to every deployer of a high-risk AI system. Only two types of deployers are covered: public or private bodies providing public services and certain financial service providers. According to Article 27, deployers of AI systems that are used for assessing and pricing the risk of nature persons in the case of life or health insurance will be subject to FRIA. Therefore, if a robo-adviser holds such a capability, their deployers must be prepared to conduct the FRIA.

To summarize, the AI Act provides a wide spectrum of mechanisms specifically for holding the operators of high-risk robo-advisers accountable. Such mechanisms include not only *ex ante* legal requirements but also duties and obligations through the operation process. In addition, necessary transparency and record-keeping measures must be ensured throughout the lifetime of a high-risk robo-adviser. What the AI Act does not clearly address, however, is how to allocate the liability among various accountable persons, where a harmful consequence has occurred. For this issue, liability regime serves as the proper mechanism to clarify.

3.5 Literacy

The discussion so far unveils how the AI Act utilizes different types of mechanisms to necessitate the accountability of AI systems. The mechanism contains not only traditional legal requirements and obligations but also emerging meta-regulations, such as standards and risk assessment. Noticeably, the AI Act also stresses the role of AI literacy in promoting trustworthy AI.

On this basis, Article 4 of the AI Act further clarifies that providers and deployers of AI systems shall take measures to make sure that their staff are employed with a sufficient level of literacy in terms of operating the AI system. To achieve this objective, all relevant methods, such as education and professional training, shall be offered. AI literacy is crucial for accountability, because it prepares the necessary level of knowledge and techniques to help staff to better understand their responsibility and obligation in the course of operating and monitoring an AI system.

Unlike other mechanisms, AI literacy in the AI Act is very much principle-based. This means that the Member States shall further develop their own AI literacy rules.

[42] Mantelero (2024).

Also, industries and companies can introduce concrete guidelines to implement AI literacy. When implementing the AI Act, insurance authorities shall work closely with insurance industry to set out sufficient guidance on AI literacy in the insurance sector.

4 Accountability for Robo-Advisers: An Example of the Recent Liability Reform

The discussion so far mapped out the accountability of robo-advisers through the lens of the new AI Act. What makes the AI Act remarkable is that various mechanisms have been developed and combined to cover different operators throughout the lifetime of robo-advisers. The AI Act, however, has no intention to address the liability issues resulting from the damage caused by robo-advisers.[43] The objective of this section is to discuss the accountability of robo-advisers from the perspective of liability. In particular, the discussion extends to the recent liability reform at the EU level

A proper allocation of liability is crucial, as it will not only influence the incentives of relevant parties but also determine the effectiveness of compensation.[44] The basic question in the context of robo-advisers is: who should be liable for the damage caused by robo-advisers? The answer to this question can be further distinguished into two folds depending on the role of stakeholders. On the one hand, we need to clarify the liability for the providers of robo-advisers; on the other hand, we need to clarify the liability for the deployers of robo-advisers.

4.1 The Liability for the Providers of Robo-Advisers

According to the 1985 product liability directive (i.e., 1985 PLD[45]), producers shall be liable for the damage caused by the defect of their products.[46] With regard to the liability for the providers of robo-advisers, it is not surprising that people may question whether providers could be comparable to the producers of normal products. From a positive legal analysis, however, there are some barriers to justify the applicability of product liability for the providers of robo-advisers.

[43] Li and Schütte (2024).

[44] Li and Faure (2024).

[45] Council Directive 85/374/EEC of 25 July 1985 on the approximation of the laws, regulations and administrative provisions of the Member States concerning liability for defective products. OJ L 210, 7.8.1985, p. 29–33.

[46] Article 1, 1985 PLD.

First of all, a robo-adviser may not be qualified as the 'product' defined in the 1985 PLD. Product in the 1985 PLD refers to movable products.[47] The CJEU further clarified that movable goods should refer to tangible goods.[48] Robo-advisers *per se*, however, are standalone AI applications, meaning that they look nowhere like the traditional products.

Secondly, the damage caused by robo-advisers may not be compensable under product liability. As 1985 PLD clearly listed, the interests protected by product liability include a person's life, physical integrity as well as their property.[49] Other interests, such as mental health as well as other fundamental rights (e.g., fairness, non-discrimination, personal data) are thereby not protected by product liability. Robo-advisers, however, are remote from causing damage to the aforementioned protected interests. The main consequences of using robo-advisers are pure economic losses or non-material damage resulting from violating fundamental rights. Therefore, robo-advisers are not well covered by the existing product liability framework, if we delve into the damage caused by them.

Thirdly, as other AI applications, there are procedural obstacles preventing victims from smoothly claiming the liability of providers. When establishing the liability of providers, victims must prove the existence of defectiveness and that there is a causal link between the defectiveness and the damage. The proof of defectiveness and causation, however, is not an easy task for victims, because they may lack the necessary information as well as the capability to do so.[50]

The discussion in this part so far disclosed the substantive and procedural obstacles of holding the providers of robo-advisers liable under product liability. On 12 March 2024, the European Parliament adopted a proposal to revise 1985 PLD.[51] The revised PLD (rPLD) was finally published in the Official Journal on 18 November 2024.[52] The rPLD adapted product liability rules to the new challenges caused by digitalization. In the aftermath of rPLD, the question remains: to what extent can the providers of robo-advisers be held liable within the rPLD?

First of all, the rPLD significantly extends the scope of product to intangible goods, such as software, AI and 3D printing.[53] By doing so, robo-advisers will be clearly covered by the rPLD.

What is more, the rPLD provides some concrete rules to help victims to prove defectiveness and causal link. Victims can request the defendant to disclose relevant

---

[47] Article 3, 1985 PLD.

[48] C-65/20, VI v Krone Verlag, ECLI:EU:C:2021:298.

[49] Article 9, 1985 PLD.

[50] Jacquemin (2024).

[51] European Parliament legislative resolution of 12 March 2024 on the proposal for a directive of the European Parliament and of the Council on liability for defective products. COM(2022)0495 – C9-0322/2022 – 2022/0302(COD).

[52] Directive (EU) 2024/2853 of the European Parliament and of the Council of 23 October 2024 on liability for defective products and repealing Council Directive 85/374/EEC, OJ L, 2024/2853.

[53] Article 4(1), rPLD.

evidence in the case that they have 'presented facts and evidence sufficient to support the plausibility of the claim for compensation'.[54] When certain conditions are met, defectiveness and causal link can also be presumed.[55]

The challenging issue of holding the provider of robo-advisers under the rPLD lies in the scope of compensable damage. Although the rPLD extends the scope of personal injury to 'medically recognized damage to psychological health', the scope of protected interests is not significantly expanded, e.g., to other fundamental rights.[56] Therefore, in the end, whether the damage caused by the defect of a robo-adviser can be held accountable under the rPLD is very largely determined by the type of damage caused by it.[57] If robo-advisers caused one of the following damage, i.e., death, personal injury (including medically recognized damage to psychological health) and property, then their providers might be held liable given the successful demonstration of other factors.

To summarize, there is a large chance that the damage caused by robo-advisers may not be recoverable under the product liability regime. In order to be compensated, the harm must fall under the scope damage defined by the rPLD and it must be caused by the defectiveness of the robo-advisors. If these conditions are not met, for example, the damage was caused by the fault of manufacturers rather than defectiveness of the robo-advisor, the rPLD may not apply. As a result, holding providers accountable would be less applicable via product liability regime. In this scenario, fault-based rules are an important complementary regime for holding the providers of robo-advisers accountable.[58]

4.2 The Liability for the Deployers of Robo-Advisers

Besides providers, the activity of deployers can also significantly contribute to harmful consequences due to their carelessness in operation and supervision. Holding deployers liable will incentivize them to take proper precautionary measures and reduce accidents. Traditionally, deployers are subject to fault-based liability, meaning that they will be liable where they fail to take the due level of care as expected. The failure to take due care level can be verified from both subjective and objective perspective: from the subjective perspective, they are negligent in triggering harmful consequences through their activities; from the objective perspective, it means that they failed to comply with regulatory requirements.

---

54 Article 9, rPLD.

55 Article 10. rPLD.

56 Article 6, rPLD.

57 Li and Schütte (2023).

58 Li and Schütte (2023).

Several elements need to be successfully demonstrated when relying on fault-based liability to hold deployers of robo-advisers accountable. First and foremost, the claimant must prove that the deployer had a *fault*. As aforementioned, the proof of fault can be established from both subjective and objective dimensions. One visible benchmark of the fault of deployers are the failure of complying with the obligations of deployers listed in the Article 26 and 27 in the AI Act. If an insurance distributor failed to comply with one or these several obligations (e.g., proper assignment of human oversight and data governance), it can be an important source of demonstrating their fault. Secondly, the claimant must prove the *damage*. The concept of damage can be defined very differently from one Member States to another.[59] The claimant needs to check the extent to which the damage suffered by them is compensable in a given legal regime. Thirdly, the claimant must prove the *causal link* between the fault of the deployer and the damage.

The elements of fault liability are not self-evident in a given case. Claimants shall take the burden of proof toward these elements. However, in reality they are very likely to encounter difficulties in establishing these elements. The products and services empowered by AI and digital technologies will even worsen this situation, considering the opacity of its operation. Since 2022, the European Commission started with a proposal to set up the liability of AI systems (i.e. AI Liability Directive, AILD).[60] Considering the huge divergence of the Member States in terms of the substantive issues, such as concept of fault, causation and damage, the AILD proposal does not intend to provide a harmonized liability regime at the EU level at the moment. Alternatively, the main purpose of the AILD is requiring the Member States to ease their procedures to facilitate the claims that are based on non-contractual fault liability.[61] In specific, the AILD requests national courts to require defendants to disclose the evidence to facilitate their claims.[62] In addition, the causal link between fault and damage shall be presumed when certain conditions are met.[63] Therefore, the AILD aims to set up minimal harmonized rules for the Member States.[64] The Member States can of course introduce or maintain their higher requirements in their national laws.

The proposal for the AILD, however, was criticized concerning its clarity and added-value.[65] The Member States like France also questioned the necessity of this directive. Under this background, the AILD was withdrawn by the Commission in February 2025. After the withdrawal, it is expected that in the following years national-based rules will play a crucial role in reshaping the liability rules of AI.

---

[59] Li and Faure (2024).

[60] European Commission (2022).

[61] Li and Schütte (2024).

[62] Article 3, AILD.

[63] Article 4, AILD.

[64] Hacker (2023).

[65] Li and Faure (2025).

To summarize, the liability for the deployer of robo-advisers is very largely shaped by national laws. The recent proposal for AILD shows the determination of the EU authorities to establish harmonized rules. Nevertheless, although it only aimed for a minimal harmonization and only targeted procedural issues rather than substantive ones, the AILD was ultimately withdrawn due to strong objection from the Member States. There is still a long way to explore the liability mechanism in the future.

5 Conclusion

To conclude, this chapter reflected the theoretical and practical arguments on the accountability issue relating to robo-advisers that are used for insurance distribution. The analytical framework of accountability requires policymakers to map out several key elements (i.e., dimension, person, stage and mechanism) in the legal rules. The discussion in this chapter further clarified how the recent legislation, including the AI Act, the rPLD and the (withdrawn) AILD, has been reframed to accommodate the different elements into concrete legal rules. It showed that the accountability for robo-advisers depends largely on the practices and purposes that a specific robo-advisers intends to apply to. Robo-advisers that adopt biometric systems and that are used for assessing the risk in the case of life and health insurance will be subject to a more comprehensive accountability rules: (1) there are more requirements and obligations; (2) the accountability concern extends to the lifetime of such applications and (3) various mechanisms (e.g., obligations, risk assessment, by design and literacy) are introduced to ensure accountability. From an *ex post* perspective, important updates are also observed in the liability sphere. However, as discussed, the reform in liability may provide little help to strengthen accountability for the providers and deployers robo-advisers. Victims may face unsurmountable barriers when identifying the liable persons and proving the liability. This chapter concludes that there is still a loophole of holding robo-advisers accountable from the *ex post* perspective.

References

Almada, M. (2023). Regulation by design and the governance of Technological futures. *European journal of risk regulation* 14(4): 697–709.

Almada, M., & Petit, N. (2025). The EU AI Act: Between the rock of product safety and the hard place of fundamental rights. *Common market law review*, 62(1): 85–120.

Baker, T., & Dellaert, B. (2017). Regulating robo advice across the financial services industry. *Iowa Law Rev* 103: 713.

Coombs, C., & Redman, A. (2018). The impact of robo-advice on financial advisers: a qualitative case study. UK Academy for Information Systems Conference Proceedings.

Dong, H., & Chen, J. (2024). Meta-Regulation: An ideal alternative to the primary responsibility as the regulatory model of generative AI in China. *Computer Law & Security Review* 54: 1–16.

Ebers, M. (2024). Truly Risk-Based Regulation of Artificial Intelligence – How to Implement the EU's AI Act, First View: 1-20.

EIOPA (2022). EIOPA letter to co-legislators on the Artificial Intelligence Act.

EIOPA (2024). Report on the digitalisation of the European insurance sector.
European Commission (2021). Proposal for a regulation of the European Parliament and of the Council laying down harmonised rules on Artificial Intelligence (Artificial Intelligence Act) and amending certain legislative acts. COM/2021/206 final.
European Commission (2022). Proposal for a Directive of the European Parliament and of the Council on adapting non-contractual civil liability rules to artificial intelligence (AI Liability Directive). COM(2022) 496 final.
Hacker, P. (2023). The European AI liability directives–Critique of a half-hearted approach and lessons for the future. *Computer Law & Security Review* 51: 1–42.
HLEG (2019). Ethical guidelines for trustworthy AI.
HLEG (2020). Assessment List for Trustworthy AI.
Infosys BPM (2018). The insurance advisor of the future: how robots are set to reshape the value framework in insurance. Available at: https://www.infosysbpm.com/mccamish/resources/Documents/insurance-advisor-of-the-future.pdf. Accessed on 31 May 2025.
Jacquemin, Z. (2024). Product Liability Directive: Disclosure of Evidence, the Burden of Proof and Presumptions. *Journal of European Tort Law* 15(2): 126–139.
Larsson, S., & Heintz, F. (2020). Transparency in artificial intelligence. *Internet policy review* 9(2): 1–16.
Laux, J., Wachter, S., & Mittelstadt, B. (2024). Three pathways for standardisation and ethical disclosure by default under the European Union Artificial Intelligence Act. *Computer Law & Security Review* 53: 1–13.
Li, S., & Faure, M. (2024). The Revised Product Liability Directive: A Law and Economics Analysis. *Journal of European Tort Law* 15(2): 140–171.
Li, S., & Faure, M. (2025). Does the EU Need an Artificial Intelligence Liability Directive? *Insights from the Economics of Federalism. Revue économique* 76(1): 115–139.
Li, S., & Schütte, B. (2023). The proposal for a revised Product Liability Directive: The emperor's new clothes? *Maastricht Journal of European and Comparative Law* 30(5): 573–596.
Li, S., & Schütte, B. (2024). The Proposed EU Artificial Intelligence Liability Directive: Does/Will Its Content Reflect Its Ambition?. *Technology and Regulation*, 143–151.
Long, D., & Magerko, B. (2020). What is AI literacy? Competencies and design considerations. Proceedings of the 2020 CHI conference on human factors in computing systems.
Mantelero, A. (2024). The Fundamental Rights Impact Assessment (FRIA) in the AI Act: Roots, legal obligations and key elements for a model template. *Computer Law & Security Review*, 54: 1–13.
Marano, P. (2019). Navigating InsurTech: The digital intermediaries of insurance products and customer protection in the EU. *Maastricht Journal of European and Comparative Law* 26(2): 294–315.
Marano, P. & Li, S. (2023). Regulating robo-advisors in insurance distribution: Lessons from the insurance distribution directive and the ai act. *Risks* 11(1): 1–13.
Novelli, C., Taddeo, M., & Floridi, L. (2024). Accountability in artificial intelligence: what it is and how it works. *AI & Society* 39(4): 1871–1882.
RapidValue Solutions (2017). The Rise of Robo-Advice in Insurance Companies. Available at: https://rapidvalue.medium.com/the-rise-of-robo-advice-in-insurance-companies-ef21d2ed8a0
Shavell, S. (2004). *Foundations of Economic Analysis of Law*, Harvard University Press.
Ulfbeck, V., & Verbruggen, P. (2022). Online Marketplaces and Product Liability: Back to the Where We Started? *European Review of Private Law* 30(6): 975–998.
Van Bekkum, M. S., Borgesius, F. J. Z., & Heskes, T. (2025). AI, insurance, discrimination and unfair differentiation. An overview and research agenda. *Law, Technology and Innovation* 17(1): 177–204.
Wendehorst, C. (2020). Strict liability for AI and other emerging technologies. *Journal of European Tort Law* 11(2): 150–180.

Chinese Perspective on Representation Duty in Blockchain-Based Insurance

Can Luo

1 Introduction

As a distributed database or ledger shared among the nodes of a computer network, blockchain is best known for its crucial role in cryptocurrency systems where it maintains a secure and decentralized record of transactions. However, its applications extend beyond cryptocurrency. In China, the term "Blockchain+Insurance" typically refers to the use of blockchain technology by insurance firms to optimize efficiency and security, a concept known as blockchain-based insurance. Because of the transparency that blockchain offers, transactions recorded on it are permanent and no data can be modified once written. One of the most common applications is in anti-fraud. Additionally, Chinese insurance firms hope using blockchain for all stages, from the pre-contract stage to post-contract stage. Since 2018, a few Chinese firms have collaborated to develop a health insurance which is the world's first to require all insurance obligations to be performed on blockchain. It is easy to imagine that the representation of a consumer would be an essential issue. For consumers, blockchain that is expected and developed by insurance firms to reduce their legal risks, is being a new situation that they have to encounter when making representations. How should this new situation be considered? How might it significantly impact existing law? How can the interests between insurers and policyholders be rebalanced in the pre-contract stage with the implementation of blockchain? These are the questions this article tries to answer.

As for the representation duty in Chinese law, the main legal rule is Article 16 of the Insurance Law of the People's Republic of China 2015 (the 2015 Act), including the definition, the breach of the duty, the insurers' remedies and the applicants' defenses. How do Chinese judges apply these rules in practice? By visiting Chinese local courts and reviewing the Chinese PKU Law database, the author has collected

C. Luo
School of AI and Law, Southwest University of Political Science and Law, Chongqing, P.R. China
email: luocan-1985@163.com

P. Marano (ed.), *Emerging Legal Frontiers in Insurance*,
AIDA Europe Research Series on Insurance Law and Regulation,
https://doi.org/10.1007/978-3-032-09716-3_3

494 samples of appeal and retrial cases in which consumers made a misrepresentation. Unexpectedly, insurers had a minority of chance of winning which is about 20% because many Judges used the judicial discretion to support consumers. These cases indicate that Chinese insurance firms are facing significant legal risks, which also explains their eagerness to adopt blockchain technology.

From a positive perspective, using blockchain can reduce the number of lawsuits related to misrepresentations. Insurance firms may be able to verify whether misrepresentations exist on the blockchain and refuse to underwrite at the first place. Thus many lawsuits focuses on misrepresentation would never happen. However, blockchain may not be beneficial to solving all problem particularly when the root cause lies in legislative deficiencies.

Besides existing problems, new legal issues will emerge in blockchain-based insurance, A typical example is individualized insurance products based on blockchain. By collaborating with social media platforms, insurance firms can get almost all material facts of potential clients, reducing reliance on their representations. It would be unnecessary for applicants to make representations. They may simply check and confirm if there is a mistake on proposal forms. This may lead to a new trend where the representation duty would be replaced by others such as the confirmation duty in blockchain-based insurance. Under what circumstances can be exempted from the duty of representation need to be strictly defined, to better rebalance the interests of two parties. In future, insurance applicants will require greater protection when acting on blockchain.

2 Blockchain-Based Insurance and Representation Duty in China

As one of the most promising technologies in the world, blockchain is expected to optimize the efficiency, security and transparency of insurance industry. When talking about "Blockchain+Insurance" in China, it usually refers that insurance firms use this technology to optimize the efficiency and security which is exactly called blockchain-based insurance. There have been more and more insurance firms, such as Ping An in China, Dynamis in the UK, AXA in France and Lemonade in the US, using it to deal with problems mainly in payment, reinsurance and risk management. One of most common use cases is anti-fraud. Because of the transparency blockchain can offer, transactions done on it are permanent and no data can be modified once written. It is noteworthy that a few Chinese firms has been providing blockchain-based insurance and everything from pre-contract stage to after-contract stage can be done on blockchain. It is believed that it may become one of the most popular use cases for "Blockchain+Insurance" in future.[1] Typically, the first step for applicants is to make representations on blockchain when entering a contract. This

[1] Qian Li, "Block chain + Insurance is booming", Shanghai Financial News, December 6,2019.

is what insurance firms aim to achieve, as pre-contract information from the insured is crucial. With the help of blockchain, insurers believe they can significantly reduce potential legal risks.

Before analyzing the impact of the technology on the duty of representation, it is necessary to outline the current legislation in China. The primary legal rule is Article 16 of Insurance Law of the People's Republic of China 2015 (the 2015 Act), which includes three key provisions:

First, applicants must answer questions honestly, which is like the rules in many other countries. According to Article. 16(1) of the 2015 Act, the applicant is required to represent only regarding the information specifically requested by the insurer on the proposal form. Even if the applicant fails to disclose material information, the insurer may not rescind the contract if such information is beyond the scope of the questions raised in the proposal form.

Second, how is a breach of the duty defined, and what constitutes a qualifying misrepresentation? When an applicant is deliberate, it is a qualifying misrepresentation as long as their answers are untrue or misleading. In cases of gross negligence, a misrepresentation is considered qualifying only if the untrue or misleading answer is related to the claim. For example, a man with a liver problem get a liver cancer. In response to a misrepresentation, an insurer's remedy is to rescind the contract. Article 16 (2) states: "The insurer shall have the right to rescind the insurance contract where the applicant fails to fulfil the duty of representation deliberately or by gross negligence so that the failure of misrepresentation shall sufficiently influence the insurer's decision on whether he will accept the insurance or raise the premium rate." Article 16 (4) specifies: "When the applicant makes the misrepresentation deliberately, the insurer shall not be liable for losses that occur prior to the rescission of the contract and shall not refund the premium." Article 16 (5) further states: "When the applicant makes the misrepresentation by gross negligence, the insurer is not liable for losses that occurred prior to the rescission of the contract if the fact misrepresented materially impacts the occurrence of the insured events, but the insurer must refund the premium."

Third, applicants are afforded legal defenses when insurers seek to rescind the contract. Article 16 (3) states: "The right to rescind an insurance contract as prescribed in the preceding paragraph shall be annulled after the lapse of 30 days or more from the day when the insurers know the cause of rescission. After the lapse of two years or more from the day when an insurance contract is entered into, the insurer cannot rescind the contract; where an insured incident occurs, the insurers shall be liable for paying indemnity or insurance benefits." Article 16(6) specifies: "Where the insurer knows the truth which the applicant fails to represent when they enter into an insurance contract, the insurer shall not rescind the contract, and if an insured incident occurs, the insurer shall pay indemnity or insurance benefits."

How does Chinese judicial practice operate when Judges apply these rules? There are 494 samples of cases in which consumers made misrepresentations from 2017 to 2023. As shown in Table 3.1, insurers lost in 396 cases, accounting for 80.2 %. Regarding these 396 cases, there are primarily two judicial decisions.

One is there is no qualifying representation, related to Article 16 (3) and 16 (6). The other is, the insurer cannot rescind the contract even though there is a qualifying misrepresentation, related to Article 16 (4) and 16 (5). When applying these rules, insurers have a minority chance of winning, reflecting that Chinese

Table 3.1 Results of 494 samples of cases in which the applicant made a representation in China

Cause	Applicable Articles	Result	Number		Percent		Judges' Views
The consumer had made a representation.	Article 16 (3) of of the 2015 Act	The insurer lost	54	**396**	10.9%	**80.2%**	The insuer cannot rescind the contract and should pay to the insured. Because the right of rescission should have been claimed either within 30 days from the day when the insurers know the misrepresentation or within two years from the day when an insurance contract is entered into. And the insurer has missed the two periods during which the remedy can be protected.
	Article 16 (6) of the 2015 Act	The insurer lost	50		10.1%		The insurer cannot rescind the contract and should pay to the insured. Because the representative of the insurer had known the truth which the applicant failed to represent correct information when entering into an insurance contract, and the insurer is deemed to know the misrepresentation.
	Article 16 (4) or (5) of the 2015 Act	The insurer lost	292		59.2%		See Table 3.2
	Article 16 (4) or (5) of the 2015 Act	The Insured lost	98		19.8%		See Table 3.2

(data elaborated by the author)

insurance firms are facing great legal risks and explaining why they are eagerly seeking to use blockchain.

3 How Blockchain Can Benefit Insurers When Applicants Make Representations in China

Will blockchain be helpful to insurers? The answer may be positive when applying Article 16 (3) and 16 (6).

Article 16 (3) allows an insurer to rescind an insurance contract within a certain period as a remedy against the misrepresentation of an applicant. The other side of the coin is that insurers will lose the right of remedy once they do not rescind the contract within such a period. It is known as the incontestable provision.

The purpose of the article is to urge insurers to exercise their rights as soon as possible. If they do not find the misrepresentation in time, they are supposed to be liable for the payment. However, many Chinese insurers have been unable to exercise this right effectively because of the incontestable provision. And in many cases, it is too late for them to find incorrect pre-contract information from consumers. Among cases with high loss rates for insurers, 54 were attributed to the incontestable provision in Article 16 (3), accounting for 10.8 % of cases.[2] Although insurers have realized the problem, it may always be difficult to be aware of it in time. Taking health and life insurance as an example, it is too costly for insurers to check applicants' representations after entering the contract because of a huge number of applicants. As a result, insurers usually fail to identify misrepresentations within the two-year period and are compelled to make payments even when applicants act dishonestly.

It may be expected that blockchain can break down the information barrier. By collaborating with relevant institutions or platforms, insurers can get insured's pre-contract information more easily. The earliest attempt in Chinese market was the service of "Health Recommendation" launched by Sunshine Insurance Group in 2018.[3]

[2] Parts of the Judgment Numbers are: Administrative Appeal Judgment No.1528 in Shandong Province 2023; Administrative Appeal Judgment No.2448 in Fujian Province 2022; Administrative Appeal Judgment No.6832 in Anhui Province 2022;Administrative Appeal Judgment No.2448 in Fujian Province 2022; Administrative Appeal Judgment No.2561 in Jilin Province 2021;Administrative Appeal Judgment No.3534 in Hubei Province 2021;Administrative Appeal Judgment No.226 in Sichuan Province 2020; Administrative Appeal Judgment No.1850 in Inner Mongolia Autonomous region 2020, Administrative Appeal Judgment No.314 in Sichuan Province 2020, Administrative Appeal Judgment No.2014 in Henan Province 2020, Administrative Appeal Judgment No.5543 in Henan Province 2019, Administrative Appeal Judgment No.2438 in Yunnan Province 2019; Administrative Appeal Judgment No.553 in Jiangxi Province 2018; Administrative Retrial Judgment No.88 in Hubei Province 2018.

[3] In 2018, based on the blockchain built by Bubi Network Technology Co., Ltd. and Beijing Belink Information Technology Co., Ltd., Sunshine Insurance Group launched the "Health Recommendation" as the first one to get personal health data in the blockchain in China. First, a consumer needs to authorizes the insurer to access to his personal health data from medical examination centers. Second, the medical examination center sends the data to the insurer after confirming the authority. Finally, the insurer is able to immediately know the real situation of the applicant and decide whether to undertake the risk.

With the client's consent, the insurer can directly correct information from medical examination centers. In other words, the insurer can detect a misrepresentation promptly and refuse to enter into a contract. With the advent of blockchain-based insurance products, insurers can pursue more effective remedies against applicants' misrepresentation, reducing the likelihood of missing critical legal deadlines.

In addition to offering more effective remedies for insurers, blockchain could also reduce legal risks caused by representatives of insurers. According to Article 16 (6), any representation made to the representative is deemed to be known to the insurer.

It is common in the Chinese market for representatives to proceed with an insurance contract even after identifying a misrepresentation. What's worse is that the representative may even collude with the applicant. However, the insurer is still required to provide coverage, as they are legally deemed to be aware of the misrepresentation, despite lacking actual knowledge. Table 3.1 indicates that there are 50 cases focusing on Article 16 (6), accounting for about 10.1 percent.[4] In these cases, the insurer lost because the representative had known the misrepresentation when entering the contract. In the Chinese market, this issue is considered nearly as problematic as that of the incontestable clause, although this kind of cases account for a smaller proportion in Table 3.1. Although the insurer has been aware of it for a long time, there are few legal provisions directly for regulating representatives because legislators believe that it should belong to internal management of an insurance firm.[5] However, insurance firm fails to effectively monitor its representatives, usually only must penalize them after the claim occurs, when they may have resigned.[6]

Blockchain appears capable of addressing this problem immediately. Based on the above "Health Recommendation" service, Sunshine Insurance Group has been providing coverage for female-specific diseases. Before entering into an insurance contract, consumers should demonstrate health and eligibility based on data from medical examination center. It's evident that the consumer's data can be directly collected by the insurer, bypassing any intermediary representative. Both the consumer

[4] Parts of the Judgment Numbers are: Administrative Appeal Judgment No.14945 in Guangdong Province 2023; Administrative Appeal Judgment No.713 in Beijing City 2023; Administrative Appeal Judgment No.713 in Liaoning Province 2023; Administrative Appeal Judgment No.5216 in Shandong Province 2022; Administrative Appeal Judgment No.3768 in Shandong Province 2021;Administrative Appeal Judgment No.3768 in Shandong Province 2021;Administrative Appeal Judgment No.3409 in Liaoning Province 2021; Administrative Appeal Judgment No.2296 in Henan Province 2020;Administrative Appeal Judgment No.1132 in Hunan Province 2020, Administrative Appeal Judgment No.20276 in Sichuan Province 2020, Administrative Appeal Judgment No.8762 in Guizhou Province 2019, Administrative Appeal Judgment No.590 in Anhui Province 2019, Administrative Appeal Judgment No.9589 in Yunnan Province 2019, Administrative Appeal Judgment No.47 in Hubei Province 2018, Administrative Appeal Judgment No.63 in Guangdong Province in 2018, Administrative Appeal Judgment No.4370 in Guangdong Province 2017; Administrative Appeal Judgment No.1289 in Jilin Province 2017, Administrative Appeal Judgment No.3185 in Shandong Province 2017, Administrative Appeal Judgment No.6801 in Hubei Province 2017.

[5] The Insurance Salesman Regulation 2013 focuses on the qualifications, obligations and liabilities of a representative. Both the insurer and the representative are stipulated to be liable for the damage of customers. But there is no rules on the liability of the representative to the insurer.

[6] See *Shiyang Wen, Insurance Law (Law Press, 2016), pp.98.*

and the representative have limited capacity to conceal information, because the insurer can find it promptly and will not take the risk. Therefore, the representative, who is exactly only a service assistant on behalf of the insurer, is unable to help the consumer to make a misrepresentation. In this way, insurers can more effectively monitor their representatives in blockchain-based insurance.

The above functions of blockchain may become particularly advantageous in some high-risk insurance sectors. Not only does it mitigate the legal risks of misrepresentations, but it is also considered to be able to efficiently promote some high-risk insurance business. In Chinese market, verifying pre-contract information for insured parties has been particularly challenging, especially within agriculture insurance. Taking the poultry husbandry as an example. There are so many unpredictable risks such as a plague that can cause huge losses to farmers. Authorities have been urging insurance firms to provide coverage.[7] Therefore, it is a huge challenge for insurers to meet the needs of farmers. The crux is the difficulty of checking the actual situation of the poultry. Due to such a large amount and a short feeding procedure, it would not be easy to exactly confirm the insured quantity in pre-contract stage. The cost of settling claims is too high. Moreover, a lot of high-cost investigations may bring new risks to epidemic prevention. Evidently, significant uncertainties persist at every stage of poultry husbandry insurance. Therefore, less than 3% of farmers can have the coverage for their poultry in some provinces including Shandong. It is usual that most farmers are rejected by insurance firms because of the excessive and uncertain risks.

Now the situation is being solved in blockchain-based insurance. A notable milestone in China was the launch of the "Blockchain-based Insurance of Duck Farming" (BIDF) in 2018 by AnHua Agricultural Insurance Company Ltd. Specifically, the insurer builds a blockchain system and set up smart claim settlements on it. The applicant should be a farmer who would supply ducks to be slaughtered to a local leading enterprise under a contract. As the party placing the ordering and carrying out slaughtering and sales, the leading enterprise implement standardized management in the whole process. Prior to underwriting, the leading enterprise who is liable for collecting a part of material facts from the farmer, should also sign the insurance contract to ensure the authenticity of the data. Records on blockchain should include the number of deaths, feed consumption, vaccination records, and other relevant details provided by the farmer and the number of ducklings supplied by the leading enterprise. When it is time for the ducks to be slaughtered, the slaughterhouse of the leading enterprise also records the relevant information. When a claim is filed, the data of each group from different parties is calculated to verify the truth including the number of deaths per day. Consequently, the data

[7] Since the beginning of this century, the State Council, China Insurance Regulatory Commission and other relevant authorities have issued a series of guidelines and rules for the development of agricultural insurance especially in the area of the poultry husbandry, including the *Several Suggestions on the Reform and Development of the Insurance Industry* in 2006, the *Announcement on the Further Development of Agricultural Insurance* in 2009, the *Regulation of Agricultural Insurance* in 2013, and the *Guidance on Speeding Up the High-quality Development of Agricultural Insurance* in 2019, which explicitly encourage and require insurance firms to provide products and upgrade their business.

processing results can be trustful and serves as the basis for payment decision. The excessive and uncertain risks that insurers worried about are believed to be significantly mitigated.

Unlike previous practices that only required farmer to provide pre-contract information, the leading enterprise, who should also responsible for recording crucial data, rarely produces incorrect records. In addition to being bound by the agreement with the insurer, as the ordering party, the leading enterprise would prefer there is no misrepresentation. With the help of blockchain, data from the two parties can be analyzed to verify the truth. Therefore, insurers can more readily detect any misrepresentation within the data processing results and exercise the remedy right. It would significantly support the insurer in developing this high-risk business. Currently, an increasing number of similar products, such as coverage for chicken and goose farming, are being explored in the Chinese market.[8] This trend suggests that agriculture can become a huge emerging market for blockchain-based insurance.

4 Potential Impacts of Blockchain-Based Insurance on Judicial Issues in China

Will blockchain be helpful to insurers when applying Article 16 (3) and 16 (6)? The response to this question may not be entirely affirmative. As shown in Table 3.1, there are 390 cases focusing on Article 16 (4) or (5) are telling that the insurer may be also in a disadvantageous position during trial even if the applicant made a misrepresentation without any defenses. Insurers lost in 292 cases, significantly contributing to their high loss rate. It indicates that so many insurers remain at a disadvantage although they are not at fault in many cases. Furthermore, it is essential to further analyze the underlying reason for this judicial phenomenon, as illustrated in Table 3.2. Article 16 (2) states that the insurer shall have the right to rescind the insurance contract where the applicant breaches the duty of representation deliberately or by gross negligence. Pre-contract information required from the applicant is often referred to as 'material fact'.[9] Article 16 (4), (5) provide remedies for qualifying misrepresentations. In brief, there are four situations that will lead to different decisions for misrepresentations.

First, for deliberate misrepresentations, the insurer can rescind the contract and should be exempted from payment for the loss of the insured accident whether or not there is no causal connection between the occurrence of the insured event and the misrepresent fact.

---

[8] Linhao Qian, "Can Blockchain Solve Problems of Farming Risks", Financial Times, September 12, 2018.

[9] See Zili Ren, Xuefeng Zhou, *Insurance Law: Principles and Cases (Tsinghua University Press, 2010), pp.60.*

Second, in cases of grossly negligent misrepresentation, the insurer can rescind the contract and should be exempted from payment for the loss of the insured event if there is causal connection between the occurrence of the insured event and the misrepresent fact, although the premium must be refunded.

Three, for misrepresentations by gross negligence, the insurer cannot rescind the contract and should be liable for the loss of the insured event if there is no causal connection between the occurrence of the insured event and the misrepresent fact.

Four, for innocent misrepresentations, the insurer cannot rescind the contract and should be liable for the loss of the insured event.

Table 3.2 presents six types of cases with different main views of Judges. It is necessary to consider the first three type, which are the most numerous and controversial. In the first type, 52 cases show judge's ruling that the applicant deliberately made a misrepresentation, but not regarding a material fact, resulting in a lost for the insurer lost, accounting for 13.3%.[10] It seems that the judge consider the false information that the applicant represent as non-material fact, so it is not a qualifying misrepresentation though the insured is deliberate.[11] However, the definition of a material fact that would sufficiently influence the insurer's decision to accept the insurance or adjust the premium rate, may usually depends on the insurer's judgment. Most questions that insurers require applicants to answer are material facts. This suggests that the applicant should be deemed to have misrepresented the material fact if they deliberately give an incorrect answer on the proposal form. However, Judges believe they can decide what should be a material fact. For example, some chronic diseases such as diabetes and heart disease those insurers think would affect their decisions and specifically ask the applicant to represent are ruled as non-material facts by a lot of Judges. Similar issues arise in the second type of cases. In 84 cases, representing 21.5%, judges are inclined to deny the causal connection between the occurrence of the insured event and the misrepresent fact although when such a connection is readily apparent from both common sense and

[10] Parts of Judgment Numbers are: Administrative Appeal Judgment No.1133 in Jilin Province 2023; Administrative Appeal Judgment No.11810 in Guandong Province 2023; Administrative Appeal Judgment No.2687 in Hubei Province 2022; Administrative Appeal Judgment No.3837 in Neimenggu Province 2022; Administrative Appeal Judgment No.4547 in Jiangsu Province 2021; Administrative Appeal Judgment No.4547 in Jilin Province 2021; Administrative Appeal Judgment No.4275 in Shandong Province 2020; Administrative Appeal Judgment No.760 in Zhejiang Province 2020; Administrative Appeal Judgment No.283 in Liaoning Province in 2020; Administrative Appeal Judgment No.3572 in Hebei Province 2020; Administrative Appeal Judgment No.2889 in Anhui province 2020; Administrative Appeal Judgment No.895 in Henan province 2018; Administrative Appeal Judgment No.89 in Jilin province 2018; Administrative Appeal Judgment No.739 in Fujian province 2018; Administrative Appeal Judgment No.1160 in Sichuan province 2017; Administrative Appeal Judgment No.1160 in Sichuan province 2017.

[11] For example, the consumer answered no when the insurer asked him if he had any major illness, in fact he had been diagnosed with cancer. However, the Judge decided that the represented information is not not material fact. See China Ping an life Insurance Co. Ltd V. Jinkui Wang,Administrative Appeal Judgment No.5140 of Chifeng Intermediate People's Court of the Inner Mongolia Autonomous region in 2019. https://www.pkulaw.com/ [Accessed 1 March 2025].

professional knowledge.[12] Common examples include thyroid nodules and thyroid tumors,[13] renal insufficiency and uremia.[14] And in many cases where applicants are clearly deliberate, judges often classify their actions as gross negligence.[15] As for the third type in which there are 134 cases, applicants often argue that insurers are also at fault when it is difficult to find good reasons for their dishonesty.[16]

[12] Parts of Judgment Numbers are: Administrative Appeal Judgment No.855 in Jilin province 2023; Administrative Appeal Judgment No.871 in Shanxi province 2023; Administrative Appeal Judgment No.1056 in Liaoning province 2023; Administrative Appeal Judgment No.4678 in Sichuan province 2022; Administrative Appeal Judgment No.1707 in Beijing City 2022; Administrative Appeal Judgment No.2893 in Shandong province 2020; Administrative Appeal Judgment No.1987 in Inner Mongolia Autonomous region 2020; Administrative Appeal Judgment No.1133 in Zhejiang province 2020; Administrative Appeal Judgment No.902 in Hunan province 2020; Administrative Appeal Judgment No.2718 in Jiangsu province 2020, Administrative Appeal Judgment No.1045 in Shaanxi province 2019; Administrative Appeal Judgment No.2587 in Henan province 2019, Administrative Appeal Judgment No.4649 in Henan province 2019; Administrative Appeal Judgment No.287 in Jilin province 2018; Administrative Appeal Judgment No.430 in Anhui province in 2018, Administrative Appeal Judgment No.249 in Shanxi province 2018; Administrative Appeal Judgment No.3763 in Henan province 2017; Administrative Appeal Judgment No.6045 in Guangdong province 2017.

[13] For example, the consumer took out a disease insurance misrepresenting the fact that she had been diagnosed with thyroid nodules, and she suffered from thyroid cancer a year later. The Judge ruled that the insured did not breach the duty of representation because there is no causal connection between the thyroid nodules and thyroid cancer.See Hengqin Life Insurance Co., Ltd V. Zhang Xiuqin, Administrative Appeal Judgment No.2118 of Dezhou Intermediate People's Court of Shandong Province in 2020. https://www.pkulaw.com/ [Accessed 1 March 2025].

[14] For example, the consumer did not represent that he suffered from renal insufficiency when entering into the contract, and later he was diagnosed with uremia. The Judge ruled that the insured did not breach the duty of representation because the insurer could not prove that the uremia was caused by the renal insufficiency. See China people's Life Insurance Co., Ltd. V. Luo Weiguo, Administrative Retrial Judgment No. 454 of High People's Court of Jiangxi Province in 2020. [Accessed 1 March 2025].

[15] For example, the consumer bought a disease policy concealing that he had just been treated for lung cancer. But the Judge believed that the consumer made a misrepresentations by gross negligence. See China Pacific Life Insurance Co., Ltd. V. Mr. Xu, Administrative Appeal Judgment No.2118 of Tonghua Intermediate People's Court of Jilin Province in 2018. https://www.pkulaw.com/ [Accessed 1 March 2025].

[16] Parts of Judgement Number are: Administrative Appeal Judgment No.1089 in Gansu province 2023; Administrative Appeal Judgment No.403 in Jilin province 2023; Administrative Appeal Judgment No.6032 in Henan province 2022; Administrative Appeal Judgment No.17550 in Liaoning province 2022; Administrative Appeal Judgment No.3419 in Shandong province 2021; Administrative Appeal Judgment No.8601 in Guangdong province 2021; Administrative Appeal Judgment No.4207 in Henan province 2021; Administrative Appeal Judgment No.4122 in Hebei province 2020; Administrative Appeal Judgment No.2312 in Hunan province 2020, Administrative Appeal Judgment No.1112 in Guizhou province 2020; Administrative Appeal Judgment No.815 in Xinjiang Uygur Autonomous region 2020; Administrative Appeal Judgment No.1113 in Guizhou province 2020; Administrative Appeal Judgment No.3638 in Hebei province 2020; Administrative Appeal Judgment No.25032 in Henan province 2019; Administrative Appeal Judgment No.3344 in Heilongjiang province 2019; Administrative Appeal Judgment No.2738 in Henan province

Although these claims are often unreasonable – such as requiring insurers to ask questions both orally and in writing[17] – they are frequently upheld by judges. In some instances, judges insist that insurers should verify the authenticity of representations and would be liable if inaccuracies are present.[18] The third type accounts for 34.5 percent, which occupies more proportion than either the first or second type. The total number of these three types of cases amount to 270, constituting 69.3% as shown in Table 3.2. This may indicate that many judges are subjected to using the judicial discretion to protect the insured.

What will happen to this judicial issue when blockchain-based insurance comes? Some insurance firms believe that blockchain may provide a solution. This is because the judicial problem appears to be in fact-finding rather than applying provisions. As observed in the controversial cases, many judges usually draw conclusions unfavorable to insurers at the fact-finding stage. When applying the law, they strictly adhere to the provisions and made no inconsistent interpretation at all. It is conceivable that all relevant facts will be presented very clearly for the judge because all records are immutable and traceable as electronic evidence. The causal connection

Table 3.2 Details of 390 sample of cases focusing on Article 16 (4) or (5)

Judge's main views	Number		Percent	
The applicant deliberately made a misrepresentation but not for material fact.	52	292	13.3%	74.9%
The applicant was grossly negligent but there was no causal connection between the occurrence of the insured event and the misrepresent fact.	84		21.5%	
The applicant breached the duty but the insurer was also at fault.	134		34.5%	
The applicant was innocent.	22		5.6%	
The applicant deliberately misrepresented material fact.	60	98	15.4%	25.1%
The applicant was grossly negligent but there was causal connection between the occurrence of the insured event and the misrepresented fact.	38		9.8%	

(data elaborated by the author)

2019; Administrative Appeal Judgment No.2424 in Yunnan province 2019; Administrative Retrial Judgment No.1887 in Xinjiang Uygur Autonomous region 2019; Administrative Appeal Judgment No.96 in Henan province 2018; Administrative Appeal Judgment No.801 in Ningxia Hui Autonomous region 2017; Administrative Appeal Judgment No.16566 in Henan province 2017; Administrative Appeal Judgment No.1817 in Hubei province 2017; Administrative Appeal Judgment No.3342 Hubei province 2017.

[17] According to main views of insurance and theory in China, insurer can ask questions either orally or in writing. See Zili Ren, Xuefeng Zhou, supra note 9 at 59.

[18] See China life Insurance Co. Ltd V. Taichang Wang, Administrative Appeal Judgment No.7787 of Nanyang Intermediate People's Court of Henan province in 2019. https://www.pkulaw.com/ [Accessed 1 March 2025].

between hepatitis and liver cancer, for example, can easily be found on blockchain. Thus, Judges seem to be better positioned to address these issues because they may only need to consider how to apply laws before making a decision. This is indeed another prominent use case in which blockchain is helping courts handle electronic evidence.[19] Insurers expect that their disadvantageous position in judicial practice will gradually improve.

However, blockchain cannot fundamentally solve the judicial problem. Because the root of the problem lies in the legislation rather than in fact-finding. Why do so many judges use judicial discretion to protect applicants? The 2015 Act imposes severe penalties on applicants once they are found to have made misrepresentations, namely, contract rescission, no matter how much impact the misrepresentation has had on the insurer. In other words, applicants would lose their coverage even for gross negligence, despite the insurer potentially entering the insurance contract under different terms or at higher premiums. The judge in a case knows there would be only two results, either a complete loss of coverage for the consumer or full payment by the insurer. This is indeed a choice of win or lose all, making it difficult to balance the interests between the two parties even when the conflict is not particularly intense. Judges in many cases hope for more flexible solutions according to different situations. Current law only asks judges to make such a difficult choice of win or lose everything. As a result, judge often exercise judicial discretion to protect the insured rather than the insurer. It can be concluded that the root of such a judicial problem may come from current legislation. In this way, blockchain fails to address the root of the problem. This technology may be able to present the facts of the case clearly, but it cannot solve the problem of conflict caused by existing legislation.

Moreover, blockchain may exacerbate the problem. Furthermore, conflicts of interest between parties would be more exposed in blockchain-based insurance. Since all immutable and traceable information in it can serve as evidence showing what has happened in pre-contract stage, both the intention and behavior of the applicant will be clearer at a glance. Similarly, insurers believe that an applicant who makes a qualifying misrepresentation can hardly have a good reason to deny it. And it is more difficult for judges who are inclined to protect applicants during fact-finding to exercise judicial discretion. As evident in other similar problems in Chinese insurance law, it is foreseeable that judges will have to exercise judicial discretion in applying the law, which diverges from what the insurer expected, requiring them to interpret provisions inconsistently with their stipulated meanings. Therefore, the existing judicial problems may be aggravated in blockchain-based insurance because the legal effect of stipulated articles may be weakened. The problem of the legislation itself, which would be highlighted in blockchain, still requires improvements in the legal system and cannot be solved by technological development alone.

[19] For example, the Supreme People's Court in China enacted the Regulation on Certain Questions Concerning the Trial by Courts of the Internet in September 4, 2018. Article 11 of the regulation defines the legal effect of electronic data as electronic evidence in blockchain.

5 Future of the Representation Duty in Blockchain-Based Insurance

As for the representation duty, some Chinese scholars have proposed improvements to it since 2015,[20] and it would be extremely urgent when the wave of blockchain comes. Where should the focus of reform lie? As mentioned above, the key point of the problem is the remedy of the insurer in cases of qualifying misrepresentations under Article 16. Chinese insurers usually have only one option, that is to rescind the contract, even if they would have agreed to the contract under different terms or at a higher premium. Meanwhile, applicants' misrepresentations may not be serious enough to warrant rescission, but they still risk losing coverage entirely. A lot of conflicts between the insurer and the applicant, could have been addressed through a series of compromise plans. Therefore, offering a variety of remedies for the insurer would be of vital essence to reconciling this conflict in the future.

According to laws in many countries, including the UK, Germany, Italy and Switzerland, it has been popular to expand remedial options for insurers. The insurer's remedy is typically determined by what action it would have taken if the applicants had complied with their duty in cases of careless qualifying misrepresentation. In addition to rescinding the contract, there are compromises that keep the insurance contract valid without causing undue losses to the insurer, if the insurer would have entered into the contract. They include treating the contract as if it had been entered into under different terms specified by the insurer under the terms the insurer would have set (excluding terms relating to the premium)[21] and proportionately reducing the amount to be paid on a claim if the insurer would have charged a higher premium.[22] For China, the first step could be to introduce the proportionate reduction in payment under Article 16 of the 2015 Act. Specifically, the insurer may proportionately reduce the amount to be paid on a claim if the insurer would have entered the insurance contract but at a higher premium, as it may be the most feasible approach. Apart from the UK, this rule has been implemented in many other countries such as Germany,[23] France,[24] Italy.[25] Another important reason is that there is a proportionate reduction in payment under Chinese law. Article 32 of the 2015 Act allows the insurer to reduce the amount proportionately only when the misrepresentation of the insured's age does not substantially affect the validity of the contract. However, this claim by the insurer is not easily supported in judicial

---

[20] Can Luo, "Remedies of the Insurer for Misrepresentations in China", Financial Law Forum (2015) 90 215–228.

[21] See Consumer Insurance (Disclosure and Representation) Act 2012 in UK, Schedule 1, Article 6.

[22] See Consumer Insurance (Disclosure and Representations) Act 2012 in UK, Schedule 1, Article 7.

[23] See Section 157 of Insurance Contract Act in Germany.

[24] See Article L113-9 of Insurance Code in France.

[25] See Article 1893 of Italian Civil Code.

practice because many judges think that it conflicts with Article 16. There is not much room for applying this article because people's age information is often open in China.[26] Nevertheless, it is of great meaning as a good basis on which the rule of proportionate reduction in payment to be more widely applied. With the existing problem that is going to aggravate in blockchain-based insurance, this necessary reform would be particularly urgent.

What should be more concerned is a series of new issues caused by technology.

Blockchain-based insurance also benefits clients with the development of individualized service. As one of the most promising products in blockchain, the individualized insurance products is becoming a popular choice for applicants. When entering into an insurance contract, applicants may not need to represent material information because the insurer has processed their personal information on blockchain.[27] A typical example is Hongfu Health Insurance (HHI) in China. It is the world's first blockchain-based insurance product, in which every step from entering into a policy to reinsurance can be completed on the blockchain. Now that the insurer, who can collect a large amount of personal information in advance, does not rely on representations by applicants. It may not be necessary for applicants to make representations. Could they be exempted from this duty under these new circumstances? Current legislation in world is nearly absent on this question. In terms of the legal purpose, the duty was designed to enable insurers to efficiently gather material facts they need to know. When the blockchain technology is fully capable of solving the information asymmetry between parties, applicants' burden could be eased, especially for consumers who may become more vulnerable in the

[26] In China, the information of one's age including a woman's age is always open, which can be accessed by a lot of ways, such as visiting the website of her employer and other relevant institutes.

[27] The HHI has been developed since 2018, on a cooperation of Huatai Insurance Group as the insurer, China Property Reinsurance Co., Ltd as the reinsurer, and Beijing Fun In Funding Network Technology Co., Ltd who offers data support. By sharing trustworthy data on the blockchain, information of parties can be transferred between the various links and process. Relying on its famous program of Fun in Funding as one of the most popular social platform in China, the Fun In Funding company can easily get personal data of at least 550 million users. And these huge amounts of data would also be speedily accessed by the insurer in the blockchain. As a result, the insurer has been able to collect almost all material facts of their potential clients before entering the insurance contract, not needing to ask the applicant to answer a series of questions on a proposal form. Depending on a precise portrait for every potential insured by an intelligent analysis of the data, the insurer would directly provide the most suitable personalized insurance terms according to the needs of every client. For applicants, it would be a great product as they do not have to answer questions, just need to correct and confirm the personal data of their own. It looks much more convenient because consumers may skip the procedure of filling out the proposal form and just wait for a individualized insurance contract. Moreover, this individualized product is paid for a lower price with more coverage than general products of the same kind. The reason is that the transparency of information has greatly reduced a lot of costs. As one of the most outstanding achievements in "blockchain + insurance", such individualized product has been predicted to be one of the most competitive and popular products in future. There are, in fact, more gradually emerging in Chinese market.

new market. New rules on blockchain-based insurance are necessary to deal with such a new situation, including when and how the applicants can be exempted from the duty.

What will happen next? Will any new pre-contract duty replace the representation? Like HHI, the insurer may ask the applicants to correct and confirm material facts when entering into the contract. It seems that this confirmation, currently a business practice, could potentially become a new duty. Future laws ought to answer a series of new questions focusing on the new duty if its legal status is established. For example, how to handle the problem that the applicants fail to point out incorrect information when confirming it? The applicants who act deliberately should be punished and the insurer should have remedies such as rescinding the contract. As for reckless and careless confirmation, it may be considered unfair to punish the more vulnerable consumers especially given that reasonable care requirements are lower, as mentioned above. Could the insurer rescind the contract? Further legal discussion in the future will be required to balance the new conflicts of parties according to the development of the market. How to regulate data controller who always play a vital role in blockchain-based insurance? They should be regulated by both insurance and data laws, and how these laws should cooperate with each other must be considered. Individualized insurance will probably reconstruct the legal relationship between insurers and applicants at the pre-contract stage and blockchain-based insurance may be regarded as a new type of insurance contract.

6 Conclusion

Representation in blockchain-based insurance is likely to become a new issue in the future. It must be noted that these issues are only part of legal reforms in the future. More new issues of the representation duty will probably emerge with the growth of this evolving market. It will reflect a legislative process from sporadic articles to systematic laws. China's insurance law should urgently settle existing issues caused by current regulations before starting to think about new legislation. From this point of view, blockchain-based insurance is not only a serious challenge, but also a great opportunity for legal reform and improvement. Moreover, the contrast between powerful insurers and vulnerable consumers will be more highlighted on blockchain, completely different from the era of "utmost good faith" based on Marine Insurance Act 1906 in UK. With the use of blockchain technology, insurers may become exceedingly powerful. For example, they would not only hold an overwhelmingly dominant position in the insurance contract but also serve as controllers or processors of personal data. Should they be regulated strictly to meet the standard of "utmost good faith"? Will a new era of "utmost good faith" emerge?

The Impact of Copyright Law on Insurance Distribution: The Development of the Insurance Market Within Economic Efficiency/Inefficiency of Copyright Monopolies

Aleksandra Nowak-Gruca

1 Introduction

There is a tendency to expand the catalog of items protected by copyright to include products, such as an insurance package or an insurance project, which may constitute part of the so-called insurance product (in the broad sense of this concept). The question arises whether we can talk about a new category of copyright-protected items, such as insurance works, and what impact this may have on the insurance market and its distribution?

The subject of copyright is a work. In the legal systems of states, members of the Berne Convention and in the jurisprudence of the Court of Justice of the European Union (CJEU), it is assumed that a work is a new and individual intellectual product, characterized by originality. The concept of a work refers to an intangible good. A separate subject of law is the thing in which this good is recorded. However, EU doctrine and case law point to the lack of sufficiently precise criteria to distinguish works from other intellectual products that do not deserve copyright protection. Specifying the criteria for the subject of copyright protection in the legislation in

The publication/article presents the results of the Project no 033/EPC/2023/POT financed from the subsidy granted to the Krakow University of Economics.

A. Nowak-Gruca
Cracow University of Economics, College of Economics, Finance, and Law, Institute of Law, Poland
e-mail: nowaka1@uek.krakow.pl
ORCID: 0000-0003-2657-1939

P. Marano (ed.), *Emerging Legal Frontiers in Insurance*,
AIDA Europe Research Series on Insurance Law and Regulation,
https://doi.org/10.1007/978-3-032-09716-3_4

this field encounters numerous difficulties. The issues of deciding on the status of a work have been transferred to the courts, which means that most justifications in this matter are based on purely intuitive criteria and not on meeting a specific cognitive paradigm. This results in copyright protection for products containing a small amount of creative work and characterized by even a small degree of originality and individuality.

When determining the status of an "insurance product" as a work within the meaning of copyright law, an analysis should be carried out taking into account various aspects and layers of this product. For the purposes of this paper, an insurance product will be understood as a service defined in the insurance contract that includes the insurance protection provided to the client, along with additional services and the formal aspects of the product (e.g., the method and form of delivering the policy). In this context, we will consider which elements of this product and under what conditions (and when these conditions are met) may be covered by copyright protection.

The aim of the chapter is to examine the impact of copyright monopolies on the distribution of insurance. The research used the economic analysis of law (EAP) method. Therefore, first of all, it will be necessary to briefly present the EAP method itself and the concept of copyright monopoly in the context of assessing its economic effectiveness. Then I will be able to move on to the issues of copyright protection rules in the context of insurance products and the insurance distribution market. This, in turn, will enable the assessment of the impact of copyright law on the insurance market. Therefore, it will be possible to identify opportunities and threats related to extending copyright protection to insurance products (in the broad sense of this concept).

The economic analysis of law (EAL) uses the perspective of efficiency to evaluate legal norms. Therefore, the analyses undertaken in the text will be based on the assumption that in order for the law to „work" it must meet the requirement of at least a minimum level of economic efficiency. These functions belong to the primary functions of law. The extent to which these functions are realized will determine the final efficiency of the law and, consequently, the possibility of its implementation.

The principle of protection adopted in the paper refers to the universal principles of copyright law derived from the Berne Convention, which sets a minimum level of protection for its member states. Although the legal systems of individual countries differ in their methods of defining the concept of a work, the lack of clear criteria to distinguish protected works from other intellectual objects remains a common problem. In this context, the analyses conducted in the text can be generalized, and the conclusions drawn from the economic analysis of law (EAL) can be considered universal. Assuming that copyright encompasses the totality of rights ensuring creators' protection of their personal and economic interests arising from the creation of a specific work, economic analysis of law is a helpful method in determining the socially desirable (efficient) level/scope of these rights.

2 A Few Comments on the Research Method (EAL) and the Issue of the Effectiveness of Copyright Law

2.1 EAL

Considerations about the relationships between law and economics have appeared for centuries in philosophical and political works, for example, those of Machiavelli, Hobbes, and Smith. Although they are characterized by significant diversity, it can be stated that the fundamental question these thinkers sought to answer was how property rights and other rights were established – in a historical and functional sense, in various societies.

The paper employs the economic analysis of law (EAL). In the literature, it is assumed that EAL deals with the theory of rational choice in a world regulated by law (Kermestre 1999, p. 384). The concept of „law" is understood not only as norms of positive law of statutory rank but also as court rulings or customary law. The economic analysis of law also describes the ways in which law is created and the impact that law has on human behavior. EAL addresses the question of what effect the application of legal solutions will have in a reality where rational individuals adjust their actions to legal regulations when they encounter such regulations in their activities (Friedman 2000, p. 1). It also seeks to answer whether the effects of legal solutions meet societal needs. The economic analysis of law allows for the examination of the impacts of legal solutions both before the introduction of regulations (*ex ante*) and after their implementation (*ex post*) (Kaplow & Shavell 1999, p. 1) A key problem for economics is the question of how society can utilize limited resources to achieve the highest level of satisfaction for its needs. When such a level is reached, the economy is said to be efficient. The economic analysis of law uses the perspective of efficiency to evaluate legal norms. And the economic efficiency perspective will be adopted in this paper.

In traditional legal theory, a legal solution is considered effective when it achieves the goal that the legislator intended by adopting that solution. This understanding is often called formal because it does not specify what particular goal the law should achieve, only that the goal is realized. On the other hand, the economic understanding can be called material, as it defines the objective of the law. Economists set this objective by using the concept of efficiency, which refers to the value produced by society within limited resources. In the context of law, efficiency means that it should be designed to minimize the wastage of resources.

The structure of the legal system determines the functioning of the market: if this system is not well-designed and law enforcement is not effective, the market will not function properly. Economic literature identifies several conditions that are particularly important for the efficient functioning of the market. These include, primarily: stable property rights, rules governing the flow and access to information, and institutionalized rules and standards for conducting transactions. It is emphasized that the justification for state intervention in the economy, primarily through the establishment of laws, is market failures. The main causes of market failures include public goods, externalities, imperfect competition, and imperfect information. Therefore, the legal system becomes a necessary element in solving problems that arise in situations of free market failures. Importantly, from an economic point of view, people create specific rules of conduct when it brings them greater benefit than acting without such rules.

2.2 Diagram of an Economic Approach to Copyright

The subject of copyright is the work (creation). This concept refers to an intangible good. A separate subject of law is the object in which this good has been fixed. From the perspective of EAL, the most significant aspect is that the work is intangible and differs from other goods in two specific ways. First, the use of a given work does not diminish the amount available to others, so the marginal cost of providing the good to an additional person is zero. Second, the ability to exclude others from consuming the work is severely limited. These characteristics indicate that works can be classified as public goods, as opposed to private goods, which are characterized by rivalry in consumption and exclusivity in consumption. Private goods are allocated by the market to the consumer who is able to pay the market price (equilibrium price) for them.

For the economic analysis of copyright, it is significant that public goods, due to the aforementioned characteristics, are one of the causes of market failures because the free market is unable to supply an optimal quantity of them. In simple terms, this situation can be presented as follows: An individual creator will be interested in supplying only the quantity of works for which their private marginal benefit equals the price (marginal cost) of creating the work. This means that they will not consider the benefits that others gain from the creator supplying the work to the market. Works as public goods are characterized by non-excludability from consumption, or more precisely, the costs of excluding others from consuming these goods are very high. In the case of works, there are objective conditions that lead to avoiding the cost of producing the good, because it can be obtained without payment. This situation is known in economic theory as the free-riding problem. In the absence of legal protection, due to the nature of the work, creators practically have no means to prevent other members of society from consuming their work. There is therefore a significant risk that they will lack sufficient incentives to create, especially when there are many free-riders, as the prices paid by non-free-riders will not cover the costs of creation. The economic rationale for granting legal protection to creators can be explained as follows: if the economic interest of creators is not protected by law, they will lack sufficient motivation to create, as they will not recover the costs associated with their creative endeavors.

From the perspective of EAL, the fact of the law being in force generates various types of costs. Firstly, it is necessary to mention those related to maintaining the state apparatus and enforcing the law. Additionally, the protection granted by copyright law gives the creator monopolistic power over the created work. From the EAL perspective, monopolistic power over a work generates social loss due to monopoly, associated with producing an inefficient level of creativity. As a monopolist, the creator will demand a price for the work that exceeds the marginal cost of its production. The monopoly granted to the creator also generates other costs. Due to the fact that creativity is generally cumulative in nature, works often arise due to inspiration from existing works. Thus, due to the requirement to obtain the consent of the original creator to dispose of and use derivative works, the costs of creativity increase because of its cumulative nature, which can negatively impact the level of creativity in the future. This type of cost is referred to in the literature as the cost of reducing the future level of creativity due to its cumulative nature. Another type of cost is the so-called trading cost, associated with the expenses that a potential creator must incur to ensure that the work they intend to create is not already covered by copyright. Additionally, there are costs resulting from behaviors described in economics as „rent-seeking". The existence of economic rent is often caused by legal restrictions on entry into the industry. This is also the case for creators, to whom copyright grants monopolistic power over their works. Therefore, it is possible that in a situation where protection is threatened or abolished, the rights holders will be willing to spend significant resources to maintain their privileged position. From society's point of view, this type of expenditure is a social loss because it does not reflect the actual costs of creativity and does not lead to an increase in the number of works.

Following W.J. Gordon and R.G. Bone, the framework of the economic approach to copyright can be reduced to the following seven core conditions (Wendy, Gordon & Bone 2000):

1. The costs of creative activity are very high.
2. The cost of creating a „copy" of the work is lower than the cost of creating the original work incurred by the creator.
3. The difference between the costs of copying a work and the costs of creating it is so significant that the market price of the non-original work ("copy") will be much lower than the price the creator should set to recover the costs of creating the work.
4. Copies are perfect substitutes for the original work.
5. If there is no possibility of recovering the costs of creative activity, no creator will undertake this activity.
6. The creator can only recover the costs incurred in creating works through agreements for the transfer of economic copyrights and agreements for the use of the work (license agreements).
7. The creator does not have a market advantage over those distributing their works.

These assumptions seem to support arguments for providing legal protection to creators. Although many of them are highly debatable, formulating them serves as an excellent starting point for research on the economically efficient level of protection for creative works.

3 The Crisis of the Concept of a Work and the Problem of Copyright Protection Boundaries

Traditionally, within the scope of copyright law, personal rights and economic rights of the creator are distinguished. The differences in justifying the motivation for granting copyright protection have led to the development of two fundamental systems: the Romanic and the Anglo-Saxon. The French term „droits d'auteur" emphasizes the personal nature of the creator's rights. In this system, primary importance is given to protecting the personal bond between the creator and their work. On the other hand, the English term „copyright" primarily reflects the author's rights to exploit their work. The Anglo-Saxon system prioritizes the benefits to society as a whole over the interests of the author, with the emphasis placed on the right of the rights holder to grant or deny permission for copying and using the work.

In the literature on copyright law, the issue of defining the subject of protection repeatedly arises with varying intensity. For instance, it is pointed out that "the concept of a work has been blurred, copyright law has been devalued, and not only creative freedom but also freedom of economic activity has been restricted by creating numerous copyright monopolies" (Jasińska 2009). The difficulties in delineating the boundaries of copyright protection have been shifted to the courts, resulting in most justifications for recognizing or denying recognition as a work under copyright law being based on purely intuitive criteria rather than meeting a specific cognitive paradigm. There is noticeable terminological inconsistency in the case law. This is evidenced by the inclusion of creations with minimal creative input and characterized by even a slight degree of originality and individuality under this protection. Courts use various terms referring to the criteria for copyright protection and the work as the subject of protection: protectability, originality, individuality, individual character, creativity, novelty, manifestation of intellectual effort, intellectual product, creation. Furthermore, they present different concepts regarding the definition of protection criteria, such as the concept of objective novelty, subjective novelty, non-repeatability of sufficiently significant differences, or, as in the CJEU case law, "creative choices"[1]

The primary sources of problems in defining a work under copyright law are circumstances such as the great diversity of copyright objects, the difficult measurability of the necessary characteristics of a work, and the lack of precision in terms and criteria provided in copyright law. It is undoubtedly clear that the lack of precise features distinguishing objects protected by copyright from those that belong to the public domain results in significant legal uncertainty. In turn, legal uncertainty reduces the effectiveness of the law.

[1] See the CJEU rulings in the Infopaq case – C-5/08, or Football Association Premier League – C-403/08 and C-429/08.

4 Insurance Package and Other Forms of 'Insurance Products' as Works in Selected Court Decisions

In copyright law, whether we are referring to continental law or the Anglo-Saxon system, the principle is established that copyright protects the expression of ideas, but ideas, concepts, and principles themselves are not subject to legal protection. This means that the mere idea of an innovative insurance product will not be protected by copyright law. The ideas and concepts contained in the product can be used by competitors. Protection in the form of expression will apply to the formulations and formats used in the insurance product. The subject of copyright protection is a work that must exhibit originality in its mode of expression. According to the established doctrine, it must originate from a human and be a subjectively new product of intellect. Copyright is divided into personal rights and economic rights. Personal rights are non-transferable and can only be held by the creator. According to the established principle in copyright law, the creator must be a natural person – an individual human being. Economic rights are time-limited (in European Union countries, they expire 70 years after the creator's death). Economic rights are transferable and subject to inheritance. They may belong to the employer (cesio legis) if the work was created as part of the obligations arising from an employment relationship. In such cases, we refer to employee copyright.

Insurance products are most often created by insurance companies or insurance distributors. Such a work may have more than one creator, and from the perspective of copyright law, we would then discuss co-authorship. A joint work exists when two or more individuals contribute their individual and original input to create the work. The creation of a joint work may arise from factual actions, such as participating in and collaboratively executing the work, or it may result from an agreement, including a relevant contract.

Regarding the potential attribution of copyright in the case of insurance works, according to the principle that only a natural person can be a creator, personal copyright rights will belong to the individuals responsible for creating the work. Economic rights may belong to the insurance company, for example, if the work was created as part of obligations arising from an employment relationship or as a result of the transfer of copyright by the creator (co-creators). Economic rights may also belong to the agent or broker who created a specific insurance product that meets the characteristics of individual creativity. If the insurance distributor acts as a co-producer, the principles regarding product oversight and management should take into account issues related to the potential authorship of the work or those fragments that meet the necessary criteria for protection through creativity. However, as previously indicated, there is a lack of sufficiently precise criteria to distinguish protected works from those intellectual objects that do not meet the originality criteria.

Insurance plays a crucial role in the financial market. The insurance activities, which involve the execution of insurance operations related to offering and providing protection against the risks of unforeseen events, differ significantly from the nature of services offered by other financial institutions such as banks, investment fund companies, or brokerage firms. The specific characteristics of insurance products – namely their intangible nature and complex structure – complicate the assessment regarding the applicability of copyright protection.

When evaluating insurance products from the perspective of copyright law, it is essential to consider the established principle that ideas, concepts, and notions are not subject to legal protection. Only the expression of a work can be protected by copyright. Therefore, in the case of a work derived from a broad range of insurance products, it is necessary to distinguish between the business idea, concept, or notion and its method of expression. As noted by *A. R. Luciano*, another important factor in the context of insurance policies is that much of the terminology can be classified as "specialized insurance terms". When the only original (or copyrightable) aspect of a work resides in its literal expression (rather than its fundamental essence or structure), a significant degree of similarity, approaching identity, is necessary to establish copyright infringement. In conducting copyright qualifications, the author proposes the application of a "sliding scale" analysis. Utilizing this approach in the context of an insurance policy could aid the court in differentiating between unprotected ideas and protected expressions, as well as in appropriately balancing competitive policies. For instance, certain insurance provisions, such as definitions or specific clauses regarding the scope of coverage, may be articulated in a limited manner due to their established legal significance or consequences. Consequently, even a literal reproduction of these provisions may not be sufficient to constitute an infringement. Conversely, other provisions may be expressed in diverse ways. In such cases, according to the "sliding scale" analysis, these provisions would warrant greater protection, as the idea and its expression are more easily separable (Luciano 1984, pp. 419–434).

When determining the status of an "insurance product" as a work within the meaning of copyright law, it is necessary to conduct an analysis that considers various aspects and layers of this product, especially in the context of the creation of such a product. The criteria for distinguishing an "insurance product" should encompass the marketing aspect, the legal aspect (understood as the structure of the insurance contract and general terms of insurance), and the economic-mathematical aspect (concerning economic efficiency, the amount of premiums, and the size of benefits) (Sokołowska 2013, p. 84).

In case law, there have been approaches granting copyright protection to insurance product or its elements. The originality of such intellectual objects manifested, for example, in the creative combination of insurance products, which involves their specific selection and integration into a whole, as well as the creation of a special, simplified, and entirely new tariff structure for them, and also in giving the package a simplified and useful form for agents. In assessing whether the criteria for copyright protection were met, it was also crucial that the project had no counterpart in the insurance market, although the general formula of an insurance package is well-known in that market.[2]

[2] See Judgment of the Supreme Court of Poland, February 3, 2017 (Case No. II CSK 400/16).

In the case of Dorsey v. Old Surety Life Insurance Co.,[3] the court articulated that the copyright associated with life insurance policies does not pertain to the right to use specific words or to employ the ideas they convey. Instead, it encompasses the unique arrangement of words chosen by the author to articulate those ideas. Moreover, copyright protection does not cover <<isolated ‘key words,’ ‘themes,’ ‘arrangements,’ or ‘plans’>>. These elements represent abstract ideas rather than tangible expressions and, in a technical context, offer minimal, if any, protection.

In the context of judicial precedent, a innovative idea involving combining two different types of insurance into a single package with a new tariff and service approach (a ready-made insurance package project) may be recognized as a work, despite the technical knowledge of bundling insurances into packages being known previously. The originality was found in the fact that the insurance package project extended beyond a simple combination of two packages. The preparation of the project took considerable time (several months), involved collaboration among several individuals, and initially included a licensing fee for its use. This package resulted in a specific product ready for sale and presentation in training sessions to employees and agents, rather than just being a conceptual idea. Furthermore, in the court’s assessment, the qualification of the plaintiff’s development as an insurance product under current regulations was irrelevant for granting copyright protection.[4]

The insurance project, constituting the general terms and conditions of comprehensive insurance for the consequences of accidents and cyclist’s liability, has also been recognized as a work within the meaning of copyright law.[5] In this case, we are dealing with the aforementioned insurance project, which is the subject of the lawsuit, as an independent work and an inspired work created based on it (the general terms of cyclist insurance). It is worth noting that the court of first instance did not recognize the insurance project as a work, stating that it lacked individuality; however, this position was not upheld in subsequent rulings. Therefore - interestingly and significantly from the perspective of the issue addressed in the article - the matter of qualifying the insurance project, constituting the general terms and conditions of comprehensive insurance for the consequences of accidents and cyclist’s liability, for copyright protection in its unfinished form (where only sketch proposals were placed alongside the finalized clauses), as well as the matter of such qualification for the subsequently created insurance product based on the consolidated forms of the template (project), was not in doubt.

First of all, it should be noted that the opinion of court-appointed experts was of significant importance for judicial decisions. Additionally, in determining the necessary feature of a work, namely the feature of creativity with an individual character,

[3] See Dorsey *v.* Old Surety Life Ins. Co., 98 F.2d 872 (10th Cir. 1938).

[4] Judgment of the Court of Appeal in Szczecin, February 11, 2016 (Case No. I ACa 722/15).

[5] See judgment of the Supreme Court of the Republic of Poland of February 27, 2009 (Case no V CSK 337/08).

the courts used the criterion of statistical uniqueness. This criterion was formulated in German doctrine by M. Kummer (Kummer 1968, p. 30), and it seems that due to its potentially objective nature, it has gained popularity in judicial decisions regarding the granting or denial of copyright protection. According to M. Kummer's concept, the so-called statistical uniqueness test requires, in the first stage, determining whether an identical object has been created before. An affirmative answer eliminates the individual character of the work, while a negative answer moves the examination to the next level. Here, it must be determined, using statistical methods, whether it is likely that an identical work could be created by another person in the future. In the aforementioned decisions, the courts, citing this criterion, do not sufficiently explain why it has been met in the given case. They merely limit themselves to the laconic statement that there is no likelihood of the given creation being made by another person. With such an approach, it is difficult to consider that the granting of copyright protection has been adequately justified in the cases in question. It must be emphasized that merely stating the presence of the feature of creativity (originality) or individuality in a given creation, without explaining the reasons/circumstances of its occurrence, cannot be considered sufficient for granting or denying copyright protection. In this context, the granting of protection to an insurance package or insurance projects can hardly be considered adequately justified. Nonetheless, beyond the issue of the lack of a methodologically consistent method of justifying the qualification for copyright protection, meeting a certain cognitive paradigm, the cited decisions highlight a highly significant social issue: the creation of exclusive rights to human intellectual creations in the context of the excessive monopolization of broadly understood creative efforts. It should be noted that the liberal approach to broadly defining the feature of creativity with an individual character is present not only in the jurisprudence of Polish courts but also in other countries. This approach can also be seen in the stance of the CJEU (Rosati 2013, p. 97).

Interestingly, in the literature on insurance law, the inclusion of insurance packages and other components of broadly understood insurance products under copyright protection has been met with favorable assessments. In contrast, in the doctrine of copyright law, the excessive expansion of the scope of such protection is met with strong criticism. In my opinion, this divergence of views may stem from a misunderstanding of the nature of copyright protection, and most importantly, the economic consequences arising from this fact.

The cited rulings seem to expand the catalog of works protected by copyright to include creations such as an insurance package, an insurance project, or even the terms of reference, which, in a broad sense, can be a component of the so-called insurance product. This raises the question of whether, in the future, we will be able to speak of a new category of copyrightable objects, such as insurance works.

From the perspective of economic analysis, a work, due to its intangible nature, differs from other goods in the economic sense in two specific ways. First, the use of a given work does not reduce the amount available to others, so the marginal cost of providing the good to another person is zero. Second, the ability to exclude others from consuming the work is severely limited. These characteristics indicate that works can be classified as public goods, which contribute to market failures because the free market is unable to supply an optimal quantity of them. In simple terms, this situation can be described as follows: an individual creator will be interested in providing only such a quantity of works where their private marginal benefit equals the price (marginal cost) of producing the work, meaning they will not consider the benefits others derive from their work being available on the market.

The protection granted by copyright gives the creator monopolistic control over the produced work. The assumption that the creator has monopolistic control implies that they will supply a quantity of works where the price is higher than the marginal cost. Therefore, when the creator behaves like a monopolist, the price of the supplied works is higher, and their "production" is lower. As a result, consumers are in a worse situation than if the creator operated in a competitive market.

Economic research clearly shows the inefficiency of monopolies, and copyright protection, in addition to the inequities resulting from monopolies, generates a range of other costs, including the significant issue of access to knowledge. The costs of operating such a protection system are greater when there is more uncertainty regarding the application of the law, especially when the subject of protection cannot be precisely defined.

In the case of works where the criterion of individual creativity is replaced by the criterion of novelty, such as insurance packages, the risk of restricting the freedom to conduct business through the creation of copyright monopolies appears to be significant. In situations of uncertainty about the ability to use an insurance project or other elements of a broadly understood "insurance product", due to the costs of enforcing the law, there is a serious risk of refraining from economic activity (the so-called chilling effect). Copyright holders can increase their profits by blocking competitors from conducting business activities merely by possessing exclusive rights. For example, an insurance distributor, often a broker, includes a clause in the agreement stating that the policy draft they have prepared is protected by copyright. This aims to prevent the client from seeking another policy draft and entering into a contract through a different intermediary.

However, courts must refrain from the error of reflexively denying protection in situations where such denial would not contribute to incentivizing the creation of new works or preserving the underlying idea within the public domain. While it is unlikely that exact duplication of any segment of standard insurance products would suffice to support a finding of infringement, courts should nonetheless be prepared to employ the analytical flexibility necessary to balance all relevant interests (Luciano 1984, pp. 419–434).

5 Summary

Insurance plays a very significant role in the financial market. The insurance activity, which involves performing insurance operations related to offering and providing protection against the risks of unforeseen events, differs significantly from the services offered by other financial institutions, such as banks, investment fund companies, or brokerage houses. The specificity of insurance product – intangible form and complex structure – complicates issues related to assessing whether copyright protection applies or not.

In assessing the status of an "insurance product" as a work under copyright law, it is imperative to undertake a comprehensive analysis that takes into account the diverse aspects and dimensions of the product, particularly regarding its creation. The criteria for defining an "insurance product" should incorporate the marketing dimension, the legal framework (which includes the structure of the insurance contract and the general terms of insurance), as well as the economic and mathematical considerations (related to economic efficiency, premium amounts, and benefit levels).

The problem of establishing criteria that will allow for precisely delineating the limits of copyright protection has been raised for years in the copyright doctrine. The clear approach in court decisions, also at the European level, to lowering the requirements for granting the status of a work to given works is also widely criticized. Although it is impossible to resolve these dilemmas in the article, in the light of the latest rulings creating exclusive rights to components of broadly understood insurance products (such as, for example, an insurance package or an insurance project), it was worth pointing out the economic consequences of such decisions.

Lowering the level of creativity required by the courts to cover a given product of the human mind with copyright protection results in the fact that the private benefits for the copyright holder (and often it will not be the creator himself) do not correspond to the social benefits. The so-called privatization of knowledge may lead to serious distortions of competition. In the case of works with a negligible level of creativity and individuality, the social costs of legal protection significantly outweigh the benefits of its introduction, therefore the recently observed tendency to extend copyright protection towards information protection should be considered an economically ineffective solution, which in a broader perspective may limit the development of the insurance market and seriously impede the free movement of insurance intermediation services.

In the light of the ever-increasing legal complexities related to the financial market, from the perspective of the economic efficiency of law, we should strive for the greatest possible legal certainty and transparency. As shown in the article, the most serious problem facing copyright today is the problem with defining protection and distinguishing objects protected by copyright from those that belong to the public domain. Introducing copyright protection to the financial market does not seem to be a good idea because, as EAL shows, the social costs of these solutions may turn out to be too high. The uncertainty related to the granting/refusal of copyright protection may result in long, complicated and costly court disputes as to whether a given business idea can actually be legally protected. The copyright doctrine is well acquainted with the problem of ineffectiveness of protection related to ideas, ideas and concepts. This approach significantly limits the number of creative initiatives and shifts the competitive struggle from the market to courtrooms. Therefore, it is important to demonstrate the ineffectiveness of authorial monopolies, especially where we are not dealing with art, but rather with works of the so-called references. Leaving broadly understood insurance products and their components in the public domain seems to be a more effective solution from the perspective of EAL. In the context of access to knowledge, technology, and intangible goods, from the perspective of economic analysis of law (EAL), leaving certain resources in the public domain can lead to significant social benefits and mitigate the negative effects of knowledge monopolization. These effects include the reduction of transaction costs, the distortion of competition, the chilling effect on knowledge utilization, and the increased social costs associated with legal uncertainty. Keeping insurance products within the public domain allows for a balance to be struck between protecting authors' rights and serving the public interest.

This does not mean that intellectual property protection should be completely abandoned in the insurance market. Nevertheless, copyright does not seem to be the best protection instrument. Copyright protection seems to be risky due to the social costs mentioned in the article, related to the search effect, chilling effect and others related to the general inefficiency of copyright monopolies. However, courts should avoid the mistake of automatically denying protection in cases where such a denial does not effectively promote the creation of new works or safeguard the underlying ideas. Although it is improbable that the precise replication of any component of standard insurance products would warrant a determination of infringement, it remains essential for courts to maintain the analytical flexibility required to weigh all pertinent interests appropriately.

It is also worth paying attention to the possibilities of protection under trademark law or possibly patent law. The conditions for this protection are much more transparent, applications are filed upon request and under the control of patent offices, and require a fee. Therefore, investments in this area can be more thoughtful and establish exclusivity where it is needed from the perspective of market strategy.

References

Friedman, D. (2000). *Law's order: what economics has to do with law and why it matters*, Princeton University Press, p. 1..

Gordon, W. J., & Bone, R. G. (2000). Copyright, in: 2 *Encyclopedia of Law and Economics* 189 (B. Bouckaert & G. De Geest ed.).

Jasińska, K. (2009). Glosa do wyroku SN z dnia 27 lutego 2009 r., V CSK 337/08, LEX/el. 2009. https://sip-1lex-1pl-1ym3yi90k0381.hanbg.uek.krakow.pl/#/publication/385984757/jasinska-katarzyna-glosa-do-wyroku-sn-z-dnia-27-lutego-2009-r-v-csk-337-08?keyword=K.%20Jasi%C5%84ska,%20Glosa%20do%20wyroku%20SN%20z%20dnia%2027%20lutego%202009%20r.,%20V%20CSK%20337%2F08&cm=SFIRST (dostęp: 2025-11-26 20:36)

Kaplow, L., & Shavell, S. (1999). *Economic analysis of law*, Working Paper Nr 6960, National Bureau of Economic Research, Cambridge, p. 1.

Kermestre, H. (1999). *Methodology: General, [w:] Encyclopedia of Law and Economics*, B. Bouckaert, G. De Geest (red.), p. 384..

Kummer, M. (1968). *Das Urheberrechtlich Szűtzbare Werk*, Berlin, p. 30.

Luciano, A. R. (1984). Copyright protection for insurance policies, The Forum (Section of Insurance, Negligence and Compensation Law, American Bar Association). *JSTOR* vol. 19, no. 3, pp. 419–434.

Rosati, E. (2013). *Orginality in EU Copyright, Full Harmonization through Case Law*, p. 97. Cheltenham: Edward ElgarPublishing.

Sokołowska, D. (2013). "Produkt ubezpieczeniowy" jako przedmiot prawa autorskiego, *Wiadomości Ubezpieczeniowe* no. 3, p. 84.

Part II
Jurisdictional Perspectives and Cross-Border Insurance Market Dynamics

Cross-Border (Life) Insurance Business: A Constant Goal with (Almost) Impossible Legal Obstacles

Stephan Stolz

1 Introduction

Already thirty years have passed since the liberalization and the associated opening of the insurance market in the European Union on 1 July 2024.[1] One of the main objectives of the European Union has been being ever since the realization of a single European market. Better rates, lower costs and access to a broader, more diverse, more innovative and, more recently, a more sustainable product range are among the benefits often attributed to the single European market.[2] These targets should also be achieved for customers of insurance products, while at the same time creating market and growth opportunities for companies in the insurance sector. The policy of minimum harmonization initially pursued in this context has been abandoned in

The author is an in-house counsel of a life insurance company and a PhD student at the University of Exeter. The (legal) views expressed in this article represent solely the personal views of the author.

[1] Comprehensive information on the deregulation of the European insurance market: Schäfer, (2020) 11; Littbarski,(2024) 28; Basedow, (2014) 1; European Consumer Centre Germany, 'The European Single Insurance Market -Cross-Border Insurance Contracts: Conclusion or Exclusion? What Does the Market for Cross-Border Insurance Products Look like for Consumers in the Year 2014?' <https://www.cec-zev.eu/fileadmin/Media/PDF/publications/Etudes-Rapports_FR/Etude_Assurances-resume_EN.pdf> accessed 16 March 2025; Gamarra (2008), I; Mark J Boléat and Marc J Boléat, (1995) 45.

[2] European Commission, 'EU Single Market - The Single Market: Europe's Best Asset in a Changing World' <https://commission.europa.eu/document/download/fa404637-9fde-446d-a9b0-cab136d8acd3_en?filename=factsheet_single_market.pdf> accessed 16 March 2025; Giordano Mion and Dominic Ponattu, 'Estimating Economic Benefits of the Single Market for European Countries and Regions' <https://www.bertelsmann-stiftung.de/fileadmin/files/BSt/Publikationen/GrauePublikationen/EZ_Study_SingleMarket.pdf> accessed 16 March 2025.

S. Stolz
University of Exeter, Exeter, United Kingdom
email: ss1161@exeter.ac.uk

P. Marano (ed.), *Emerging Legal Frontiers in Insurance*,
AIDA Europe Research Series on Insurance Law and Regulation,
https://doi.org/10.1007/978-3-032-09716-3_5

favor of complete harmonization; at least partially in insurance supervisory law due to the increasing support for internationally oriented supervisory standards, particularly following the experiences of the financial crisis. In this regard, the European legislator stated in recital 11 of Directive 2009/138, better known as 'Solvency II'[3]: *'It is therefore appropriate to bring about such harmonisation as is necessary and sufficient to achieve the mutual recognition of authorisations and supervisory systems, and thus a single authorisation which is valid throughout the Community and which allows the supervision of an undertaking to be carried out by the home member state.'*[4] As a result, the European Union has addressed the harmonization and strengthening of the European insurance market by initiatives such as PRIIPs Regulation,[5] IDD Directive,[6] and, most recently, the comprehensive ESG legislation,[7] as well as PEPP Regulation[8] to name just the major regulations governing life insurance.

Although insurance companies based in a member state of the European Union have been authorized to offer their products in other member states for 30 years now, both by the Lisbon Treaty and by various regulations and directives, under the freedom of establishment and/or the freedom to provide services, from a consumer's point of view, even in 2024, insurance markets are still largely strongly dominated by national insurance products.[9]This is especially due to the fact that insurers mainly offer their products only in their home markets. This article argues that legal obstacles are still a major hurdle for (life) insurers to offer their products cross-border.

Concerning life insurance, broader access to products seems particularly important from a customer's point of view. Life insurance has various functions. For example, it provides financial resources to support the policyholder's family after death. However, it also provides financial resources for support (through investments)

---

[3] Directive 2009/138/EC of the European Parliament and of the Council of 25 November 2009 on the taking-up and pursuit of the business of Insurance and Reinsurance (Solvency II).

[4] ibid.

[5] Regulation (EU) No 1286/2014 of the European Parliament and of the Council of 26 November 2014 on key information documents for packaged retail and insurance-based investment products (PRIIPs).

[6] Directive (EU) 2016/97 of the European Parliament and of the Council of 20 January 2016 on insurance distribution (recast)Text with EEA relevance.

[7] European Commission, 'Sustainability-Related Disclosure in the Financial Services Sector' <https://finance.ec.europa.eu/sustainable-finance/disclosures/sustainability-related-disclosure-financial-services-sector_en> accessed 16 March 2025; 'EU Taxonomy for Sustainable Activities - European Commission' <https://finance.ec.europa.eu/sustainable-finance/tools-and-standards/eu-taxonomy-sustainable-activities_en> accessed 16 March 2025.

[8] Regulation (EU) 2019/ of the European Parliament and of the Council of 20 June 2019 on a Pan-European Personal Pension Product (PEPP).

[9] For example, the number of insurers operating in Germany with a European passport has declined significantly over the last ten years, as shown in a recent presentation by BaFin and the German Insurance Association. According to BaFin, the service and/or branch office business of EEA insurers accounted for just 5.1% of the total direct insurance business in Germany in 2021, Theis, (2023).

during the policyholder's life in conjunction with a death benefit.[10] In addition, life insurance has an essential function as security for loans. Above all, however, the focus is on providing financial resources for the policyholder's retirement phase (old-aged provision). As part of the publication of the PEPP Regulation, the European legislator once again pointed out that although households in the EU have the highest saving rates worldwide, most of these savings are available at short notice in bank accounts. Old-age pensions which are typical for life insurance in many member states or are at least regularly available as an option for capital life insurance products, represent a significant proportion of pensioners' income. Moreover, for many people, adequate old-aged provision makes the difference between a comfortable life and poverty in old age. If more of the savings available in the European Union could be channeled into long-term investment products, such as voluntary pension products aimed at long-term retirement savings, both the whole economy (not only insurers) as well as individuals would profit massively. Individuals would in this regard especially benefit from higher returns and more adequate old-aged provision.[11] According to the European Commission, a more extensive European market for private pension provision would also help to ensure that more funds are available for institutional investors and investment in the economy.[12] In this context, the European Commission once again explicitly emphasized that the single market for private pension products is still not working.[13] _The example of life insurance, in particular, underscores the significant challenges in achieving a harmonized European single insurance market; a goal which has yet to be achieved. Instead, recent developments sometimes seem to be going in the opposite direction, as insurers shy more and more away from offering their products cross-border.[14]

Whether consumers have access to life insurance products from foreign insurers in their national market ultimately results from the entrepreneurial decision of individual insurers based in other member states of the European Union. They decide to offer a particular product across borders on the same basis as they decide for (purely) national product launches. They make a business decision based on all opportunities and risks associated with it. Decisive parameters include the target market's size and potential customers' purchasing power. However, experience in recent years has also shown that the high legal hurdles that still exist for cross-border product launches in the European Union represent a significantly greater challenge than in a purely national environment and often lead to cross-border business being abandoned in cases of doubt or - at least initially - being put on the back burner behind other company projects. This paper provides an initial overview of the legal

[10] BaFin, 'Lebensversicherungen' <https://www.bafin.de/DE/Verbraucher/Versicherung/Produkte/Leben/lebensversicherung_node.html> accessed 16 March 2025.

[11] Recital 13 Regulation (EU) 2019/ of the European Parliament and of the Council of 20 June 2019 on a pan-European Personal Pension Product (PEPP).

[12] Recitals 7 and 11 ibid.

[13] ibid.

[14] J David Cummins, María Rubio-Misas and Dev Vencappa, (2017) 68.

challenges that arise in these decision-making processes of insurance companies. In addition, this paper identifies potential improvements from a legal perspective that could help to strengthen the cross-border life insurance business. Moreover, to provide the reader with a complete overview, the Paper emphasizes briefly legal issues the European regulator needs to address reviewing the PEPP regulation.

2 Regulatory Aspects of Cross-Border Life Insurance Business

2.1 Single License Principle

From the insurance company's perspective as a product provider in cross-border business, the first question is what is required to be authorized to offer products in another member state of the European Union. If an EU or EEA member state grants a licence to an insurer to do business, this licence is valid in all EU or EEA states (Art. 14 and 15 Solvency II). It is, therefore, a 'European passport' (so-called 'single licence principle').[15] The single licence principle is based on the mutual recognition of authorizations and supervisory systems within the EU.[16] An authorization granted from the supervisory authority of one member state entitles the insurance company to operate in all member states within the insurance lines for which it has been granted authorization.[17] The single licence principle is a key component of harmonizing insurance supervisory law in the EU and promotes the freedom to provide services ('FoS') and the freedom of establishment ('FoE') in the insurance sector. It enables insurance companies to operate across borders without having to apply for a separate licence in each member state. The supervisory authority of the home state is responsible for the financial supervision of the insurance company, which includes solvency criteria and the formation of technical provisions.[18] This principle was introduced as part of the third generation of directives and is now regulated in

[15] Diehl, (2022) 111; Mönnich, (2015) 49; BaFin, 'EU/EEA Insurers' <https://www.bafin.de/EN/Aufsicht/VersichererPensionsfonds/Zulassung/EU-EWR-Versicherer/eu_ewr_versicherer_node_en.html> accessed 16 March 2025; FMA Austria, 'EU-Pass für Kreditinstitute, Versicherungen und Wertpapierfirmen' <https://www.fma.gv.at/glossar/eu-pass-fuer-kreditinstitute-versicherungen-und-wertpapierfirmen/> accessed 16 March 2025; Baranowska-Zając, (2014).

[16] Companies domiciled outside the EU or a contracting state of the EEA (third-country companies are not subject to the single license principle like EU/EEA insurers). Instead, they require a license from the relevant supervisory authority in each EU member state in which they wish to conduct insurance business.

[17] Authorization is granted separately for each class of direct insurance in accordance with Annex I Part A or, as far as life insurance is concerned, Annex II Solvency II. It shall cover the entire class in each case unless the applicant intends to cover only part of the risks of that class.

[18] In this context, the German Federal Administrative Court has also determined that the supervisory authority of the home Member State is solely responsible for all reorganisation and liquidation measures. The home country authority must exclusively apply the substantive law of the home Member State. (*BVerwG, 23 3 2011 - 8 C 47/09* [2011] BVerwG 8 C 47/09, 2011 NJW-RR 1250).

the Solvency II Directive. It forms the basis for the realization of a single European market for insurance, which is based on the FoE/FoS and the harmonization of legal systems. The supervisory authority of the country of domicile is primarily responsible for ongoing supervision within the EU. It is also primarily authorized to intervene. However, in addition, the supervisory authority of the host country is – within the framework of general legal supervision – to a limited extent responsible for supervising the business activities of an insurance company under FoS and FoE. If necessary, the host country supervisory authority may carry out checks and requests the insurance company to take appropriate measures. In the event of non-compliance, the supervisory authority informs the authority of the home state. If the latter also fails to take binding measures against the insurance undertaking, the authority of the host state may, as a last resort, make binding decisions against the insurance undertaking in accordance with Art. 155 Solvency II.

If an insurance company domiciled in an EU member state wishes to offer its life insurance or capitalization products in another member state, it first is necessary following the provisions of the Consolidated Life Insurance Directive 2002/83/EC, which was incorporated into Solvency II, for the company to conduct a notification procedure.[19] The conditions for the acceptance include the insurer's notification that it wishes to establish a branch in the territory of another member state (or offer its products under freedom of services)[20] which requires inter alia the submission of certain documents required by the respective supervisory authority as part of this notification procedure.[21] The purpose of the notification procedure is to provide the supervisory authorities of both the home and the host ember State with the information required for joint supervision;[22] it is mainly similar to the procedure for notifying the commencement of the freedom to provide services.[23] The supervisory

[19] The European fundamental freedoms, including FoS and FoE, imply a ban on discrimination and are committed to creating a level playing field in the single market. The freedoms also prohibit restrictions, which are intended to ensure access to the markets of other member states for (life) insurers based in the Union and facilitate the corresponding cross-border demand.

[20] Whether the company should conduct its business activities in the host country under FoE or FoS must be assessed on a case-by-case basis. The demarcation in this respect is not always easy. In abstract terms, the demarcation criterion can be described as whether the production itself - then establishment - or only the insurance product - then services - crosses the border, Manuel Baroch Castellvi, 'VAG § 57 Versicherungsgeschäfte Über Niederlassungen Oder Im Dienstleistungsverkehr' in Oliver Brand and Manuel BarochCastellvi (eds), *Versicherungsaufsichtsgesetz* 2nd edn, (2024) 10.

[21] 'Notification Procedure: BaFin, Exchange of Information among EU/EEA Insurance Supervisors' <https://www.bafin.de/SharedDocs/Veroeffentlichungen/EN/Fachartikel/2018/fa_bj_1805_Notifikation_en.html> accessed 16 March 2025; BaFin, 'Hinweise für die Tätigkeit in den EU/EWR-Staaten' <https://www.bafin.de/SharedDocs/Veroeffentlichungen/DE/Merkblatt/VA/mb_100208_taetigkeiteuewr_va.html > accessed 16 March 2025; Diehl, (2020) 18.

[22] If an insurance company violates this provision, this does not affect the validity of the insurance contracts under civil law.

[23] In principle, FoS and FoE exist side by side. The difference between establishment and freedom to provide services lies in the different notification procedures (e.g. by § 58 or § 59 of the German

authority of the home state checks whether the requirements (e.g. the reliability of the authorized representative of the branch) for granting the licence are met in the case of an intended establishment of a branch in another member state and then informs the supervisory authority of the state of the branch about the granting of the licence.[24]

2.2 *Applicable Supervisory Law and Competent Supervisory Authority(ies) for Cross-Border Business*

Once these formalities, which are manageable from the product provider's perspective, have been completed, the insurance company is faced with the question of the legal structure of the products. The first step is to clarify which law applies to the design of the products. A distinction needs to be made between supervisory law and private law. In accordance with the single licence principle, the supervisory law of the home member state should always and fully apply to the company and the product, as indicated above in the quote from the European legislator. The reasoning behind is that the supervision of the entire business of an insurer domiciled in a member state, including the business which is written in another member state under FoE or FoS, is and remains the responsibility of the home country supervisory authority, i.e. supervisory authority at the company's registered office (so-called home country control). This comprehensive regulatory framework is further underscored by the three-pillar model of the Solvency II supervisory regime,[25] which assigns the qualitative requirements for insurance companies' capitalization and governance system to supervisory law. The same applies to the regulations on reporting and disclosure obligations both to the supervisory authority and to the public. Solvency II requires insurance and reinsurance companies to maintain an effective governance system that ensures their business activities' sound and prudent management.[26] The main objective of

Insurance Supervision Act (VAG)), the different dates of the earliest permissible start of activity and the higher organisational requirements for an establishment. Whether an insurance company can (still) operate in the host country under FoS or requires a branch is likely to be assessed on a case-by-case basis according to the criteria of duration, frequency, regularity and continuity of activity.

[24] Beckmann and Matusche-Beckmann (2024), 15. Wandt (2018) 103.

[25] BaFin, 'Solvency II' <https://www.bafin.de/EN/Aufsicht/VersichererPensionsfonds/Allgemeines/SolvencyII/solvency_II_node_en.html> accessed 30 September 2024; EIOPA, 'What Is Solvency II?' <https://www.eiopa.europa.eu/browse/regulation-and-policy/solvency-ii_en> accessed 16 March 2025.

[26] Art. 41 Directive 2009/138/EC of the European Parliament and of the Council of 25 November 2009 on the taking-up and pursuit of the business of Insurance and Reinsurance (Solvency II).

regulating and supervising insurance and reinsurance companies under Solvency II is the appropriate protection of policyholders and beneficiaries.[27]

For the supervisory authority of the country of operation, supervision is – as implied above – limited to the 'general legal supervision apart from that'.[28] Therefore, the host country supervisory authority is only supposed to check whether the insurer complies with the relevant legal provisions that serve the 'general interest', i.e. compliance with consumer protection aspects for policyholders living in the host country.[29] In principle, this indicates a clear separation between supervisory and private law, which goes hand in hand with a clear separation of tasks between home and host country supervision. The supervisory objective of both host and home country supervision is to adequately safeguard the interests of policyholders,[30] insured persons and beneficiaries in every respect.[31] This obligation continues throughout the entire duration of an insurance company's business operations. For example, according to the German Federal Administrative Court case law, the interests of policyholders and insured persons are not sufficiently safeguarded if the interests of the insured persons worthy of protection are impaired. The impairment of the interests as a whole and the unique features of the class of insurance concerned is considered unreasonable and so severe that official intervention is justified.[32] Nevertheless, supervision is limited to the extent that it may only be exercised in the public interest. Any further optimization is not permitted.[33]

The regulations on the framework conditions for product development and product design are assigned to insurance supervisory law. Product design is an area where few harmonized standards at the European level exist, and national supervisory regulations dominate. In particular, supervisory laws of the member states of the EU reveal a broad spectrum of regulations on overall accounting, surplus participation

---

[27] Recital 16 ibid.

[28] Recital 77, 85 and Art. 146 Abs. 3, 156, 180, 206 Abs. 1 lit. a ibid; Dreher, (2024) 294; Schäfers, (2024) 30.

[29] However, as will be made clear below, this is by no means a trivial matter.

[30] In the opinion of the German Federal Administrative Court, for example, the interests of the insured persons are not sufficiently safeguarded if the interests of the insured persons worthy of protection are impaired. This impairment is to be regarded as unreasonable, taking into account all the interests involved and the unique features of the branch of insurance concerned. It is so serious that official intervention is justified.

[31] Recital 14, 17, 43, 60 Directive 2009/138/EC of the European Parliament and of the Council of 25 November 2009 on the taking-up and pursuit of the business of Insurance and Reinsurance (Solvency II). It should be noted that Art. 27 II Solvency II leaves it to the discretion of the member states as to how the supervisory authorities ensure the protection of policyholders.

[32] *BVerwG, 21042021 - 8 C 620* [2021] BVerwG 8 C 6.20.

[33] In this respect, it is the task of the authorities to prevent insurers from exploiting their structural superiority over the insured persons by unilaterally realising their interests and thereby unreasonably disadvantaging the insured persons. The supervisory authority does not have to ensure that - positively - the interests of the insured persons receive the best possible consideration or even the best possible consideration, but only - negatively - to prevent unreasonable prejudice to the interests of the insured persons (ibid.).

systems, fund-based products, and risk minimization techniques. As a result, life insurance products are also structured differently, initially promising a broad market from the consumer's perspective. Insurance companies design their products based on the supervisory law of their home country and bring these products across the border as part of their single licence. Consequently, the home country's supervisory authority has to ensure that product development is carried out in accordance with the national supervisory regulations as well as that the insurance company does not engage in non-insurance business. However, it is important to note that product monitoring and control or better product oversight and governance (POG) has been harmonized through European initiatives.[34] As part of the product-specific product approval process, which applies both to new insurance products and to significant changes to the product, companies must define the target market and determine and assess the relevant risks for the target market. These tasks must also include corrective measures for insurance products that are disadvantageous to the customer. Furthermore, insurers must define an appropriate sales strategy for the respective target market and provide the relevant necessary information to the respective sales partners. These measures are not least intended to ensure the respective insurance product is sold to the specific target market. Only products that are compatible with the needs, characteristics, and objectives of the customers belonging to the target market can be marketed by the product providers. When assessing whether an insurance product is compatible with a target market, product providers have to take into account the level of information available to the customers belonging to that target market and their financial literacy. In addition, the insurance company must define the process for monitoring and regularly reviewing the insurance product. These requirements ensure that insurance products are always designed considering customers' interests and characteristics and preventing negative effects on customers at the earliest possible stage and at any time. Thus, it can be summarized that the standardized requirements for POG ensure that the interests of customers (throughout Europe) are prioritized already in product design and throughout the entire life cycle of a product.[35] All product providers, and moreover all

[34] Marano, (2021) 68; Marano, (2016) .

[35] When designing products, POG requires manufacturers to identify a target market, i.e. the group(s) of customers for whom the manufacturer is designing the product and for whom the product is considered suitable. In order to clarify a target market for which the product is not considered suitable, it is also necessary to better define the boundaries of the target market for which the products are intended. In addition, manufacturers must conduct a product analysis to assess the expected product performance in different stress scenarios. They need to ensure that the personnel involved in the product design have the necessary skills, knowledge and experience to understand the key features and characteristics of the product and the interests and characteristics of the target market (Directive (EU) 2016/97 of the European Parliament and of the Council of 20 January 2016 on insurance distribution). Marano highlights with regard to cross-border insurance business that '*although the activity plan does not have to be submitted when an insurer notifies the start of its activity under FoE or FoS, the relevant home country authorisation procedure should be in line with the objective of the POG*', Marano, 'The Contribution of Product Oversight and Governance (POG) to the Single Market: A Set of Organisational Rules for Business Conduct' (n 35) 72.

distributors,[36] in the European Union are obliged to comply with these almost standardized requirements throughout the European Union, regardless of the country in which the product is ultimately offered.[37] As a result, Insurance Based Investment Products (IBIPs), for example, have similar, if not identical, content, so the products do not differ significantly, and product providers have (anyway) no economic interest in these products differing significantly.[38] Therefore, if a cross-border insurance company (intends to) offer them throughout Europe, there will be no significant differences from the product provider's point of view, at least in the national markets where the potential customers have similar characteristics. Nowadays, these differences are based in particular on necessary adjustments due to national insurance laws applicable to the insurance contract (see III. Below).[39]

The final responsibility for monitoring the rules regarding POG in cross-border business has still not been clarified. From a product providers point of view, it makes sense that the supervision of the POG regulations falls under the supervision of the home country. This is also supported by the fact that the IDD is only a directive and not a regulation, and it is open to national legislators, also those in the countries where the insurers are based in the respective transformation acts,[40] to go beyond the directive provisions. And indeed, although it is not clear from the provisions of the IDD on the POG that the home country supervisory authority is also responsible for monitoring distribution in the host country, the author's experience at least shows that the home country supervisory authority does inquire about the distribution of products abroad that have been withdrawn under domestic supervisory law.

[36] Moreover, as Marano expressed rightfully, '*POG is a tool that increases transparency to the supervisory authorities by improving their ability to understand and assess the process of manufacturing and distributing insurance products*', Marano (2021) 65.

[37] '*POG aims at anticipating customer protection at the design stage for product marketing, and it enables supervisory authorities to have a clearer picture of the businesses processes that are behind the products marketed to customers*', ibid 56. In this respect, it must further be noted that POG does not only affect (life) insurers due to its implementation within the framework of the IDD Directive. The regulations are modelled on the MiFID legislation and extend far beyond the insurance sector. Customers across all financial sectors should be provided with adequate and similar protection, ensuring that the same level of protection applies regardless of the channel through which customers purchase an insurance or investment product.

[38] From the insurer's point of view, the following applies: Independent of country and target market, the same product and processes (as similar as possible), thus achieving maximum scaling effects and, as a result, cost and time savings.

[39] Marano (2021) 68.

[40] '*A convergent understanding of the set of rules on POG between* [the different European] *authorities would reduce the legal uncertainty for supervised entities and facilitates the cross-border activities*', ibid 71. A common understanding of EU legal acts, not only of directives such as the IDD but also of regulations that are, in any case, to be interpreted and understood uniformly and autonomously, would be desirable in principle. Unfortunately, from the author's experience, especially concerning the PRIPP regulation, different national interpretations still exist.

Certainly, complementary to the IDD's product and oversight governance provisions (although they precede the provisions of the IDD in terms of their publication date and validity) are product classification systems under Solvency II. Consequently, products that a life insurer intents to offer must also be classified, at least on a general basis, according to Annex II of the Solvency II. As part of the notification procedure, insurers must indicate which class of products under Annex II of Solvency II they wish to sell in the respective member state.[41] Although Annex II of Solvency II specifies standardized classes throughout Europe without restricting the scope for product developers too much, individual national legislators and supervisory authorities may have drafted parallel or supplementary regulations on classifications.[42] In this respect, it can prove challenging for insurers operating across borders to categorize their product, developed and classified by the national supervisory law of their home country, in the product classification scheme of the host country. On the one hand, such categorization is usually requested by the host country's supervisory authorities when the product is launched. On the other hand, the national regulation on pre-contractual information sometimes also requires the national classification to be mentioned in particular (pre-)contractual documents, which are often additionally required due to national legislation.[43] Moreover, additional processes, such as supervisory or customer notification processes, might be linked to the national categorization. If modern foreign product concepts have yet to be known in the host country – currently, modern dynamic hybrid concepts can be named as an example – categorization is already tricky. Arising thereby: the processes and obligations linked to the national categorization, which are not or only partially compatible with the new (foreign) product concepts, prove to be a

---

[41] If insurers have not initially notified all classes for a particular member state and wish to extend their offer beyond the notified classes, a new notification and a new notification procedure are required.

[42] One example of such a national classification is the Italian Ramo classification 'Rami Assicurativi Vita | COVIP' <https://www.covip.it/per-il-cittadino/educazione-previdenziale/glossario/rami-assicurativi-vita> accessed 16 March 2025. These national classifications are usually based on Annex II Solevency II. However, some differences arise in the national interpretation of the classes.

[43] For example, the product provider must mention the Italian Ramo classification in the additional pre-contractual document called DIP (acronimo di Documento Informativo Precontrattuale) or IPID (Insurance Product Information Document) which needs to be provided additionally for the Italian market. DIP Life is the pre-contractual information document for 'pure term life insurance policies', where the capital payment is only made when the insured event occurs. The DIP Life contains essential information about the product, such as information about the type of risk insured, the main exclusions and limits of cover and the conditions for premium payment. The DIP Vita is provided for and regulated by the Private Insurance Code and IVASS Regulation No. 41/2018 (Art 12. Regolamento IVASS N. 41 del 2 agosto 2018.), according to the same standardised scheme used at European level for non-life products (IVASS, 'Distribuzione Prodetti Assicurativi Semplificazione e Standardizzazione Delle Informazioni' <https://www.ivass.it/normativa/focus/distribuzione-assicurativa/approfondimenti/INFORMATIVA_PRECONTRATTUALE.pdf> accessed 16 March 2025.).

significant hurdle.[44] As a result,, the purpose of the nationally implemented obligation or processes and associated the added value for the customer cannot be achieved since the documents may not be meaningfully adapted to the product concepts and thus the actual purpose of the documents might be lost. Moreover, the fulfilment of the additional obligations increases the difficulties associated with the product launch. This leads to higher implementation costs on part of the product provider, including additional lengthy coordination rounds, necessary costly legal opinions, and discussions with supervisory authorities. This, in turn, results in higher costs for the life insurance products, which are likely to be borne by the customer. In economic terms, this makes the insurer's product less attractive to customers and reduces competitiveness compared to national products.

The single license principle is the basis for cross-border life insurance business. The formalities for entering cross-border business are straightforward and make sense from a consumer protection point of view. The supervisory authorities need to know which insurers operate in their country to protect their policyholders effectively. The basic applicability of the law of the insurer's domicile to insurance supervisory law is also beneficial in terms of a functioning single market. Solvency II and, in particular, the POG Process regulations published as part of the IDD Directive provide a solid basis for product development and monitoring, especially in the cross-border insurance business. However, national interpretations of European directives and regulations by national legislators and supervisory authorities significantly impede cross-border product launches, particularly concerning regulatory requirements. This is evident not least in national product classifications deviating from Solvency II and the associated processes or documentation obligations. Moreover, the responsibilities of supervisory authorities are not always clearly defined. Hence, it is worth discussing, not only with regard to European harmonization or standardization initiatives such as PRIIP or IDD, if it is still necessary that national legislators or regulators require specific nationally regulated processes or the obligation to create additional customer documents

3 Challenges from the Area of Private Law

Once the regulatory hurdles have been overcome, the product provider must turn its attention to private law and clarify which private law regulations apply to the insurance contract. This initially concerns questions of private international law and then national insurance contract and consumer protection law, as well as other regulations that are to be applied based on national supervisory orders.

[44] These are often also documentation obligations under private law, which will be discussed in detail later in section II.2.2.

3.1 International Private Law

3.1.1 Choice of Law: Art. 7 Rom I Regulation

The applicable private law is determined by Regulation 593/2008[45] on the law applicable to contractual obligations (Rome I Regulation). Life insurance contracts are contracts for mass risks (Article 7(3) of the Rome I Regulation) as they do not fall under category 'contracts for major risks' within the meaning of Article 7(2) of the Rome I Regulation in conjunction with Article 5(d) of Directive 73/239/EEC. This limits the choice of law (and thus also private autonomy) to those legal systems in which the specified connecting criteria suggests a connection to the specific insurance contract.[46] The options in Article 7(3) subpara.1 (a) to I of the Rome I Regulation are on an equal footing.[47] By restricting the freedom of choice of law and thus private autonomy, the legislator sought to protect the policyholder as the weaker part. The contracting parties can decide which option they wish to use if several alternatives are relevant. As a rule, the law applicable to life insurance contracts will be the law of the member state[48] in which the risk is located in accordance with Art. 7 (3) subpara. 1 (a) of the Rome I Regulation.[49] When determining the location of the risk, the time of the conclusion of the contract is always decisive.[50] Accordingly, a relocation of the insured risk to a non-member state after the conclusion of the contract is irrelevant to the applicability of the conflict of law rules under Art. 7 Rome I Regulation. In the case of life insurance contracts, Art. 7 para. 6 Rome I Regulation locates the risk in the state of the obligation within the meaning of Art. 13 no. 14 Solvency II Directive.[51] Accordingly, the member state of the obligation is generally the state in which the policyholder has his habitual residence.[52] If the

[45] Regulation (EC) No 593/2008 of the European Parliament and the Council of June 2008 on the law applicable to contractual obligations (Rome I).

[46] The European legislator introduced this system, which affects not only insurance law but all private law to protect the weaker party.

[47] Lüttringhaus (2024) 108.

[48] Member state within the scope of Art. 7 is to be interpreted broadly based on Solvency II and includes the EEA states of Norway, Iceland and Liechtenstein.

[49] With regard to life insurance, Art. 7(3)(a) and (b) will always lead to the application of the same law since Art. 7(6) Rome I Regulation places the risk at the policyholder's habitual residence anyway.

[50] In the interests of legal certainty, stabilising the connecting factor prevents a subsequent change in the location of risk from leading to a change in the articles of association.

[51] Staudinger, (2018) 71.

[52] It should be noted that the concept of habitual residence should not be mixed up with that of domicile. Habitual residence depends solely on the actual circumstances. A legal intention to establish or maintain a habitual residence is not required. The habitual residence is the center of life. It is the center of a person's activities and the center of social integration in an established environment. The law does not allow a person to have several habitual residences or one habitual residence in several places simultaneously. In this respect, the center of life must also have a certain permanence or regularity. For example, relocation of habitual residence by a person must also

policyholder is a legal entity, partnership or other association, the member state of the undertaking or establishment to which the insurance contract relates is decisive in this regard.[53] Alternatively, under Article 7(3) subpara. 1 (c) of the Rome I Regulation, only the law of the member state of which the policyholder is a national may be chosen for life insurance policies.[54] The rationale behind the provision in Article 7(3) subpara. 1 (c) of the Rome I Regulation is that the policyholder usually remains bound to his home state even if he now has his habitual residence in another state.[55] In practice, there is hardly any other choice of law in life insurance apart from the alternatives described. Art 7 (3) subpara. 1 Rome I Regulation itself does not contain a conflict of laws provision but refers in Art 7 (3) subpara. 2 Rome I Regulation to the private international law of the member states. The provision, therefore, even contains an opening clause.[56]

Although the European legislator has, in principle, created the possibility for member states to create a choice of law options, hardly any member state has made use of this possibility to date, particularly concerning life insurance, and it is currently unlikely that this will change soon.[57] Only the Italian legislator has endeavored to enshrine a corresponding choice of law for life insurance contracts in Art. 181 of the Italian Private Insurance Act. In addition, Austrian law, for example, also provides in Section 35 para. 1 IPRG that the parties may choose any other law in the cases of Art. 7 para. 3 subpara. 1 (a), (b) al(e) Rome I Regulation, provided that the choice of law does not result in the policyholder being deprived of the protection afforded by the mandatory provisions of the law applicable without a choice of law (Section 31 para. 1 IPRG). However, the Austrian Supreme Court has ruled concerning the provisions of § 35 IPRG that life insurance policies are explicitly mentioned in Art 7 para 3 (c) Rome I Regulation.[58] Thus, according to the Austrian Supreme Court, the parties may only choose the law of the member state of the policyholder's nationality following Art. 7 para. 3 lit. c Rome I

---

reflect their intention to establish the permanent or habitual center of their interests there to give it permanence. In principle, a certain duration of residence is also required in this respect. A minimum period of around six months is usually cited as a guide. Overall, the duration of the stay, the social connections and the intention to establish a (new) center of existence must be considered.

[53] From the perspective of the EU conflict on laws for life insurance contracts, the habitual residence of both the insured and the beneficiary is irrelevant.

[54] Art. 7 para. 3 subpara. 1 lit. c Rome I Regulation does not regulate the point in time relevant to the determination of nationality. However, the systematic connection to lit. a and sub-para 3 makes it clear that the conclusion of the contract should also be taken into account in this respect.

[55] Lüttringhaus (2024) 116; Staudinger (2018) 37; Looschelders (2024) 117.

[56] Lüttringhaus (2023) 128.

[57] At most, supervisory authorities in smaller countries with a small or no substantial life insurance market are currently likely to be prepared to make exceptions in individual cases to enable customers in their country to access foreign products.

[58] *OGH 7Ob19/21a.*

Regulation.[59] Hence, it can be concluded that the Austrian Supreme Court is of the opinion that the extension of the choice of law option according to Section 35 (1) IPRG should not apply to life insurance policies.[60] Overall, it is worth discussing whether there is a need for such a substantial restriction of private autonomy for life insurance contracts. The discussion should take into account that policyholders, unlike investors, inevitably transfer some or all of the investment risks to the insurer due to the insurance mechanism behind.

The restriction on the freedom of choice of law also applies to all contracts under the term ‘life insurance’. The term ‘life insurance contract’ within the meaning of Art. 7 Rome I Regulation is to be interpreted autonomously with recourse to other acts of the European Union. Art. 7 Rome I Regulation also refers to this (secondary) legislation in other contexts, a definition based on the life insurance branches listed in Art. 2 para. 3 no. 1 lit. a (i-iii) and no. 2 (i-ii) Solvency II Directive could be evident. This means that Art. 7 (3) subpara. 1 Rome I Regulation extends to life insurance which comprises assurance on survival to a stipulated age only, assurance on death only, assurance on survival to a stipulated age or on earlier death, life assurance with return of premiums, marriage and birth insurance, annuity insurance and supplementary life insurance. According to a widespread but unconvincing view, this should also apply directly to capitalization products, as these are also mentioned in Art. 2 (3) No. 1 lit. a (i-iii) and No. 2 (i-ii) Solvency II Directive. According to Art. 2 (3) no. 1 lit. b (ii) Solvency II Directive, capitalization products are products whose development and distribution are permitted for life insurance companies. Capitalization products are products in which the single or recurring premiums fixed in advance and the obligations assumed are determined by duration and amount using a mathematical method.[61] Capitalization products are, therefore, life products, but not life insurance contracts in the traditional sense. In this respect, it is argued that it is at least worth discussing whether the protective framework of Art. 7 Rome I Regulation must apply to capitalization products from the customer’s perspective or whether the European or national legislation should allow an exception to the strict corset of Art. 7 (3) subpara. 1 Rome I Regulation concerning life insurance, at least for capitalization products. At least with regard to the term ‘life insurance contract’, the question must be asked whether the biometric risk that characterizes life insurance contracts, namely the life, death or longevity of the insured person, should not play a decisive role in the context of Art. 7 para. 3 subpara. 1

[59] ibid.

[60] ibid. Critical on this: Gruber/Konwitschka: In the opinion of the authors mentioned, the court’s reasoning is based on a misunderstanding of the interaction of Art 7 para 3 sub-para 2 of the Rome I Regulation and § 35a para 1 IPRG. The Supreme Court did not take into account in its interpretation that Article 7(3)(1)(c) of the Rome I Regulation opens up an additional choice of law option, which the opening clause under Article 7(3)(2) of the Rome I Regulation is not restricted. The parties can, therefore, also make a choice of law for life insurance contracts in accordance with Article 7(3)(1)(a) (location of risk) or (b) (habitual residence of the policyholder) of the Rome I Regulation, Gruber and Konwitschka, (2022), 69.

[61] Pickartz and Stegmann, (2024) 12.

Rome I Regulation. However, such a biometric risk is not inherent in capitalization products. The current treatment of this legal issue has resulted in an artificial synchronization between supervisory and private law at this point,[62] with the indirect consequence that national supervisory authorities (still) declare insurance contract law to apply, at least in part or principle, to capitalization products.

3.1.2 Extent of the Choice of Law: Art. 10 to 12 Rom I Regulation

In accordance with the provisions of Art. 10 and 12 of the Rome I Regulation, the law appointed to apply under Art. 7 of the Rome I Regulation decides in principle on all substantive legal issues relating to the insurance contract. It follows from these provisions that the contract statute covers all questions relating to the formation of the contract, its validity, interpretation, performance and termination (cancellation, rescission, avoidance or termination). Furthermore, the insurance contract statute also decides on the inclusion of the general insurance conditions (GIC) and on the claims, duties and obligations resulting from the contract.[63] The form of the insurance contract is determined in accordance with the alternative link of Art. 11 Rome I Regulation. Accordingly, life insurance contracts must fulfil the formal requirements of the contract statute or the formal requirements of the law at the place of performance.[64] Art. 6 Rome I Regulation plays a crucial role in determining the form of consumer contracts. It stipulates that the form is determined by the law of the policyholder's habitual residence (Art. 11 para. 4 Rome I Regulation).

3.1.3 Overriding Mandatory Provisions: Art. 9 Rom I Regulation

Irrespective of the choice of law, it should also be noted that in the event of a direct conflict, such provisions, which are often regarded by a country as decisive

[62] A reference to Art. 2 para. 3 in conjunction with Annex II Solvency II does not seem appropriate in this respect. While Art. 2 para. 3 in conjunction with Annex II Solvency II determines which transactions life insurance undertakings are permitted to conduct, Art. 7 Rome I Regulation serves the special and significant protection of policyholders and insured persons as a class of consumers particularly worthy of protection.

[63] The breach of pre-contractual information obligations is not covered by the Rome I Regulation but is instead linked to the contract by Art. 12 para. 1 of the Rome II Regulation and is subject to the (possibly hypothetical) contractual statute. The term *'non-contractual obligations arising out of negotiations before the conclusion of a contract'* is intended to cover the breach of pre-contractual disclosure obligations (recital 30 of the Rome II Regulation).

[64] The place of performance is the place where the acceptance of the offer is declared. If the insurer declares acceptance, the insurer's registered office is, therefore, decisive with regard to the form. If the contract is concluded between absentees, the place of receipt of the declaration of acceptance is also irrelevant in this respect.

for safeguarding its public interest in social organization, can even be regarded as overriding mandatory provisions within the meaning of Art. 9 para. 1 Rome I Regulation.[65] Art. 9 Rome I Regulation is, therefore, a necessary valve through which the conflict of laws opens up for fundamental state regulatory concerns, but at the same time, it always has an exceptional character to the unitary connection according to Art. 3 et seq. Rome I Regulation, and thus also to Art. 7 Rome I Regulation.[66] The basic requirement for the application of a provision as an overriding mandatory provision in the sense of Art 9 Rome I Regulation is the mandatory nature of this provision. To this end, the legal provision must fulfil several requirements. At the first level, the rule in question must not be at the disposal of the contracting parties within the framework of the legal system to which it belongs. Whether this is the case is not determined by Art. 9 Rome I Regulation but solely by the regulatory content of the provision in question and must be determined by its interpretation. The national interpretation standards of the respective enacting legislation are decisive.[67] In addition to its mandatory nature, the respective provision must have an international claim to validity.[68] With their effect of breaking through the contractual statute, overriding mandatory provisions thus have a considerable influence on the basic principle of modern private international law, which assumes the fundamental equivalence and interchangeability of all private law systems and, therefore, subjects the international situation to the law that is most appropriate in terms of territory. In this respect, it can be argued that Art. 9 of the Rome I Regulation already provides sufficient protection for policyholders.

Despite these possibilities, which are or better would be in particular resulting from a correct utilization of Art. 9 Rome I Regulation, the European legislator has so far adhered to the strong restriction of private autonomy in the area of private international law in the insurance sector, as laid down in Art. 7 (3) subpara. 1 Rom I Regulation. This is certainly one reason why cross-border life insurance business is only successful to a limited extent. It is obvious that the applicability of only one legal system for its products would not only save costs for the insurer in terms of product development, but also in terms of ongoing contract management, which would then also be governed by a single national law, and consequently without having to adjust documents and processes to different legal systems.

[65] Staudinger (2024) 105, Martiny (2021)105.

[66] Therefore, the provision contains an opening clause in favor of mandatory international standards that apply regardless of the contractual statute (Staudinger (2024) 1.).

[67] Insofar as a provision's mandatory nature is sufficient, its legal source is irrelevant for the application of Art. 9 Rome I Regulation; it is therefore irrelevant whether it is a provision of written statutory law, a statutory provision concretised or developed by the courts, customary law, or pure case law.

[68] Staudinger (2024) 3.

3.2 General Good Requirements

3.2.1 General Good Requirements: Backgrounds

Beyond the challenges on cross-border life insurance imposed by the Rom I Regulation, the so-called 'general good requirements' (GGR) (or 'general good rules') also pose a considerable challenge from the perspective of the product provider. The European Commission's interpretative communication on the freedom to provide services and the general good in the insurance sector (2000/C 43/03)[69] stipulates that the host country may lay down certain provisions of its national law that EU companies operating in its territory under FoS or FoE (based on the Single license principle) must comply with when carrying out their activities (Articles 146(3), 156 and 180 Solvency II).[70] As the GGR can restrict or hinder FoS and the FoE, the European legislator has specified that a national provision can only be classified as a provision of general interest if it fulfils the following conditions:[71]

- The legal norm must relate to a non-harmonized area and pursue an objective that is in the general interest. In addition, the standard must not be discriminatory.
- The purpose it pursues must be objectively necessary and the restriction imposed by the standard must be proportionate to the objective pursued.
- Finally, the public interest objective must not be guaranteed by the rules to which the provider is subject in the member state in which he is established.

The supervisory authorities of the host member state shall publish these general product rules on their websites. The supervisory authorities should inform insurers established in other member states of the relevant national public-interest legislation, particularly consumer protection rules, which must be observed when selling

[69] 'Official Journal of the European Communities -Information and Notices (C43)' <https://eur-lex.europa.eu/legal-content/EN/TXT/PDF/?uri=OJ:C:2000:043:FULL> accessed 16 March 2025.

[70] In this respect, it should also be noted that the European legislator has once again taken up the issue of GGR as part of the IDD legislation regarding the advice provided by intermediaries. The host country supervisory authorities also publish on their websites the regulations that intermediaries operating in the host country must comply with while acting under FoS or FoE. The host supervisory authorities are also responsible for monitoring. This applies, in particular, to the information provided to policyholders. Although the primary aim of the regulations is to ensure that the intermediary provides appropriate and extensive advice. The 'IDD GGR' - like the other GGR - also apply to the insurer. This is because, albeit not in all cases, intermediaries are often or, for the most part, in the 'insurer's camp'. In other words, the insurer will likely be responsible for the intermediary's advice. This applies almost invariably to the documents provided to the customer. In the vast majority of cases, the documents originate from the insurer.

[71] The insurance sector is a particularly sensitive area regarding the protection of consumers as policyholders and beneficiaries; moreover, contracts are concluded by such a large number of policyholders that the protection of the insured's interests affects almost the entire population. Therefore, this sector has overriding reasons in the public interest for restricting the fundamental freedoms (see ECJ, judgment of 4 December 1986 - C-205/84, Commission v Germany - para. 30 et seq.).

insurance products in that member state. Looking at the extensive and sprawling lists of the GGR that can nowadays be found on the websites of the (host country) supervisory authorities,[72] the question must be allowed as to whether all of the provisions listed there actually fulfil the stated criteria. This is particularly doubtful when supervisory authorities list entire or almost entire codes of law and do not refer specifically to individual regulations. The comprehensive lists are sometimes difficult for foreign companies to oversee. In addition, the legal provisions listed there are adapted in unregular intervals, i.e. due to changes and amendments to the law. For foreign insurers, this means that law firms operating in the host country would generally have to be permanently mandated in order to not miss any changes and to be in a good position to make necessary adjustments. Product providers urgently need to comply with the GGR, since according to Article 180 of the Solvency II, neither the home, nor the host state may prevent policyholders from concluding a contract with an insurer authorized under freedom of service as long as the conclusion of the contract is not contrary to the legislation listed in the GGR of the member state.

3.2.2 General Good Requirements: Application Cases

The GGR are always applicable when an insurance-related situation arises in the host country, governed by FoS or FoE. In this respect, it should also be noted that the European legislator has not made any reference to the choice of law provisions of Art. 3 et seq. of the Rome I Regulation. What this means in detail can be illustrated by the following brief examples: As long as, for example, a German life insurer wishes to sell a life insurance policy to a Spanish citizen whose center of life is in Madrid, Spain, this has no significant impact purely in terms of the applicable private law provisions published in the list of the GGR by the Spanish supervisory authority, as Spanish (private) law[73] will apply according to the Rom I Regulation to the contract anyway (see above). If the same German life insurer wishes to sell a life insurance policy developed in accordance with German law to a German citizen

[72] By way of example: 'IVASS - General Good Provisions for Foreign Operators' <https://www.ivass.it/normativa/nazionale/norme-int-gen/index.html> accessed 16 March 2025; BaFin, 'General Good Requirements in Germany' (*BaFin*) <https://www.bafin.de/SharedDocs/Veroeffentlichungen/EN/Merkblatt/VA/mb_110308_zulassung_eu_liste_vorschriftenallgemeininteresse_va_en.html> accessed 16 March 2025; 'General Good Rules (GGR)' (*Banque de France*, 12 April 2023) <https://acpr.banque-france.fr/en/authorisation/insurance-sector-procedures/general-good-rules-ggr> accessed 16 March 2025.

[73] It is likely disputable whether the choice of law pursuant to Art. 7 para. 3 subpara. 1 Rome I Regulation also leads to the application of individual supervisory provisions or whether this requires the applicability of the provisions by way of the 'diversions' of the GGR. At the very least, it should be indisputable that these supervisory provisions, insofar as they serve to enforce the general welfare-related legal policy interests of the respective legal system, but which are nevertheless suitable for influencing contractual obligations, are at least applicable via Art. 9 Rome I Regulation (Maultzsch, (2024) 26.).

who has his center of life in Madrid, he can do so, as shown above, by concluding a life insurance contract with him to which German law applies per Art. 7 para. 3 subpara. 1 I Rome I Regulation. However, the fact that the German national has his center of life in Spain means that insurers who wish to sell to nationals and the law of the policyholder's nationality is chosen must take into account the GGR of the host country. This may result in the fact that essential elements of the contract may have to be adapted. The reason repeatedly given is that the insured person needs to be protected by the laws of the member state in which the commitment was entered into. This also means, for example, that pre-contractual information obligations specified in the GGR of the host country prior to the conclusion of the contract must also be fulfilled. In this context, it is also unclear what happens if the provisions of the laws specified in the GGR of the host country conflict with those of the home country applicable to the insurance product. It remains to be seen whether a solution can always be found in the policyholder's best interests.[74]

3.2.3 General Good Requirements and the 'Correspondence Insurance'

Similarly, the situation is unclear in the case of so-called 'correspondence insurance'. The correspondence insurance refers to a situation in which a policyholder contacts an insurance company in another member state on its own initiative.[75] Let us assume a French customer living in Brussels, Belgium, who contacts a French insurance company on his own initiative. In this respect, it is debatable and still not finally clarified whether these cases are subject to FoS or FoE at all or whether the correspondence insurance should initially be an exceptional case in that it should be regarded as purely domestic business.[76] The fact that the insurer's business is not focussed on the 'host country' in the case of correspondence insurance certainly speaks in favor of the correspondence insurance being out of the scope of FoS. This is supported by the fact that there are generally no targeted advertising measures conducted or websites designed specifically with the 'host member' state in mind. Additionally, there is also usually no translation of documents or advertising materials. The freedom of supervision with regard to the 'host country supervision' of correspondence insurance can probably also be justified by the fact that a policyholder who deliberately approaches an insurance company abroad cannot expect

---

[74] K. Noussia's reference to intermediaries in one of her papers is also very interesting in this context. She points out that in connection with the 'national law governing the advisory situation', the IDD's legislators apparently believe that the (stricter) national provisions of the customer's habitual residence are always decisive. Consequently, this would inevitably lead to contradictory or at least 'strange' legal situations. Such situations would always arise if the parties determined the law of the policyholder's nationality (Article 7(3) subpara. 1 (c) of the Rome I Regulation) as the law applicable to the insurance contract and the policyholder has his center of life in another country when the contract is concluded, Kyriaki (2021) 82.

[75] Grote, (2024) 40; Pohlmann, (2019) 32.

[76] Grote (2024) 40.

the supervisory authority of his home country to supervise the insurance company abroad. By actively acting across the border, the policyholder deliberately places himself in the hands and under the supervisory regime of the insurance company's home country. Irrespective, this should not be detrimental within the EU, whose supervisory regime is, as shown, largely fully harmonized under Solvency II. On the contrary, Solvency II aimed to facilitate cross-border insurance business within the EU (and also the EEA). If one assumes, contrary to the view expressed here, that the cases of correspondence insurance also are subject to FoS or, as is sometimes formulated, a so-called 'passive freedom to provide services', this would initially mean that in the example mentioned above, the French insurer would have had to notify the regulatory authorities of the commencement of the freedom to provide services in Belgium before concluding the contract. Furthermore, and generally much more critical for insurance companies, the question then arises as to whether this would also have the consequence that this life insurance contract, which would only be concluded because the French citizen actively approaches the French insurer (across the national border) in order to obtain insurance cover, would also mean that the Belgian GGR would apply (in full) to this contract. For the insurer, this is likely to mean that, in case of doubt, it will not be able to conclude the corresponding contract – at least not without a significant delay and effort –, as the insurer is unlikely aware of any possible consequences for its insurance contract regarding the GGR published by the Belgian supervisory authority; at least not without conducting a comprehensive review of the GGR (and adjusting the contract). For the policyholder, this is inevitably associated with an (unnecessary) narrowing of the available product range.

3.2.4 General Good Requirements and the 'Departure or Relocation Cases'

Furthermore, it has not been conclusively clarified whether the GGR extend to so-called departure or relocation cases.[77] If, for example, a German citizen with

[77] According to the view expressed here, it is preferable not to assume that this case is subject to FoS. In these departure cases, it seems appropriate to require a voluntary element on the part of the insurance company or to focus exclusively on the time of the conclusion of the contract. Thus, a subsequent departure of the policyholder would not require providing services abroad within the meaning of the European regulation. This view is also supported by the fact that the "intended" commencement of the provision of services must be notified. If relocation cases are regarded as services requiring notification, conducting insurance business within the EU/EEA would be more difficult. The mere relocation of the policyholder does not constitute an intention on the part of the insurer. At best, an intention could be justified by the maintenance of the contract, i.e. the expiry of the first cancellation option after notification of the move. However, concerning life insurance policies in Germany, for example, it should be noted that life insurance policies in Germany are subject to cancellation restrictions according to § 171 S.1 in conjunction with § 166 VVG. Thus,

a center of life in Germany or an Italian citizen with a center of life in Germany each conclude a life insurance contract with an insurance company based in Germany, the contracting parties can in both cases choose German law. Suppose both parties decide to relocate their center of life to France after a few years of the contract duration. In that case, the question arises as to whether the insurance contracts are subject to the freedom to provide services and, therefore, also to the application of the French GGR, as the GGR, unlike the Rome I Regulation, does not recognize the time of conclusion of the contract as a regular connecting factor.[78]

3.2.5 General Good Requirements: Summary

The GGR represent a major, if not the biggest, challenge in the cross-border insurance business. Whether such a far-reaching restriction of the freedom to provide services and freedom of establishment is necessary should be reviewed by the by the EU's institutions, particularly by EIOPA. Moreover, as mentioned before, particularly with regard to the life insurance sector – and as important consumer protection, especially regarding the purposes of life insurance, undoubtedly is – Solvency II and more recent regulations such as IDD and PRIIP have created such a high level of protection for policyholders throughout Europe that it does not appear to be necessary to protect policyholders even more through national regulations. Given the strict provisions of private international law for insurance law, whether the GGR are ultimately needed might also be discussed. Moreover, as explained above, Art. 9 Rome I Regulation sets out the conditions that may nevertheless guarantee a high protection of policyholders in case of any lack of mandatory protection by national provisions in individual cases.

3.3 Requirements of National Private Law

Once it has been clarified during the product launch process which national law must be applied to the life insurance contract, the insurer operating across borders must ask what effects this will have on the insurance conditions and other pre-contractual and contractual documents originally drafted for the home

they cannot be canceled by the insurance company with the consequence of their termination. Consequently, the continuation of the contract in Germany in these cases is independent of the insurer's intention (Baroch Castellvi (2024) 34–38.).

[78] For the Rome I Regulation, this results in particular from Art. 19 Rome I Regulation.

country, the processes and whether there will even be any effects on the product as such.

3.3.1 Overview

Most insurance contract law regulations in the European Union are still the result of national legislation. National insurance contract laws are generally tailored to national supervisory law and, therefore, to 'domestic' insurance products. Many aspects of consumer protection are also anchored in national contract laws. There is no European insurance contract directive or regulation.[79] All corresponding initiatives have failed so far. The national provisions of insurance contract law often prevent the parties from opting out (mandatory provisions) or deviating to the detriment of the policyholder (semi-mandatory provisions). Such mandatory or semi-mandatory rules may restrict the insurer's freedom to provide services across borders (and thus constitute obstacles) always with the indication of consumer protection. Without any doubt, it might be argued that this is positive from the point of view of both consumers and national supervisory authorities. Consumers are most familiar with their contract law. National supervisory authorities might know their own national insurance contract law regulations best and can, therefore, best fulfil their task of protecting consumers resident in their country. However, in view of the range of products available, this certainly also has disadvantages for customers.

With regard to insurance contract law, more than ten years ago[80] the European Commission set up a group of experts to analyze the impact of differences in national contract law on cross-border insurance business under the freedom to provide services and the freedom of establishment.[81] Its final report of 24 January 2014[82] concluded that both pre-contractual information obligations and the calculation of surrender values are highly relevant to cross-border life insurance business. In addition, issues such as the diverging cancellation periods, the consequences of cancellation, various national questionnaires, the regulations regarding the payment of premiums and different cancellation regulations in individual

[79] On this already in 2014: Basedow, (2015) .

[80] The Commission's decision of 17 January 2013 established an expert group on European insurance contract law.

[81] European Commission, 'Expert Group on European Insurance Contract Law - European Commission' <https://commission.europa.eu/business-economy-euro/doing-business-eu/contract-rules/insurance-contracts/expert-group-european-insurance-contract-law_en> accessed 16 March 2025.

[82] European Commission - Directorate-General for Justice, 'Final Report of the Commission Expert Group on European Insurance Contract Law' (2014) <https://www.mpipriv.de/1102634/eicl-finalreport.pdf> accessed 16 March 2025.

European jurisdictions are often very obstructive concerning cross-border life insurance business.

3.3.2 National Provisions of General and Special Insurance Law

To give the reader a first rough impression of the variety, peculiarities, and differences in the national insurance contract law regulations, some of the divergent regulations in the national regulatory frameworks are presented below as examples.[83]

3.3.2.1 Conclusion of Contract

If product providers in cross-border business are in the process of launching a product, the first question in relation to contract law that arises, also in order to be able to set up IT processes correctly at an early stage, is the question of the contract conclusion procedure and directly associated obligations, such as formal requirements. Although differences in the actual or technical handling of the conclusion of the contract, which do not necessarily have legal reasons, always come to light at this stage, it is also obvious that the legal differences in the area of contract conclusion are significant from country to country. In Germany, the insurance contract is bilateral. The policyholder makes an offer, which the insurer accepts after a review. A special requirement of form, text form or even written form of the contract is not required, but the insurer must issue an insurance policy, § 3 para. 1 of the German Insurance Contract Act (VVG). This policy must be handed over to the policyholder in writing, i.e. at least in text form. As long as the insurer has not issued the policy, the applicant is not obliged to pay the premium (§ 33 VVG). Insurance cover can be refused if the policyholder has not paid the first premium due (cf. § 37 Para. 2 VVG). Under Austrian law, the insurance policy must be sent to the policyholder on paper or electronically, § 3 Austrian Insurance Contract Act (VersVG). In Italy, a contract is concluded following the provisions of Article 1326 et seq. of the Italian Civil Code (codice civile (CC)). Accordingly, the offer is usually made by the policyholder and is binding for 15 days. The contract is concluded when the insurer accepts the offer and communicates this acceptance to the policyholder. According to Article 1888 CC, the contract must be recorded in writing for reasons of proof. The insurer is obliged to provide the policyholder with a copy of the contract. Unless otherwise agreed, contracts must be written in Italian. Under Spanish law, the insurance contract becomes effective when the policyholder notifies the insurer of acceptance of the

[83] Many of the differences described below have already been identified or analysed to a similar or equal extent by the European Commission's expert group. However, there has been no real further development towards more harmonisation to date.

offer. There is no legal obligation to conclude the contract in a specific form.[84] The conclusion of an insurance contract in France is governed by Article L112-3 of the French Insurance Code (C.assur.). According to this article, the contract and all related information provided by the insurer must be in writing, in French and in an understandable format. The contract itself is concluded by the parties' mutual agreement, regardless of whether this is given orally or in writing. The written form is only required as proof of existence and content of the contract. If the parties agree on a different law per Article 7(3) subpara. 1 I of the Rome I Regulation, they may also choose a different language for the contract.

3.3.2.2 Information and Documentation Obligations

Once the issues relating to the conclusion of the contract have been clarified, it is then necessary to discuss whether specific information obligations exist under the national law of the host country. For example, depending on the national general insurance law, a certain clause relevant to the design of an insurance product may be declared null and void because formal requirements have not been met. According to French law, Art. L 112-4 C.assur., exclusion clauses must be printed in bold in a visible place on the policy. An insurance policy from a foreign product provider sold on the French market without complying with this formal requirement would render any exclusion clauses invalid. In some member states, national provisions of insurance contract law also require that the insurer must be able to prove that the policyholder has received, read and accepted the terms and conditions of the contract. In addition, the French Insurance Code contains several very detailed provisions on the content and form of the documents to be provided to the policyholder in the pre-contractual phase.[85] Other national regulations provide for specific deadlines to be met by the insurer, e.g. for the application of sanctions following the discovery of a non-disclosure or misrepresentation, an increase in risk or any other fact relevant to the contract. In some member states, the insurer is obliged to warn the policyholder in some instances, e.g. under the VVG, the insurer is obliged to inform the policyholder of the consequences of a breach of the duty of disclosure or misrepresentation,[86] a breach of the contractual duty to disclose and provide information about an insured event,[87] or the non-payment of the premium.[88]

[84] However, there is a special form of contract according to Article 5 LCS. It consists of the insurance plan, the general terms and conditions and any additional agreements. In this case, Article 5 LCS stipulates that the contract and any amendments or additions must be recorded in writing.

[85] Cf, e.g.: L. 132-5-1, L. 132-5-2, Art. 132-4 and Art. 132-8 C.assur.

[86] § 19 (4)-(5) VVG.

[87] § 28 (4) VVG.

[88] 37 (2) sentence two and § 38 (1) sentence 2 VVG.

3.3.2.3 National Life Insurance Law

In life insurance, product-related mandatory regulations are another point to consider for the cross-border business. If, for example, death risks are insured, as it is typically the case with term life insurance, statutory or contractual exclusion clauses, which are intended to exempt the insurer from liability in the event of the suicide of the person at risk, are often restricted by mandatory provisions. However, these differ regularly in detail. In Germany, the insurer must always pay the insured amount if the person at risk commits suicide more than three years after the contract was concluded.[89] Within the first three years of the policy term, the insurer only has to pay the insured amount if the person at risk commits suicide while lunatic (§ 161 Para. 1 Sentence 2 VVG). In contrast, the latter rule applies in Austria, for example, irrespective of the time of suicide (cf. § 169 VersVG). Another example is the written consent required under Austrian and German law from the person at risk on whose life a life insurance policy is taken out.[90]

With regard to life insurance, contractual and pre-contractual information obligations play an essential role both in a purely national context and especially in an international context. The recent developments on the European legislative stage are fundamentally positive for cross-border business transactions. For example, the PRIIPs Regulation has laid down standardized rules for pre-contractual information for IBIPs.[91] These relate to the format and content of the key information document to be prepared by PRIIP manufacturers. The aim is to enable retail investors to understand and compare the key features and risks of the PRIIP.[92] The regulation aims to provide investors with concise and clear key contractual information for pre-contractual decision-making.[93] Like other financial products, life insurance

[89] § 161 (1) Sentence 1 VVG.

[90] cf. section 159 (2) VersVG; section 150 (2) VVG.

[91] Wendt and Wendt, (2021) 17.

[92] Although these efforts are fundamentally positive, there is also criticism concerning the implementation in detail. Although the standardization of the key information documents is intended to create an advantageous situation for policyholders through optimal comparability, this goal is rarely achieved. Versatile, sometimes technically complex products are forced into a rigid corset, with the result that a very distorted presentation can arise. This becomes particularly clear when customers try to compare products across borders. In addition, standardization is often accompanied by an overload of information for the investor or policyholder that is neither helpful nor useful for their investment decision. As a result, this leads to an 'information overload' instead of targeted investor protection.

[93] Insurance distribution itself was harmonised in many areas by the IDD. Here, too, consumer protection took center stage. The European legislator, therefore, considers the sale of insurance products to be similar to the offering of financial products. Both are characterized by asymmetric information between distributors and customers, so they are similar. However, the EU legislator would also have to consider that insurance products, which allow the risk to be transferred to the insurer, are not comparable to financial products, where the customer still bears the risk.

contracts that are subject to the PRIIPs Regulation are to be explained comprehensibly, thus creating cross-sector comparability of different financial products.[94]

Despite numerous standardization and harmonization efforts, national regulations remain the key players in the field of (pre-) contractual information obligations. For instance, the French Insurance Code is home to a plethora of highly detailed regulations on the content and form of the documents that must be provided to the policyholder in the pre-contractual phase (particularly under Arts. L. 132-5-1, L. 132-5-2, A. 132-4 and A. 132-8 C.assur.) The German Regulation on information requirements for insurance contracts (VVG-InfoV) also houses comprehensive regulations that product providers must adhere to. The obligation to provide ongoing contractual information, a feature present in many legal systems, is a prime example of how a single rule can be found across all legal systems. However, the structure and level of detail pertaining to the information to be provided vary from member state to member state, highlighting the crucial need to understand and navigate the national regulations.[95] Furthermore, it can be observed that Member States have, for example, implemented EU law requirements on pre-contractual information in different ways[96] or have also issued additional requirements in order to achieve an (even) higher level of protection for national consumers in their member state, a practice often referred to as "gold plating".[97] As a result, there are still significant

[94] According to Article 1, sentence 1 of the PRIIPs Regulation, its provisions apply to the establishment and sale of packaged retail investment products and insurance-based investment products. These insurance products offer a surrender value that is fully or partially directly or indirectly exposed to market fluctuations - i.e. unit-linked life insurance policies. The range of products covered by the regulation is therefore immense.

[95] In France, the legislator has only recently issued more extensive information requirements for unit-linked life insurance contracts. According to Articles L. 522-1 and 522-5, for unit-linked life insurance contracts, the gross and net performance after costs in the last completed financial year in per cent, the costs withdrawn from the assets to cover the unit of account in the last completed financial year, the recurring costs withdrawn from the contract, the final performance of the investment after deduction of the management fees and the above-mentioned recurring costs, expressed as a percentage, as well as the proportion of costs resulting in commission rebates to the various professionals (managers, custodians, intermediaries), must be listed for each unit of account. A decree of 20 June 2024, published on 4 July, supplements the obligations: The information must now also include the annualized five-year average of the previously listed information for each unit of account.

[96] For example, the policyholder's right to withdraw from life insurance contracts is standardised in Article 186 of Solvency II. However, the directive offers member states room for maneuver for their own regulations in certain areas. This concerns firstly the duration of the cancellation period, which can vary between 14 and 30 days; secondly, the start and end of the period if the policyholder has not been informed of the right of cancellation. Thirdly, the possibility of excluding specific contracts, and fourthly, the consequences of cancellation, particularly the reimbursement of amounts paid. The member states have different regulations on these aspects. In France, for example, the cancellation period can extend for years if there is no information about the right of cancellation. In Germany, the "VVG Info Regulation" (Section 7 VVG) contains detailed specifications on the order and content of the information to be provided.

[97] Möllers, (2016), 331.

differences in legislation and case law between the member states as a whole concerning (pre-)contractual information requirements.

3.3.3 (National) Supervisory Regulations Within (National) Private Law

In addition to the provisions that are exclusively attributable to private law, the following additional aspect must be considered from the perspective of the product provider. As mentioned, the national insurance contract laws are based on the respective national supervisory law. In many jurisdictions, supervisory law and contract law are not entirely separable from each other. Instead, provisions can be found in the contract law regulations that refer to the national structures of national supervisory law. This inevitably leads to difficulties when launching products in the cross-border insurance business.

For example, Section 153 VVG grants policyholders of life insurance contracts a right to participate in the surpluses generated by the insurer (including hidden reserves). These profits must be calculated and distributed as prescribed in Section 153 VVG.[98] The right to profit-participation may be excluded in total. However, if a contract that offers profit participation is offered, a change or exclusion of the policyholder's rights as laid down in § 153 Para. 1 VVG is prohibited. The provision of Section 153 VVG, which is also included in the list of GGR published by BaFin, applies in principle to foreign insurers, in particular those based in the EU or EEA, if they conclude insurance contracts with policyholders who have their habitual residence in Germany.[99] According to the explanatory memorandum to Section 153 of the VVG, the law is to be applied to foreign insurance companies with the provision that the profit is to be determined based on the annual financial statements the company must prepare. For insurance companies domiciled in an EU member state or an EEA contracting state, the respective transposition provisions of Directive 91/674/EEC as amended by Directive 2003/51/EC and Directive 2006/46/EC apply. The annual financial statements, prepared in accordance with the relevant law of the country in which the company is domiciled, are the basis for determining the surpluses. The extension of Section 153 to foreign EU/EEA member states interferes with their product design and, therefore, restricts their freedom to provide services and freedom of establishment. Whether this restriction is justified by the interest of consumer protection, is doubtful, at least not sufficiently substantiated.

It is also noteworthy that national supervisory regulations are increasingly finding their way into the member states' respective national insurance contract laws. Another illustrative example from the recent past can be found in French law.[100] The

---

[98] Heiss, (2024) 9.

[99] ibid 14; different: Leithoff, (2022) 7.

[100] The background to the introduction of the regulation is the so-called Pacte law. The Pacte law was passed in 2019 to boost the French economy through simplification and modernisation measures. Of the numerous measures implemented, some directly impact life insurance policies. Among other things, one regulation tightens the information on the fees charged for so-called 'dynamic' life insurance contracts, i.e., partially invested in units of account.

new Article L 131-1-2 C.assur. was introduced to increase the offer of solidarity and responsible funds and green funds in life insurance contracts. Every unit-linked contract taken out from 1 January 2020 must offer at least one unit of account in its range of financial products consisting of assets that meet at least one of the following three conditions: A proportion of between 5% and 10% must consist of securities issued by authorized solidarity-based social utility companies, by venture capital companies as defined in Article1(1) of Law No. 85-695 of 11. July 1985 or by venture funds, at least 40% of whose assets consist of securities issued by solidarity-based companies, having obtained a label recognized by the State that meets the criteria for financing the energy and ecological transition in accordance with procedures laid down by decree or having obtained a label recognized by the State and meet the criteria for socially responsible investment in accordance with procedures laid down by decree (C. ass. Art. L 131-1-2 new, paras. 1 to 5).[101,102]

As a result, insurers aiming to sell their products in another member state must comply with these regulations, which are, technically, supervisory law, when designing and distributing their products. The same applies to official announcements by the supervisory authorities. These are often addressed to domestic insurers and those operating in the respective member state under the FoE or FoS. As far as purely contractual or consumer protection aspects are concerned, this may appear uncritical. However, regulations that concern essential aspects of product design, i.e. supervisory law, can easily be categorized as consumer protection. At the same time, many national contract law regulatio–s - for example, with regard to documentation requiremen–s - are very much tailored to national supervisory requirements and, therefore, to domestic products. Nevertheless, foreign insurers must comply with these requirements even though these regulations do not fit their products, and consumers often do not benefit from their compliance by foreign insurers. In addition, there are significant differences in insurance law and terminology. This

[101] Contracts concluded from 1 January 2022 must offer units of account that comply with these three modalities. From the same date, the proportion of each category of these units of account will be communicated to policyholders before the conclusion of the contract in order to encourage insurance companies to expand their catalog of units of account consisting of assets bearing a quality label (Art. L 131-1-2 new, paras. 5 and 6 C. assur.).

[102] Another example that can be cited is the recently published IVASS consultation paper 02/2024 'Outline of IVASS regulation laying down provisions on insurance contracts referred to in Art. 41. papa. 1 and 2 of the legislative Degree number 209 of 7 September 2005 - concerning the private insurance code and subsequent amendments and additions'. With reference to 'only existing minimum harmonisations in this field'. The statement provides for comprehensive regulations that should also apply, particularly to companies that offer or intend to offer unit-linked products on the Italian market. This justification is supplemented by the general statement that non-application to companies headquartered in other member states would be discriminatory for Italian companies and would not adequately protect persons based in Italy, without giving examples of disadvantages. At the very least, it should be highlighted that the GGR is certainly not intended to protect domestic companies from being disadvantaged ('IVASS - Documento di consultazione n. 2/2024' <https://www.ivass.it/normativa/nazionale/secondaria-ivass/pubb-cons/2024/02-pc/index.html> accessed 16 March 2025.).

poses a significant challenge for product design and the cross-border distribution of products. Furthermore, the issue of inconsistent terminology will likely play a significant role in the future comparability of products within the Open Finance Initiative.[103]

4 Excursus PEPP

When discussing cross-border (life) insurance business, the regulation on a Pan-European Pension Product (PEPP) has been a recurring theme in recent years. Thus, this EU initiative should as a last point at least be briefly touched.[104] The PEPP is supposed to be a private pension product of the third pension pillar that all financial service providers, authorized under European law, can market in the European Union. This includes also insurance companies. The PEPP does not harmonize existing pension products; it is an additional optional product. For product provider (and customers), this sounds promising at first. However, contrary to the EU Commission's and EIOPAs original announcements,[105] it turns out that PEPP has not become a successful model since its market launch in March 2022, and there is still no (significant) PEPP manufacturer.[106,107] Firstly, there are actuarial reasons for this, which are not least due to the provisions of Commission Delegated Regulation (EU) 2021/473 of 18 December 2020.[108]But secondly, it is also the case that the PEPP is far from being an original European product from a legal perspective. There are some deviations of the PEPP Regulation from existing European Regulations, which are not always necessary. In particular, the diverse and complicated

[103] 'Framework for Financial Data Access - European Commission' <https://finance.ec.europa.eu/digital-finance/framework-financial-data-access_en> accessed 16 March 2025.

[104] For a comprehensive overview of information on PEPP: 'Pan-European Personal Pension Product (PEPP) - European Union' (12 July 2022) <https://www.eiopa.europa.eu/browse/regulation-and-policy/pan-european-personal-pension-product-pepp_en> accessed 16 March 2025.

[105] Petra Hielkema, 'Closing Pension Gaps in Europe - European Union' (FIAP conference / Conference of the Spanish Association for Investment and Pension Funds, 28 October 2021) <https://www.eiopa.europa.eu/publications/closing-pension-gaps-europe_en> accessed 16 March 2025.

[106] Cf. on the term PEPP manufacturer: Art. 2 No. 15 PEPP Regulation.

[107] Jack Schickler, 'Brussels' Pensions Plan Is Not Working' (*euronews*, 7 March 2024) <https://www.euronews.com/business/2024/03/07/hype-over-hit-brussels-pensions-plan-is-not-working> accessed 16 March 2025.

[108] For example, the overall risk indicator to be presented in the PEPP key information document differs in essential aspects from the overall risk indicator in the PRIIP key information document. For PEPP, a stochastic simulation forms the basis for the overall risk indicator, while other methods are specified for PRIIP, which differ again depending on the PRIIP category. Differences exist concerning the scaling of the risk indicator, and even the basic methodology for determining it is different. Regarding the basic idea, the overall risk indicator of the PEPP is closer to determining the risk/reward class of Basis and Riester products in Germany than to PRIIPs (Stolz and Rieck, (2025) 41.).

references to national law, various sectoral supervisory regimes, a confusion of national and European law, legal sources of different normative quality and legal areas of different systems (supervisory law, tax law, contract law, etc.) due to the unique conception of the PEPP with so-called accounts and sub-accounts that have a deterrent effect.[109] The example of the PEPP has rather shown that the fundamental legal and tax framework must first be created before such a comprehensive, original European product can function. PEPP in its current form has so far not been the answer for a flourishing cross-border (life) insurance business. To achieve this goal in the future, the EU Commission must carefully address the points mentioned in a future review of the regulation.

5 Concluding Remarks

Insurers who want to offer their products across borders still have to deal intensively with foreign legal systems, as the existing choice of law options only generally lead to applicability of the law of the host country being applied to the contract in cross-border business. In addition, the regulations of the General Good Requirements also imply that a wide range of regulations of the national insurance contract and supervisory law of the host country are to be applied to the product or contract. Furthermore, there are still significant differences in national insurance contract and consumer protection laws, adding to the complexity of the situation. In addition, it is important to note that the variations in the implementation of directives across EU member states, along with the associated differences in supervisory practices, remain a significant issue. This was a point of contention for the EU during the 2008/2009 financial crisis, and it continues to be a challenge for the single insurance market. Despite the ongoing flood of European regulation, it has not yet been possible to standardize European competitive conditions in life insurance.[110] A genuine common market for life insurance seems desirable from the point of view of both insurers and policyholders.

Although indeed customer protection seems to be the right measure to tackle many problems which were revealed during the financial crisis, increasing complexity as highlighted in this paper clearly is not. As consequence, insurers cannot simply offer products marketed in their home country in another member state without time-consuming and costly legal analyses and often very complex adjustments to the legal requirements of the host member state. Products designed and calculated

[109] Reiner and Horvath, (2018).

[110] This is particularly regrettable in view of the possibilities of online sales. The European Commission's group of experts had already stated in 2014 - a long time ago from an IT perspective - that insurers should have the freedom to develop strategies and take commercial risks in order to sell contracts more easily in the host countries. Unfortunately, however, it is still the case that insurers generally reject applications from abroad. One of the reasons for this behavior is once again likely to be mandatory foreign (contract) law.

according to the actuarial principles applicable in the insurer's home member state may even have to be recalculated according to the 'contract law' requirements of the target market. Actuarial science, and therefore the life insurance business, is based on the law of large numbers and risk diversification. It could therefore be more efficie–t - and less costly in terms of premiu–s - if an insurer would only have to develop and market one single 'European' product (or tariff). This could certainly open up the market to a broader range of (still very well-protected) customers. However, this has not yet been possible. Irrespective of other factors, the large number of mandatory rules and their diversity in the different member states poses an operational problem for an insurer entering into a new market. Moreover, the complexity of these regulations often hinders an insurer from having the same staff and IT system dealing with these matters in different jurisdictions. The insurer has to hire specialists and maintain a separate IT system for each member state. This incurs additional costs that may prevent an insurer from becoming seriously active in other EU member states. These costs increase with the number of member states an insurer operates in. It can therefore be stated that – despite all efforts – the single licence principle is still not decisive for a noteworthy cross-border business in the life insurance sector. Admittedly, a joint European effort to achieve more flexibility in the choice of law or, even, a common unified private insurance law would open up the opportunity to truly create a European single market for life insurance. From the author's point of view, a comprehensive, targeted and perhaps completely rethought review of the PEPP regulation could be a good start.

Regulations

Regulation (EU) No 1286/2014 of the European Parliament and of the Council of 26 November 2014 on key information documents for packaged retail and insurance-based investment products (PRIIPs)

Directive 2009/138/EC of the European Parliament and of the Council of 25 November 2009 on the taking-up and pursuit of the business of Insurance and Reinsurance (Solvency II)

Directive (EU) 2016/97 of the European Parliament and of the Council of 20 January 2016 on insurance distribution

Directive (EU) 2016/97 of the European Parliament and of the Council of 20 January 2016 on insurance distribution (recast)Text with EEA relevance

Regolamento IVASS N. 41 del 2 agosto 2018

Regulation (EC) No 593/2008 of the European Parliament and the Council of June 2008 on the law applicable to contractual obligations (Rome I)

Regulation (EU) 2019/ of the European Parliament and of the Council of 20 June 2019 on a pan-European Personal Pension Product (PEPP)

Cases

BVerwG, 21042021 - 8 C 620 [2021] BVerwG 8 C 6.20 (Germany)

BVerwG, 23 3 2011 - 8 C 47/09 [2011] BVerwG 8 C 47/09, 2011 NJW-RR 1250 (Germany)

OGH 7Ob19/21a (Austria)

Book Chapters

Baroch Castellvi M, 'VAG § 57 Versicherungsgeschäfte Über Niederlassung de rim im Dienstleistungsverkehr' in Oliver Brand and Manuel BarochCastellvi (eds), *Versicherungsaufsichtsgesetz* (2nd edn, 2024).
Beckmann R and Matusche-Beckmann A, 'Versicherungsrecht' in Manfred Dauses and Ludwig Ludwigs (eds), *Handbuch des EU-Wirtschaftsrechts* (61st edn, 2024).
Diehl F, '§ 24 Europäischer Binnenmarkt' in Frank Diehl (ed), *Diehl* (1st edn, 2020).
Diehl F, Grundzüge des Versicherungsaufsichtsrechts' in Höra Höra and Schubach Schubach (eds), *Münchener Anwaltshandbuch Versicherungsrecht* (5th edn, 2022).
Dreher M, 'VAG § 294 Aufgaben' in Meinrad Dreher (ed), *Versicherungsaufsichtsgesetz* (14th edn, 2024).
Grote J, 'VAG § 67 Erlaubnis; Spartentrennung' in Meinrad Dreher (ed), *Versicherungsaufsichtsgesetz* (14th edn, 2024).
Heiss H, 'VVG § 153 Überschussbeteiligung' in Theo Langheid and Manfred Wandt (eds), *Münchener Kommentar zum VVG* (3rd edn, 2024).
Kyriaki N, 'The IDD and Its Impact on the Life Insurance Industry'. in Pierpaolo Marano and Kyriaki Noussia (eds), *Insurance Distribution Directive: A Legal Analysis* (2021).
Leithoff T, 'VVG § 153 Überschussbeteiligung' in Ansgar Staudinger, Wolfgang Halm and Domenik Wendt (eds), *Versicherungsrecht* (3rd edn, 2022).
Littbarski S, 'Vorbemerkungen Zu §§ 100–112' in Theo Langheid and Manfred Wandt (eds), *Münchener Kommentar zum VVG* (3rd edn, 2024).
Looschelders D, 'Kap. 15. Internationales Versicherungsvertragsrecht' in Theo Langheid and Manfred Wandt (eds), *Münchener Kommentar zum VVG* (3rd edn, 2024).
Lüttringhaus J, 'Rom I-VO Art. 7 Versicherungsverträge' in Beate Gsell and others (eds), *beck-online.Grosskommentar* (status: 2024).
Marano P, 'The "Mifidization": The Sunset of Life Insurance in the EU Regulation on Insurance? *Social Science Research Network* (2016).
Marano P, 'The Contribution of Product Oversight and Governance (POG) to the Single Market: A Set of Organisational Rules for Business Conduct' in Pierpaolo Marano and Kyriaki Noussia (eds), *Insurance Distribution Directive: A Legal Analysis* (2021).
Martiny D, 'Rom I-VO Art. 9 Eingriffsnormen', in Jan v Hein (eds), *Münchener Kommentar zum BGB* (8th edn, 2021).
Maultzsch F, 'Rom I-VO Art. 9 Eingriffsnormen' in Beate Gsell and others (eds), *beck-online. GGrosskommentar* (status: 2024).
Mönnich U, '§ 2. Europäisierung Des Privatversicherungsrechts' in Roland Beckmann and Annemarie Matusche-Beckmann (eds), *Versicherungsrechts-Handbuch* (3rd edn, 2015).
Pickartz U and Stegmann A, 'VAG § 52 Verpflichtete Unternehmen' in Oliver Brand and Manuel Baroch Castellvi (eds), *Versicherungsaufsichtsgesetz* (2nd edn, 2024).
Pohlmann P, 'VAG § 67 Erlaubnis; Spartentrennung' in Detlef Kaulbach, Gunne W Bähr and Petra Pohlmann (eds), *Versicherungsaufsichtsgesetz* (6th edn, 2019).
Schäfer FL, '§ 1. Duales Krankenversicherungssystem' in Jan Boetius, Jens Rogler and Frank L Schäfer (eds), *Rechtshandbuch Private Krankenversicherung* (1st edn, 2020).
Schäfers D, 'VAG § 294 Aufgaben' in Kay Uwe Erdmann, Frank S Diehl and Heinrich R Schradin (eds), *BeckOK VAG* (26th edn, 2024).
Staudinger A, 'VO (EG) 593/2008 Art. 7 Versicherungsverträge' in Franco Ferrari and others (eds), *Internationales Vertragsrecht* (3rd edn, 2018).
Staudinger A, 'Rom I-VO Art. 9 Eingriffsnormen' in Reiner Schulze (ed), *Schul–e - Bürgerliches Gesetzbuch* (12th edn, 2024).
Stolz S and Rieck T, 'Art. 28 PEPP-VO' in Robert Horvath and Martin Ramharter (eds), *Paneuropäisches Privates Pensionsprodukt (PEPP-VO)* (1st edn, 2025).
Wandt M, 'Allgemeines Versicherungsaufsichtsrecht' in Wolfgang E Halm, Andreas Engelbrecht and Frank Krahe, *Handbuch des Fachanwalts Versicherungsrecht* (6., 2018).
Wendt J and Wendt DH, 'Einleitung' in Janine Wendt and Domenik H Wendt (eds), *PRIIP-Verordnung* (1st edn, 2021).

Articles

Baranowska-Zając W, 'Freedom of Establishment on the Internal Insurance Market of the European Union in the Light of Directive 2009/138/EC (Solvency II)' (2014) *Mediterranean Journal of Social Sciences, Vol. 5* No. 5, 661–671.

Basedow J, 'Versicherungsvertragsrecht Als Markthindernis?' (2014) *Europäische Zeitschrift für Wirtschaftsrecht*, Vol. 1, 1–2.

Basedow J, 'Towards a European Insurance Contract Law? The Commission Expert Group, Its Antecedents and Consequences' (2015), Max Planck Private Law Research Paper, Vol 18, 1–17.

Boléat MJ and Boléat MJ, 'The European Single Insurance Market' (1995) 20 *The Geneva Papers on Risk and Insurance, Vol. 20*, 45–56.

Cummins JD, Rubio-Misas M and Vencappa D, 'Competition, Efficiency and Soundness in European Life Insurance Markets' (2017) 28 *Journal of Financial Stability, Vol. 28*, 6–78.

Gamarra T, 'The Effects of Liberalization and Deregulation on the Performance of Financial Institutions: The Case of the German Life Insurance Market', (2008) Thünen-Series of Applied Economic Theo–y - Working Paper, No. 93, 1–44.

Gruber M and Konwitschka M, 'Die Rechtswahl Nach § 35a IPRG Bei Lebensversicherungsverträgen' (2022) *Zeitschrift für Versicherungsrecht, Haftungs- und Schadensrecht, Vol. 3*, 65–70.

Marano P, 'The "Mifidization": The Sunset of Life Insurance in the EU Regulation on Insurance?' (2026), *Social Science Research Network.*

Möllers TMJ, 'Europäische Gesetzgebungslehre 2.0: Die Dynamische Rechtsharmonisierung Im Kapitalmarktrecht Am Beispiel von MiFID II Und PRIIP' (2016) *Zeitschrift für Europäisches Privatrecht, Vol. 2*, 19–355.

Theis DA, 'EWR-Versicherer in Deutschland: Eine Bestandsaufnahme' (2023), Economic Resear–h - Insurance Flash, Gesamtverband der Versicherer, No. 1, 1–3.

Reiner M and Horvath R, 'Das Neue Europäische Private Altersvorsorgeprodukt PEPP (Pan-European Personal Pension Product) Und Seine Markt-Gängigkeit Im Binnenmar–t - Eine Kritische Intervention', (2018), Working Paper Series by the University of Applied Sciences BFI Vienna, No. 98, 1–31.

Institutional Websites

Banque de France, 'General Good Rules (GGR)' https://acpr.banque-france.fr/en/authorisation/insurance-sector-procedures/general-good-rules-ggr, accessed 30 Sep 2024.

BaFin, 'EU/EEA Insurers' https://www.bafin.de/EN/Aufsicht/VersichererPensionsfonds/Zulassung/EU-EWR-Versicherer/eu_ewr_versicherer_node_en.html, accessed 16 Mar 2025.

BaFin, 'General Good Requirements in Germany' https://www.bafin.de/SharedDocs/Veroeffentlichungen/EN/Merkblatt/VA/mb_110308_zulassung_eu_liste_vorschriftenallgemeininteresse_va_en.html, accessed 16 Mar 2025.

BaFin, 'Hinweise für die Tätigkeit in den EU/EWR-Staaten' https://www.bafin.de/SharedDocs/Veroeffentlichungen/DE/Merkblatt/VA/mb_100208_taetigkeiteuewr_va.html, accessed 16 Mar 2025.

BaFin, 'Lebensversicherungen' https://www.bafin.de/DE/Verbraucher/Versicherung/Produkte/Leben/lebensversicherung_node.html, accessed 16 Mar 2025.

BaFin, 'Notification Procedure: Exchange of Information among EU/EEA Insurance Supervisors' https://www.bafin.de/SharedDocs/Veroeffentlichungen/EN/Fachartikel/2018/fa_bj_1805_Notifikation_en.html, accessed 16 Mar 2025.

BaFin, 'Solvency II' https://www.bafin.de/EN/Aufsicht/VersichererPensionsfonds/Allgemeines/SolvencyII/solvency_II_node_en.html, accessed 30 Sep 2024.

EIOPA, 'Pan-European Personal Pension Product (PEPP)' https://www.eiopa.europa.eu/browse/regulation-and-policy/pan-european-personal-pension-product-pepp_en, accessed 16 Mar 2025.

EIOPA, 'What Is Solvency II?' https://www.eiopa.europa.eu/browse/regulation-and-policy/solvency-ii_en, accessed 16 Mar 2025.

European Commission, 'EU Taxonomy for Sustainable Activities' https://finance.ec.europa.eu/sustainable-finance/tools-and-standards/eu-taxonomy-sustainable-activities_en, accessed 16 Mar 2025.

European Commission, 'EU Single Mark–t - The Single Market: Europe's Best Asset in a Changing World' https://commission.europa.eu/document/download/fa404637-9fde-446d-a9b0-cab136d8acd3_en?filename=factsheet_single_market.pdf, accessed 16 Mar 2025.

European Commissi–n - Directorate-General for Justice, 'Final Report of the Commission Expert Group on European Insurance Contract Law' (2014) https://www.mpipriv.de/1102634/eicl-finalreport.pdf

European Commission, 'Expert Group on European Insurance Contract L–w - European Commission' https://commission.europa.eu/business-economy-euro/doing-business-eu/contract-rules/insurance-contracts/expert-group-european-insurance-contract-law_en, accessed 16 Mar 2025.

European Commission, 'Sustainability-Related Disclosure in the Financial Services Sector' https://finance.ec.europa.eu/sustainable-finance/disclosures/sustainability-related-disclosure-financial-services-sector_en, accessed 16 Mar 2025.

European Consumer Centre Germany, 'The European Single Insurance Mark–t -Cross-Border Insurance Contracts: Conclusion or Exclusion? What Does the Market for Cross-Border Insurance Products Look like for Consumers in the Year 2014?' https://www.cec-zev.eu/fileadmin/Media/PDF/publications/Etudes-Rapports_FR/Etude_Assurances-resume_EN.pdf, accessed 16 Mar 2025.

European Commission, 'Framework for Financial Data Acce–s - European Commission' https://finance.ec.europa.eu/digital-finance/framework-financial-data-access_en, accessed 16 Mar 2025.

FMA Austria, 'EU-Pass für Kreditinstitute, Versicherungen und Wertpapierfirmemn' https://www.fma.gv.at/glossar/eu-pass-fuer-kreditinstitute-versicherungen-und-wertpapierfiren/, accessed 16 Mar 2025.

Hielkema P, 'Closing Pension Gaps in Euro–e - European Union' (FIAP conference / Conference of the Spanish Association for Investment and Pension Funds, 28 October 2021) https://www.eiopa.europa.eu/publications/closing-pension-gaps-europe_en, accessed 16 Mar 2025.

IVASS, 'Distribuzione Prodetti Assicurativi Semplificazione e Standardizzazione Delle Informazioni' https://www.ivass.it/normativa/focus/distribuzione-assicurativa/approfondimenti/INFORMATIVA_PRECONTRATTUALE.pdf, accessed 16 Mar 2025.

IVASS, 'General Good Provisions for Foreign Operators' https://www.ivass.it/normativa/nazionale/norme-int-gen/index.html, accessed 16 Mar 2025.

Office of the official publications of the European Communities, 'Official Journal of the European Communiti–s -Information and Notices (C43)' https://eur-lex.europa.eu/legal-content/EN/TXT/PDF/?uri=OJ:C:2000:043:FULL, accessed 16 Mar 2025.

COVIP, 'Rami Assicurativi Vita' https://www.covip.it/per-il-cittadino/educazione-previdenziale/glossario/rami-assicurativi-vita, accessed 16 Mar 2025.

Further Websites

Mion G and Ponattu D, 'Estimating Economic Benefits of the Single Market for European Countries and Regions' https://www.bertelsmann-stiftung.de/fileadmin/files/BSt/Publikationen/GrauePublikationen/EZ_Study_SingleMarket. pdf, accessed 16 Mar 2025.

Schickler J, 'Brussels' Pensions Plan Is Not Working' (*euronews*, 7 March 2024) https://www.euronews.com/business/2024/03/07/hype-over-hit-brussels-pensions-plan-is-not-working, accessed 16 Mar 2025.

Group Insurance in Comparative Perspective: Ensuring Fairness, Efficiency, and Beyond

Mariusz Fras

1 Introduction

The intensive development of group insurance should prompt an in-depth reflection on the legal nature of these solutions, in which the insurance coverage scheme goes beyond the classic formula of individual insurance. In spite of this, this increasingly popular and at the same time evolving form of insurance, permanently embedded in the market practice, has not lived to see its regulation in the provisions on the insurance contract in the Civil Code. There is a lack of legal regulations of substantive law of member states which, taking into account the distinctiveness of group insurance, would give it a legal framework adapted to the needs of the market and could counteract those risks that arise from the specific subjective arrangement of group insurance. There is a lack of definition at the EU level of the group insurance contract. There is only a mention in recital 49 of the Directive IDD 2016/97: "In the case of group insurance, 'customer' should mean the representative of a group of members who concludes an insurance contract on behalf of the group of members where the individual member cannot take an individual decision to join, such as a mandatory occupational pension arrangement. The representative of the group should, promptly after enrollment of the member in the group insurance, provide, where relevant, the insurance product information document and the distributor's conduct of business information". As a result, the level of protection of the interests of the group insured has not kept pace with the dynamic changes in the legal constructions on the basis of which insurance cover is offered. The legal comparative method is important in this chapter. French law was chosen as the principal subject of comparative research. It constitutes particularly fertile research material from the point of view of the purpose of this study, as group insurance in France has the broadest and most comprehensive normative regulation. Thus, French jurisprudence and science should be the starting point and basis for consideration of the normative shape of the group insurance contract. The aim of the research is to develop a "benchmark" legal regulation of the group insurance contract in order to ensure its effectiveness and to protect the weaker party in the contract.

This research was funded in whole by National Science Centre, Poland, Grant Number 2020/39/B/HS5/02631.

M. Fras
Department of Civil Law and Private International Law, Silesian University, Katowice, Poland
e-mail: mariusz.fras@us-edu.pl

P. Marano (ed.), *Emerging Legal Frontiers in Insurance*,
AIDA Europe Research Series on Insurance Law and Regulation,
https://doi.org/10.1007/978-3-032-09716-3_6

2 The Origins and Development of the Group Insurance Contract

2.1 US: Pioneer of the Group Insurance

The group insurance contract, in the presently known formula, arose at the beginning of the twentieth century in the United States of America.[1] Formation and development of group insurance was an answer to the unquestioned need to secure the interests of employees, which was not sufficiently addressed by public law solutions in the era of industrialization.[2] As opposed to European benchmarks, in the United States of America there was no organized social security system,[3] despite the greatest dynamics of industrial development in that country. It should be of no surprise that group insurance was viewed as panacea to the threats relating to the unstable economic situation and, at the same time, as instrument free from any political influence.[4]

Another factor contributing to the popularization of group insurance in the United States of America in the middle twentieth century were the legal provisions introduced at that time on minimum and maximum salaries of persons employed in the industrial sector. Employers willing to establish cooperation with qualified workforce engaged by their competition could not offer to such qualified professionals remuneration exceeding the amount of maximum salary. In search of another stimulus that might induce a valued specialist to change the place of work, industrialists turned to insurance, thanks to which they could ensure additional benefits to their employees in case of sickness or invalidity, without the need to increase the rate of the remuneration paid.[5]

In literature of the subject, an opinion can also be found that, historically speaking, the formula of group insurance had a shameful record. Certain authors point out that that the origins of group insurance should be traced back to the contracts concluded at the beginning of the nineteenth century by enslaved people traders with the intention to secure their interests in case of death of the persons transported by ships from Africa to North America. In those contracts, these were those who enslaved people that were designated as beneficiaries entitled to receive monetary indemnity.[6] Analogous contracts were concluded even several decades later with regard to the first workers sent to work at the construction of the Panama Canal.[7]

[1] F. Herdter, (2010), p. 9.
[2] K.L. Clark, (2012), p. 3.
[3] W.F. Schickinger (1988), pp. 239–248.
[4] J.M. Herrick, P.H. Stuart (2005)p. 433.
[5] K.L. Clark (2012), p. 3.
[6] R.H. Jerry, D.R. Richmond (2012), p. 916, fn 1.
[7] I.M. Field(2012), p. 916.

It seems, however, that the opinion that group insurance was formed in the circumstances mentioned above should be approached with much caution. According to certain authors, similar forms of securing the interests of those who enslaved people were known already in ancient times. They were to assume the form of insurance of owners against the escape of enslaved people.[8] That formula was closer to what presently is referred to as property insurance. Escaped enslaved people were treated as lost assets of their owner. This conclusion may just as well be referred to the above-mentioned insurance of enslaved people traders concluded in the nineteenth century. Also in that context, the slave him- or herself could not apply for insurance protection under a life insurance contract concluded individually with the insurer.

2.2 *The Origins of Group Insurance Contracts in Europe (French Example)*

Insurance contracts have a long tradition in France, which dates back to early Middle Ages.[9] However, the construction of the group insurance contract developed relatively late. Its emergence was dictated, in the first place, by the changes in the employment structure in the period of the industrial revolution which took place in France in the nineteenth century. The growth in the number of people working in factories did not translate into the improvement of safety conditions, which resulted in multiplication of the number of accidents, usually leading to permanent disablement and loss of the earning potential. The social security institutions existing at that time did not guarantee benefits that would allow to sufficiently satisfy the life's necessities of workers forced to permanently give up their professional activities. Moreover, at the initial stage of operation of this system, its beneficiaries were only a small number of employees whose income did not exceed the threshold specified in statutory law.[10]

There were attempts to make up for those shortcomings by imposing on entrepreneurs the liability for accidents at work. Because of the mass nature of such events, industrialists, for their part, were searching for solutions allowing to reduce the economic burden relating to the need of paying benefits to the injured parties.[11]

[8] W.K. Rajcher, following Aristotle, gives an example of a Babylonian official who, inconsideration of a specific amount of money, guaranteed to wealthy persons the capture and return of an escaped enslave person or payment of an equivalent the person'sworth, as specified in advance by the owner. However, this author calls into question the credibility of the report of ancient enslaved people owners' insurance against escape of their victims. W.K. Rajcher (1951), pp. 123–125,and the literature cited therein.

[9] For more on the development of insurance in France, see M. Chagny, L. Perdrix, (2012), p. 19 et seq.

[10] M. Fauque, (1971), p. 13.

[11] Ibid., pp. 11–12.

However, only the abolition of monopoly of state social security institutions did allow insurers to offer services supposed to compensate for the shortcomings of the public law social security system.[12] In that period market practice gave rise to first insurance schemes against accidents at work (*l'assurancecontre les accidents du travail*),[13] which constituted a formula of group insurance. At that time, the terms were used interchangeably of group insurance (*assurance de groupe*), collective insurance (*assurance collective*) or pension and disability insurance (*assurance de prévoyance et de retraite*).[14]

At this development stage of French law, the group insurance contract was treated as a variety of life insurance,[15] and the fragmentary legal regime related only to insurance in case of death.[16] However, there were no provisions devoted to the formation or terms of performing those contracts. In addition, this legal construction was not paid much attention by academic literature. Group insurance, which developed as a response to the existing social and economic demands, aroused more interest in the management staff and academic authors in the area of economy than among legal theorists.[17]

The development dynamics of the market for insurance services, however, implied the need to adapt legislative solutions to the needs of economic transactions. Group insurance, closest to the model presently operating in French law, were subject to normative regulation only in the 20s of the twentieth century.[18] In this period, first legislative acts were adopted governing workers' compensation insurance in which the afforded protection covered different types of risk relating to sicknesses, invalidity, death or attainment of a specific age.[19] However, only in the Act of 13 July 1930, did the legislator introduce specific solutions in respect of this form of insurance.[20] The model of group insurance adopted by the French legislator was not based on the experiences of other European countries.[21] Rather than that, inspiration was drawn from the solutions developed in the United States of America.[22] It is a kind of curiosity that the Anglo-American literature, which was

[12] E. Routel (2001), pp., 11–12; N. Marques (2000),pp. 7–8.

[13] For more, see M. Bosredon(1990), pp. 104–106; V.P. Comiti(1985), pp. 124–125.

[14] L. Mayaux(2007), p. 653.

[15] J. Voigt (1942), p. 15.

[16] F. Berdot(1980), p. 11.

[17] L. Mayaux(2007), p. 620.

[18] A. Gogueld'Allondans(2000), pp. 58–59.

[19] Ibid., pp. 58–59.

[20] Loi du 13 juillet 1930 diteGodart relative au contratd'assurances, JORF du 18 juillet 1930, p. 8003.

[21] As a consequence, already in the first decades of the XX century the French tradition of group insurance developed independently from the German experiences; see Chapter 1 item 1.3. For more on the origins of collective insurance in particular European countries, see E. Roueil (1998), p. 25 et seq.

[22] J. Voigt, (1942),pp. 10–17.

a source of strong inspirations to the French, points by itself to the ancient Roman origins of group insurance in the form they have presently assumed in the countries of *common law* tradition.[23]

The dynamics of growth of the group insurance market in France in the first half of the twentieth century are evidenced by the statistical data published in literature. Already in 1937, the total amount of benefits that potentially could be paid in case of materialization of different types of risk covered by group insurance contracts was 2 billion francs, whereas already one year later the same amount exceeded 3 billion francs.[24] However, certain authors reserve at this point that the proliferation of group forms of insurance was not correlated with an introduction of new legislative solutions. Proponents of that view emphasize that the development of the market for group insurance was possible thanks to the abolishment of the prohibition to charge lower premium in case of collective insurance schemes than it was the case with individual insurance.[25] Only in 1929 did the French legislator withdraw from the previously adopted solution imposing a requirement to apply identical tariff tables for individual and collective insurance forms.[26]

Another stage of development of group insurance in France belongs to the second half of the twentieth century. A fragmentary regime of those contracts was contained in the Decree of 24 January 1956. However, for the most part, these were norms relating to the financial and technical aspects of the activities pursued by insurers.[27]

Another step towards the currently applicable solutions was the introduction of the definition of group insurance under the Decree of 16 July 1976,[28] adopted in spite of the absence of a normative definition of the insurance contract in French law, which gap had been filled by academic literature.[29] In 1981, under the Act of 7 January 1981 on the insurance contract and capitalization operations,[30] the definition included so far in the Decree of 1976 was transposed into the Insurance Code.[31] Beyond any doubt, this legal regime set the directions for the development of the French insurance thought in the years to come.

---

[23] K.L. Clark (2012), p. 2.

[24] E. Roueil, (1998), p. 31.

[25] M. Milcamps (1956), p. 28.

[26] See Art. 2 of the Decree of 23 May 1929 (Décret du 23 mai 1929, portant modification au décret de 20 janvier 1906, modifie par les décrets des 24 juin 1916 et 22 juin 1921 sur le tarif minimum des assurances-vie, J.O. du 29 mai 1929; Semainejuridique 1929, IV, p. 162.).

[27] V. Nicolas (1996), p. 200.

[28] Décretn° 76 667 du 16 juillet 1976, relatif à la codification des textesréglementairesconcernant les Assurance, JORF du 21 juillet 1976, p. 4343.

[29] See. J. Hémard (1924), p. 73; G. Cornu (2001), p. 81.

[30] Loi relative au contratd'assurance et aux opérations de capitalisation, Loi n° 81-5 du 7 janvier 1981, JO du 8 janvier 1981.

[31] The French Insurance Code (Code des assurances; JO 1978, p. 1088, modifié).

2.3 *The Origins of Group Insurance Contracts in Europe (German Example)*

In the territory of present-day Germany, solutions characteristic of group insurance can already be identified in the Middle Ages.[32] However, the constructions applicable at the time were based on a reciprocal basis and, in the same way, closer to services provided within the operative framework of mutual insurance companies.[33] This note should be referred, above all, to associations established for the protection of common interests. Such mutual assistance organizations were established, in the first place, by craftsmen and small merchants,[34] although similar associations were formed also in peasant communities.[35] When it comes to Germanic peoples, those structures transformed over time into guilds, a part of which had the characteristics of insurance associations. They were created for the purpose of aiding the members of such associations in case of fortuitous events.[36]

Group insurance, as a method of organizing insurance for the purpose of affording insurance protection to a certain group under one contract, crystalized only in the late nineteenth and early twentieth century.[37] Originally, the group insurance construction was used to ensure protection against the risk of death. Then, it began to cover also the risks relating to inability to work, and, finally, a broader category of risks relating to the insured person's health.[38] Already under the Act of 10 April 1854, a duty was imposed on certain categories of employers to insure workers. At the same time, the Act of 1854 established a normative framework for the first nationwide workers' compensation insurance.[39]

A few decades later, emperor Wilhelm I, following Otto von Bismarck's advice, inspired legislative works on a package of acts that were supposed to make a foundation for a modern, public law system of social security. This purpose was achieved after the adoption by the Reichstag of three consecutive acts, respectively: on 29 May 1883 – the Act on health insurance,[40] on 6 June 1884– the Act on occupational accident insurance,[41] and on 22 June 1889 – the Act on insurance against invalidity and attainment of a specific age.[42]

32 K. Łyskawa (2007),p. 153.

33 K.L. Clark (2012), p. 2.

34 H. Braun (1925), p. 6.

35 J. Łazowski (1998), p. 29.

36 Ibid., p. 28.

37 D.K. Chandler (1997), pp. 2–3.

38 G. Baars, N. Sennett (1993), p. 14.

39 F. Herdter, (2010), p. 9.

40 RGBl 1883, p. 73 et seq.,the Act was promulgated on 15 June 1883 and entered into force on 1 December 1884.

41 RGBl 1884, p. 1884 et seq., the Act entered into force on 1 October 1885.

42 RGBl 1889, p. 97 et seq., the Act entered into force on 1 January 1891.

The normative solutions introduced at that time were universally applicable. This was the progressiveness of the Prussian system. However, because of the aspiration to afford insurance coverage to a relatively wide number of people, the system offered only a minimum protection level to its participants.[43] An answer to the shortcomings of the state mechanism was group insurance offered by insurance companies.

In the lack of a definition of group insurance and the respective legal regime, the direction for the development of such insurance was set by interventions of the insurance supervision. At an initial stage, those were actions intended to limit the number of so-called privileged contracts. The term is referred to group insurance contracts under which individual persons obtained preferential terms and conditions from their point of view.[44] This practice was considered harmful to the total of the insured parties because preference of specific individuals was stipulated, so to say, at the expense of other persons covered by the insurance protection. Another undesired tendency that became apparent in commercial transactions was the stipulation of commission for the policyholder in consideration of a concluded contract. It must be noted that, initially, the attempts to counteract such practices were a manifestation of self-regulation of the insurance sector,[45] which supports the conclusion that already in the late nineteenth and early twentieth century, the market for group insurance was relatively well-organized in the territory of present-day Germany.

3 Sources of Generally Applicable Law Governing the Group Insurance Contract

The entirety of norms on the relations connected with conclusion and performance of insurance contracts make up economic insurance law. Because of its objective homogeneity, it is generally treated as a separate branch of law.[46] From the dogmatic perspective, its permanent element are group insurance contracts. However, the results of a comparative law research allow to draw the conclusion that in a substantial number of legal systems the term "group insurance" is not to be found in normative acts.[47] Even in the systems recognizing the need to specifically regulate the group insurance contract, the prevalent tendency is to regulate this subject matter rudimentarily.

One of the few exceptions to that rule is France, where group insurance attracted special attention of the legislator. French insurance law is composed of a number

43 W.F. Schickinger, (1998),p. 240.

44 For more, see V. Kurzendörfer (2000), p. 443.

45 F. Herdter, (2010),p. 15.

46 M. Fras (2020)pp.179–231.,

47 L.D. Loacker (2015), p. 226.

of legislative acts,[48] which include multiple solutions distinctive against the background of other European legislations. Among solutions specific almost exclusively to French law, one can point also to the extensive regime of group insurance contracts.[49] Complications following from the application of those provisions are subject to detailed doctrinal discussion.

The contemporary catalog of sources of insurance law constitutes a very extensive system of interrelated normative acts. One may speak of coherent statutory solutions only in case of one of the types of collective insurance agreements, namely the group insurance contract. Other collective insurance contracts do not form any homogenous category and are characterized by the absence of coherent systemic solutions.

The basic legislative act covering problems of insurance law is the Insurance Code (CA)[50]. Its field of application *ratione personae* precludes recourse to the solutions envisaged in the Code in regard to contracts in which the party affording insurance protection is an entity other than joint-stock company pursuing insurance activities.[51] The provisions of the Code do not apply to contracts concluded by mutual insurance societies or social security institutions. The Insurance Code does not govern insurance law relationships concluded with the involvement of such entities.[52] This gap, however, is filled by other codes: the Mutual Insurance Code (*Code de la mutualité*)[53] and the Social Security Code (*Code de la sécuritésociale*).[54]

Beside the Insurance Code, the foundation of the modern legislation on collective group agreements, as a wider category covering among others group insurance contracts, is laid by two Acts of 31 December 1989, namely the Act No. 89-1009 reinforcing the safeguards of persons insured against certain types of risk,[55] referred to as *loiEvin*,[56] and the Act No. 89-1014, adjusting the Insurance Code to the opening of the European market,[57] referred to as *loiBérégovoy.*

[48] M. Bigot-Gonçalves (2009), p. 49.

[49] M. Bigot-Gonçalves (2009), p. 22.

[50] CA – French Insurance Code (Code des assurances; JO 1978, p. 1088, modifié).

[51] L. Mayaux(2007), p. 640.

[52] M. Bigot-Gonçalves(2009), p. 20.

[53] http://www.legifrance.gouv.fr/affichCode.do?cidTexte=LEGITEXT000006074067 (last accessed: 27 June 2024).

[54] http://www.legifrance.gouv.fr/affichCode.do?cidTexte=LEGITEXT000006073189 (last accessed: 27 June 2024).

[55] Act No. 89-1009 of 31 December 1989 reinforcing the safeguards of persons insured against certain types of risk (La loi n° 89-1009 du 31 décembre 1989 renforçant les garantiesoffertes aux personnesassuréescontrecertainsrisques, JO du 2 janvier 1990).

[56] D. Rigaud, P. Baron, X. Pignaud, Le prévoyance collective des salariés et la loi Evin, Droit social 2009, no 4, p. 465.

[57] Act No. 89-1014 of 31 December1989 adjusting the Insurance Code to the opening of the Europeanmarket(Loi n° 89-1014 du 31 décembre 1989 portant adaptation du code des assurances à l'ouverture du marché européen, JO n° 2 du 03.01.1990).

Originally, the provisions of Title IV of Book I CA were classified as default norms. Under the Regulation of 30 January 2009,[58] the ruleof Art. L. 111-2 CA was amended so that the provisions of Book I Title IV of the Code, governing group insurance contracts, were given the status of mandatory provisions (*ius cogens*)[59] Under the version currently in force of Art. L. 111-2 CA, the provisions of Book I Titles I, II, III i IV of the Code may not be modified by the intention of the parties. However, the legislator stipulates that the said principle does not relate to provisions which expressly provide for such eventuality and which were exhaustively listed in Art. L. 111-2 CA. It is significant that the norm under Art. L. 111-2 CA does not list as default norms any of the provisions of Title IV of Book I of the Code.[60] The mandatory character of the rules devoted to group insurance contracts should be of no surprise. Bearing in mind the limited possibility of members of the group of insured parties to influence the contents of the insurance contract, granting extensive contractual freedom to the parties of such contracts could infringe the interests of the collectivity covered by insurance protection.

It must be noted that the legislator introduces as well specific solutions for group insurance contracts outside Book I Title IV of the Code. Under art. L. 132-7 CA, life insurance is invalid if the insured party committed suicide in the first year of the term of such agreement. This norm, however, does not apply to group insurance contracts[61] mentioned in Art. L. 141-1 CA signed by the parties listed in Art. L. 141-6 CA. Pursuant to Art. L. 132-23 CA, in group insurance contracts in which the risk relates to the end of the working life, including supplemental insurance for public officers, it is inadmissible to stipulate the right to surrender a policy.

French law is characterized by a tendency to enact special provisions for generic categories of group insurance. The Act No. 2003-775 of 21 August 2003 introducing a pension reform,[62] referred to as *loiFillon*, established the normative framework for the operation of group insurance contracts serving as pension insurance. Another area which attracted the legislator's special attention was the sector of elective insurance of employees and persons performing work on a basis other than employment contract.[63]

On the contrary, a feature characteristic of German law is the existence of only rudimentary rules on group insurance. This may surprise, bearing in mind that the currently applicable Act on the insurance contract entered into force only on 1

[58] Ordonnance n° 2009-106 du 30 janvier 2009 portant sur la commercialisation des produits d'assurance sur la vie et sur des opérations de prévoyance collective et d'assurance, JORF no, 0026 of 31 January 2009, p. 1838 et seq.

[59] J.C. Ponge(2010), p. 57.

[60] See A. Bzdyń (2011), p. 200.

[61] This solution, however, is criticized in the doctrine. See G. Courtieu, Un suicide raté ou le législateur se tire une balle dans le pied, Gazette du Palais 1999, 8–9 janvier, p. 2.

[62] La loi du 21 août 2003 portant réforme des retraites, JO du 22 août 2003.

[63] M. Bigot-Gonçalves (2009), pp. 40 – 41.

January 2009.[64] The German legislator decided to introduce a new legislative act in view of the fact that adaptation to today's challenges of the Insurance Law Act which had been in force for nearly 100 years would not be possible by implementing minor legislative corrections.[65] The attitude of the legislator in itself to the conception of reforming insurance law augured far-reaching review of the regime of insurance relationships.

However, in the said Act, there is no comprehensive set of norms governing group insurance contracts. What is more, the German legislator did not decide to formulate a definition of group insurance although that term is used in the Act. The distinctive feature of the German legislative framework of group insurance is the legislator's care for the insured parties being guaranteed the right to continue. Only in this context does the new Act mention group insurance contracts (§ 206 and § 207 VVG).

The few legal systems in which the legislator decided to introduce a definition of the group insurance contract include as well Scandinavian countries. In Swedish law,[66] it is defined as insurance contract under which protection is afforded to a group of persons.[67] The provision of § 2 item 6 of the Finnish Act[68] defines the group insurance contract as an insurance contract in which protection is or may be afforded to members of a group specified in the insurance contract. In Norwegian law,[69] in turn, the group insurance contract is defined as insurance in which the rights and obligations of the group members are defined by an agreement concluded by the policyholder in the name or on behalf of the group members (§ 1–2 letter d of the Norwegian Act on the insurance contract).

A controversial method of regulating group insurance contracts was used by the Turkish legislator in the new Commercial Code,[70] applicable as of 1 July 2012. It must be noted that the Turkish regime is strongly inspired by the works on the uniform insurance contract law,[71] carried out with the use of comparative law research. Among the provisions on the insurance contract (Arts. 1401–1520 TTK), there is

---

[64] German Act on the insurance contract of 23 November 2007 (Versicherungsvertragsgesetz, DasBundesgesetzblatt, p. 2631).

[65] See H. Heiss (2012), vol. 5, p. 105 and the legislative materials cited therein.

[66] Swedish Act on the insurance contract 2005, Försäkringsavtalslag (SFS 2005:104), available at: https://www.riksdagen.se/sv/dokument-lagar/dokument/svensk-forfattningssamling/forsakringsavtalslag-2005104_sfs-2005-104 (last accessed: 27June 2024).

[67] J. Hjalmarsson (2008), no 1, pp. 91–92.

[68] Finnish Act on the insurance contract No. 543/1994 of 28 June 1994, Vakuutussopimuslaki 28.6.1994/543, Författningssamling 1450 (last accessed: 27 June 2024)

[69] Norwegian Act on the insurance contract, Act of 16 June 1989 No. 69, available at: http://www.aida.org.uk/pdf/NORWAY%20Insurance%20Contracts%20Act%201990-2009.pdf (last accessed: 27 June 2024).

[70] TürkTicaretKanunu, 13.1.2011, No.: 6102, ResmiGazete 14.2.2011, No. 27846.

[71] K. Atamer, New Turkish Insurance Contract Law, p. 5, study available in electronic version: http://www.aida.org.uk/pdf/Turkish%20Insurance%20Contract%20Law.pdf (last accessed: 27 June 2024).

only one article on group insurance (Art. 1496 TTK). Within the framework of that provision, the legislator attempted, at least partially, to regulate such issues which stir doubts of insurance law experts, starting from the definition of group insurance, and ending with the question of individual continuation of insurance protection. It should be remarked that the legislator recognizes the need to regulate insurance contracts more extensively. Under the delegation of legislative powers provided for in Art. 1496(5)TTK, questions expressly listed by the legislator (including but not limited to the surrender of policy or notification requirements in group insurance) and – which may surprise – "other questions material to the group insurance contract" will be regulated in secondary legislation. It does not seem that such legislative technique deserves to be followed.

Poland, on the contrary, is an example of a legal system in which the legislator does not pay attention to group insurance. Group insurance contracts are concluded under the principle of freedom of contract (Art. 353^1CC) and according to the mandatory provisions contained in Book III Title XXVII of the Civil Code.[72]

In Portuguese law, besides specific legislation concerning life insurance, general rules regarding group insurance laid down in the legal framework of the insurance contract (Articles 76–90[73]) apply to group life insurance. As such, group life insurance can either be contributive or non-contributive. Group life insurance cover risk related to a group of people who are linked to the policyholder for a certain reason not related with insurance – the group may be composed, for example, of the employees of a certain company, the lawyers of a bar association, or the teachers of a certain school.

Contributive group life insurance contracts should regulate surrender in accordance with the contribution of the insured person (Article 194[74]). In group life insurance the nomination of the beneficiary is made by the insured person – in all other aspects the rules on the nomination of the beneficiary apply also to group life insurance contracts (Article 81[75]).

In Spanish law, according to the number of insured, personal insurance can be either individual insurance or group insurance as prescribed by Article 81 of the LCS.[76] This provision states that contracts may be subscribed with the reference to risk related to one person or to a group of them.

Indeed, Article 81 of the LCS expressly allows the contract to be subscribed for the benefit of a group of persons and imposes the only requirement that the group be identified by a common characteristic different from the insurance's purpose.[77]

[72] J. Handschke, B. Kęszycka, E. Kowalewski (2007), p. 5; M. Serwach, J. Kliszcz(2010), p. 33.

[73] Decreto-Lei n.º 72/2008 de 16 de Abril, Estabelece o regime jurídico do contrato de seguro, available in electronic version: https://data.dre.pt/eli/dec-lei/72/2008/04/16/p/dre/pt/html, (last accessed: 27June 2027).

[74] Decreto-Lei n.º 72/2008 de 16 de Abril.

[75] Decreto-Lei n.º 72/2008 de 16 de Abril.

[76] Ley 80/2005, de 8 de octubre de Contrato de Seguro, BOE-A-1980-22501.

[77] J.B. Grau, N.L. Chiner, J.O. Iglesia (2014), pp. 182–183

4 The Concept of "Group"in Group Insurance Contracts

In light of the subjective configuration, which is characteristic only of collective insurance contracts, special attention should be paid to the understanding of the term "group" in insurance law.

At this point, it is worth referring to thorough investigations on the essence of the concept of "group" in foreign literature.

In French law, the term "group" is generally not to be found in the provisions of the Insurance Code. It is not used in the definition of the group insurance contract under Art. L. 141-1 CA. However, the meaning of that term may be reconstructed on the basis of the normative content of that provision. Under Art. L. 141-1 CA, insurance contract is concluded by the policyholder for the purpose of such contract being acceded by a collectivity of people who meet the criteria specified in the contract. Moreover, each of the persons acceding to the insurance must have connections of the same type with the policyholder (Art. L. 141-1(2) CA). The requirements under items (1)and (2)of Art. L. 141-1 CA allow to determine the range of persons who, at least potentially, may accede to a group insurance. As a result, they delimitate the concept of "group" when read jointly.[78]

Specification of further requirements which must be met by persons interested in accession to the insurance (Art. L.141-1(1) CA) allows to realize the principle of freedom of contract as a part of the relationship between the policyholder and the insurer. Such requirements may be expressed positively in the agreement. Then, their fulfilment by a given person will condition the possibility to accede to the group insurance and gain the status of an insured party. On the other hand, there are no contradictions to defining such requirements negatively. Then, they specify a feature which disqualifies a given person from the possibility of applying for the insurance protection.

Within the range discussed above, the French model corresponds to the solutions developed in German doctrine. Group insurance contracts are divided by the provisions of law into partial groups (*Teilgruppe*) and extended groups (*erweiterte Gruppe*). If there is a group covered bya group insurance contract within the meaning described above, it is possible to identify its parts under the contract. This involves specification of a limited group of persons according to their general characteristics. It is possible to limit the range of entitled persons within a group by such criteria as age, period of employment with the employer, place of residence or the position held in the hierarchy of a given workplace. A group insurance contract may contain a clause excluding the possibility of the protection covering, for instance, certain employee groups which, because of the character of their work, could expose the insurer to an excessive risk of paying high benefits. Consequently, like in French law, it is possible to limit the range of persons capable of applying for insurance protection by reference to negative criteria. It should be mentioned that in case of

[78] G. Sargos (2012), p. 26.;M. Fras, (2020), pp. 179–231.

extended groups within the framework of group insurance, apart from the insured party, there appear other persons directly enjoying the insurance protection.[79] These are so called co-insured parties, usually close relatives of the insured party himself, covered by the protection either under the standard agreement or under additional contracts, usually providing for a higher premium.[80]

In the provisions of the French Insurance Code, the meaning of the second prerequisite (Art. L. 141-1(2) CA), referring to the extra-insurance relation between the policyholder and the insured parties, has not been specified.[81] Analysis of the wording of the provisions of the Insurance Code does not permit any clear answer to the question if there must be a legal relationship or if a factual connection is sufficient between the person acceding to the insurance and the policyholder.[82] Besides, there are no hints allowing to determine whether the existence of such relation must predate accession to the insurance.

By textual interpretation of the provision of Art. L. 141-1(2) CA, one may formulate the conclusion that such relation must subsist at the time of accession to the contract. On the other hand, the second sentence of Art. L. 141-1 CA does not require that the connection between the interested parties exist prior to accession to the insurance agreement.[83] In consequence, a question arises if mere notification of the intention to be covered by insurance protection is sufficient for the conclusion of a group insurance contract. At this stage, one may already speak about formation of a specific relation between a group member and the policyholder.

It is essential to correctly read the intention of the French legislator since the conclusion that there must be a legal relationship between the policyholder and the insured parties would significantly restrict the scope of application of the provisions of Book I Title IV CA. For example, necessity of a legal relationship between the policyholder and the insured parties would preclude the possibility of concluding a group insurance contract for the benefit of former employees. At the time of concluding the contract, there would, in fact, be no legal relationship representing the relationship required by the second sentence of Art. L. 141-1 CA. This example is adduced by one of the authors,[84] who draws attention to the admissibility of concluding such type of insurance contract in the context of Art. 4 *loiEvin*and Art. 14 of the national inter-trade agreement of 11 January 2008 r.[85] This kind of doubt is also voiced by representatives of German legal science, for

[79] F. Herdter, (2010), p. 47.

[80] M. Szczepańska (2008), p. 127.

[81] G. Sargos (2012), p. 26.

[82] Otherwise in A. Bzdyń (2011), p. 201.

[83] L. Mayaux(2007), p. 632.

[84] G. Sargos, (2012), p. 27.

[85] L'Accord National Interprofessionnel du 11 janvier 2008 sur la modernisation du marché de travail. More on the role of inter-trade agreements and their benefits for former employees in A. Fabre, F. Lefresne, C. Tuchszirer, L'accord du 11 janvier 2008 sur la modernisation du marché du travail. Une tentative d'évaluation, Revue de l'OFCE 2008, vol. 4, n° 107, p. 8.

whom the reason to conduct research in this regard are group life insurance contracts for retired employees.[86]

A question that may raise doubts is whether membership in a given structure is in itself sufficient to conclude that the prerequisite under Art. L. 141-1(2) CA has been met. When answering the above question, one should note that the contract under Art. L. 141-1 CA may be concluded by a person running an enterprise. The discussed provision of Art. L. 141-1(2) CA does not require any connection between an insured party covered by group insurance and such enterprise. The French legislator attaches significance only to the relation between the specific persons participating in the relationship formed under a group insurance contract (policyholder and insured parties). There should be no doubt that under the French legislative framework it is insignificant if such connection exists between particular insured parties.[87]

Certain authors, however, are of the opinion that the insured parties may be in a certain relation either with the policyholder himself or with the initiative organized by the policyholder, as long as insurance protection is afforded in connection with such initiative.[88] Proponents of such interpretation of the provision of Art. L. 141-1 CA use the example of participants in a sports event who need not be connected by any legal relationship with the event's organizer for their effective coverage by the insurance protection afforded under a group insurance contract.[89] It is sufficient if they are focused "around" the policyholder or a certain undertaking.

In German literature,[90] a typology of groups is accentuated which, from the point of view of the requirement of group durability, understood as connection between the parties insured under a group insurance and the policyholders, looks similar to the French model.

The first category distinguished by German science are durable groups (*Dauergruppe*), which imply multiplicity of persons simultaneously connected by a legal relationship intended for a longer period of time. As a consequence, members of such group are subjected to a specific legal relationship. The persons especially predestined for the role of policyholder– group organizer – are employers in relation to employee groups or organizations (associations, political parties, trade unions, etc.) in relation to the groups of their members.[91]

An opposite of a durable group is a short-term group (*kurzfristige Gruppe*). By this category, one should understand a multiplicity of persons connected by

[86] See the arguments in A. Wieser, Gruppenversicherungen (2006), p. 104.

[87] M. Bigot-Gonçalves(2009), p. 19.

[88] G. Sargos (2012), p. 26–27; L. Mayaux(2007), p. 632.

[89] L. Mayaux(2007), pp. 632–633.

[90] F. Herdter, (2010), p. 43.

[91] Ibid., p. 43.

common active or passive, depending on the organizer, participation in an undertaking delimited in time and space. Participants of such undertaking are grouped, within its framework, in a specific factual situation. An example of such group may be participants and viewers of a football match. Purchase of a ticket implies admission by the organizer to participation in the mass event which can be clearly defined in terms of time and space. The concept of short-term group will not apply to mass events open for an unlimited number of people (e.g. procession). For the emergence of a short-term group for the purpose of group insurance, it is only required that a larger number of people connected by a legal relationship with the group organized take part in a mass event which can be delimited in time and space.[92]

An interesting solution has been provided for in the Finnish Act of 1994.[93] The Act defines group insurance as insurance under which insurance protection covers or may cover a group specified in the contract (§ 2 item 6). The insurance protection subsists independently of the extra-insurance relations between the policyholder and the insured parties. This does not mean, however, that this feature is irrelevant. Under the Finnish Act, there are two separate normative regimes for group insurance contracts: the former, which is basic in nature, and the latter, which applies when the group insurance relates only to a short-term stay at an agreed location or participation in an event lasting no longer than a month (§ 4).

Comparison of the normative content of the abovementioned legal systems allows to formulate the conclusion that the extra-insurance relation between the insured party and the policyholder required for the subsistence of a group is, in principle, a legal relationship. A factual relationship is a sufficient ground to afford insurance protection if it can be contained within a specific temporal and spatial framework.

In such legal systems in which no connection between the policyholder and the insured parties is required, the requirement of specificity of the group of parties insured within the framework of group insurance is expressed only in that such group should be designated by pointing to a common characteristic feature. Such solution was adopted by the Spanish legislator in Art. 81 of the Act 50/1980 of 8 October 1980 on the insurance contract,[94] stating that a group within the framework of group insurance should be designated by reference to a common characteristic distinguishing such group for the purposes of insurance.

---

[92] Ibid., p. 45.

[93] Finnish Act on the insurance contract No. 543/1994 of 28 June 1994, Vakuutussopimuslaki 28.6.1994/543, Författningssamling 1450 (last accessed: 27June 2024).

[94] Spanish Act on the insurance contract No. 80/2005 of 8 October 2005, Ley 80/2005, de 8 de octubre de Contrato de Seguro, BOE-A-1980-22501.

5 Legal Position of the Policyholder and Organizer of the Group

Article 2(3) and (5) of Directive 2002/92/EC of the European Parliament and of the Council of 9 December 2002 on insurance mediation, as amended by Directive 2014/65/EU of the European Parliament and of the Council of 15 May 2014, and of Article 2(1)(1), (3) and (8) of Directive (EU) 2016/97 of the European Parliament and of the Council of 20 January 2016, on the distribution of insurance, as amended by Directive (EU) 2018/411 of the European Parliament and of the Council of 14 March 2018, must be interpreted as meaning that the concept of 'insurance intermediary' and, therefore, that of 'insurance distributor', within the meaning of those provisions, covers a legal person whose activity consists in offering its customers membership on a voluntary basis, in return for payment which it receives from them, of a group insurance policy to which it has subscribed previously with an insurance company, where that membership entitles those customers to insurance benefits in the event, in particular, of sickness or accident abroad.

Group organizer as a distributor by terms of IDD. This is the main idea of Judgement of the Court (First Chamber) of 29 September 2022 in case C-633/20, Bundesverband der Verbraucherzentralen und Verbraucherverbände – Verbraucherzentrale Bundesverband eV v. TC Medical Air Ambulance Agency GmbH.[95]

In the justification of this judgment, the CJEU draws attention to the fact that the positive answer to the referred preliminary question is a consequence of interpretation of Directive 2002/92 and Directive 2016/97, taking into account not only the text of the provisions but also their context and purposes of the legislative instruments. In this regard, the CJEU shared the view that consumers should enjoy insurance coverage at the same level regardless of differences between the channels of insurance distribution. However, the qualification of the policyholder in the group insurance contract as insurance intermediary raises legitimate doubts of academic authors and may have major significance in the insurance practice.

Analysis of the commented judgment leads to the conclusion that the CJEU offered broad interpretation of the terms "insurance distribution" and "insurance intermediary," including the prerequisite "for consideration." In effect, the CJEU explained in very general terms in what situations and under what conditions a policyholder in a group insurance contract can qualify as insurance intermediary. In the first place, by giving expression to a broad understanding of the term "consideration," used by the EU legislator in Recital 11 of Directive 2002/92 and in Art. 2(1) item 9 of Directive 2016/97, CJEU admits that "the condition relating to the existence of remuneration must be regarded as satisfied where every membership of a customer of the legal person which subscribed to the group insurance policy with the insurance company and which pays, on that basis, the insurance premiums to that company, gives rise to a payment to that legal person".

[95] M. Fras, O. Zgonina (2023)pp.97–113

One can only agree with the opinion of the CJEU that the defendant in the main proceedings actually acted in the defendant's own economic interest and, as a consequence, the benefits obtained by the defendant fell within the scope of the term "consideration." However, it is still dubious to put an equation mark between the activities of a group's organizer, who is a party to the insurance contract, and remunerated activities of an insurance intermediary or insurance distributor.[96] A further part of the justification of the commented judgment reveals that, in the opinion of the CJEU, it is irrelevant that a legal person conducting such activities as examined in the main proceedings is in itself a party to the group insurance contract in respect of which the legal person intends to encourage its customers to make a declaration of accession (46). One should approach with criticism the lack of in-depth considerations in this respect.

In the same way, the CJEU points to two prerequisites permitting qualification of a policyholder in a group insurance contract as insurance intermediary. First of all, this is voluntary accession to the group insurance scheme, that is the possibility to make an individual decision, and the economic interest of the policyholder as organizer of the group. However, in the commented judgment, the Court did not address the difference between acquisition of membership in a particular group and the accession to the group insurance contract as such.

It seems that the decisive factor in the assessment of the prerequisite of voluntariness, as invoked by the CJEU, should be intention and purpose for which potential members of the group join the scheme. Therefore, it should be sufficient to resolve if, when joining a particular group, its members have a real possibility to withdraw from the insurance coverage offered within the framework of the group insurance contract.[97]

One should accept the opinion that the judgment of the CJEU should not be interpreted so that the policyholder in the group insurance contract must always be treated as insurance intermediary if the policyholder encourages to become members of the group organized by the policyholder, which involves the need to pay a membership fee, as a part of which members of the group obtain at the same time insurance cover under the group insurance contract concluded by the organizer of the group.[98] As an example, M. Wandt points so a sports club whose members pay a fixed membership fee, in consideration of which they obtain insurance coverage under the group insurance contract concluded by the sports club.

---

[96] C. Armbrüster, EuGH, 29.09.2022 - C-633/20: Niederlassungsfreiheit: Erlaubnis zur Versicherungsvermittlung für Versicherungsnehmer einer Gruppenversicherung, Europäische Zeitschrift für Wirtschaftsrecht 20/2022, p. 954.

[97] A. Fischer, T. Lübcke, Ende oder Neuanfang im Gruppenversicherungsmarkt? Zugleich Anmerkung zum Urteil des EuGH v. 29.9.2022 - C-633/20, Versicherungsrecht (VersR) Zeitschrift für Versicherungsrecht, Haftungs- und Schadensrecht 23/2022, p. 1480.

[98] M. Wandt, Versicherungsnehmer einer Gruppenversicherung als Versicherungsvermittler. Grund und Grenzen der Entscheidung des EuGH v. 29.9.2022 - C-633/20, Versicherungsrecht (VersR) Zeitschrift für Versicherungsrecht, Haftungs- und Schadensrecht23/2022, p. 1481 et seq.

In the case-law of the CJEU, a tendency can be noticed to treat a policyholder in a group insurance contract as insurance intermediary. In the commented judgment, the CJEU refers to an earlier judgment of 24 February 2022,[99] in which the Court held that an entrepreneur being a policyholder in a group insurance contract has a disclosure obligation to the insured party. It was explained in the cited judgment that the status of insurance distributor is not incompatible in that context with the status of a policyholder. This view was consequently upheld also in the latest judgment of the CJEU of 2 February 2023.[100]

6 Asserting Claims Under the Group Insurance Contract, Based on the Construction of Insurance Contract for Account of a Third Party – Two Models from the Efficiency Perspective

6.1 German Method of Regulation

Particular legal systems differently approach the question of asserting claims in insurance for account of a third party. Certain jurisdictions confer that right on the insured person in the form of a claim against the insurer.[101] In others, the same right is vested in the policyholder, and the insured person has a claim against the policyholder for the transfer of benefit paid by the insurer. The policyholder's right and the insured person's claim – just as the insured person's claim vis-à-vis the insurer – altogether serve the purpose of satisfying the receivables of the person insured under the contract. For example, in German law, under § 44 VVG, it has been provided that rights under the insurance contract for account of a third party are vested in the insured person. However, issue of the insurance policy may only be requested by the policyholder (Subsection 1). The insured person, without the policyholder's consent, may dispose of his rights and assert them in court proceedings as long as the insured person holds the policy (Subsection 2). Under § 45 VVG, the policyholder may, in his own name, dispose of the rights conferred, under the insurance contract, on the insured person (Subparagraph 1). If the policy is issued, the policyholder is entitled, without the insured person's consent, to receive the payment and to transfer the insured person's rights only if the policyholder holds the policy (Subsection 2). The insurer is obliged to pay benefit to the policyholder only if the policyholder proves that the insured person consented to the insurance (Subparagraph 3).[102]

---

[99] Judgement of the CJEU of 24.02.2022 r., C-143/20, LEX nr 3307852.

[100] Judgement of the CJEU of 2.02.2023 r., C-208/21, LEX nr 3480544.

[101] Polish, French, Italian and Dutch law. See, M. Kropka (2007), p. 202, and literature cited therein, footnote.

[102] VVG – the German Act on the insurance contract of 23 November 2007 (Versicherungsvertragsgesetz; BGBl. I, p. 2631)

The essence of the legal relationship between the policyholder and the insured person, as laid down in the above-mentioned provisions of the VVG, comprises the policyholder's right to claim the benefit from the insurance undertaking and the policyholder's obligation to transfer to the insured person the benefit received from the insurance undertaking.[103] Following the judgment of the German Supreme Court (*Bundesgerichtshof*, BGH) from 1973, this relation is referred to as statutory trust relationship (*gesetzlichesTreuhandverhältnis*).[104] The receivable (*Forderung*) and the substantive law claim for satisfying the receivable (*Anspruch auf Leistungsauszahlung*) under the insurance contract is vested in the insured person, and the formal right to dispose of the claim (*Verfugungsrecht*) – exclusively in the policyholder.[105] This right is exercised by the policyholder in his own name.[106] The insured person, on the other hand, has a claim against the policyholder for the transfer of the benefit rendered by the insurance undertaking (*Anspruch auf Auskehrung der Versicherungssumme*).[107] The legal basis for such claim is § 816 II BGB, which is a provision on unjust enrichment.[108] In the light of the above, the policyholder's role is that of intermediary in satisfying the insured person's receivable (*Durchgangsperson*[109]).

The statutory trust relationship is modified by the content of the legal relationship between the policyholder and the insured person, both contractual and non-contractual (*Innenverhältnis*). In this context, the contractual relationship may be a reason for concluding the insurance contract when the subject of the insurance are risks relating to the relationship (accident at work, illness of a team member). Such modification can, among others, consist in the policyholder's obligation towards the insured person to claim the payment of benefit from the insurance undertaking, conferral on the policyholder of defenses against the insured person's claim for the transfer of the benefit paid by the insurance undertaking,[110] or conferral on the insured person of a separate legal basis of that claim. An example of such relationship is employment relationship, which in practice is a frequent reason for concluding a group insurance contract. An employment relationship can both give rise to the employer's obligation to claim the payment of benefit from the insurance

[103] Judgment of the German Supreme Court (Bundesgerichtshof) of 4 April 1973, IV ZR 130/71.

[104] Judgment of 4 April 1973, IV ZR 130/71.„Neue JuristischeWochenschrift“ [hereinafter: NJW] 1973, pp. 1368–1369.

[105] J. Prölls, in: Versicherungsvertragsgesetz. Hrsg. J. Prölls, A. Martin. Munchen 2004, p. 682.

[106] Judgment of the BGH of 7 May 1975, IV ZR 209/73. NJW 1975, p. 1274.

[107] J. Prölls, in: Versicherungsvertragsgesetz. Hrsg. J. Prölls, A. Martin. Munchen 2004, p. 691; judgment of the BGH of 4 April 1973, IV ZR 130/71. NJW 1973, p. 1368.

[108] H. Sprau, in: PalandtKommentarzumBugerlichenGesetzbuch. Munchen 2007, p. 1192.

[109] Judgment of the BGH of 7 May 1975, IV Zr 209/73. NJW 1975, p. 1274.

[110] J. Prölls, in: Versicherungsvertragsgesetz. Hrsg. J. Prölls, A. Martin. Munchen 2004, p. 691; judgment of the BGH of 4 April 1973, IV ZR 130/71. NJW 1973, p. 1369.

undertaking and[111] be a separate basis for the insured person's claim against the policyholder for the transfer of the benefit paid by the insurance undertaking.[112]

The policyholder's obligation to transfer to the insured person the benefit paid by the insurance undertaking may follow from the parties' intention expressed in the contract establishing the internal relationship or from other sources of such relationship and its contents (e.g. legal provisions). An example may be the employment relationship. The parties to an employment contract may agree that the employer, throughout the period of employment, is obliged to insure the employee against consequences of personal accidents. The policyholder's obligation to transfer the benefit paid by the insurance undertaking is then based directly on the employment contract. Such obligation may also arise under the provisions of law applicable to the employment relationship even if the employment contract itself does not contain references to the insurance contract. In fact, the legal basis for the insurance claim do not have to be the legal provisions on the internal relationship.

Sections 76–77 VVG, along with other provisions of the VVG, govern the relations between the insurance undertaking, the policyholder and the insured person arising under a personal accident insurance agreement concluded for account of the insured person. The statutory trust relationship is a means to achieve the basic goal of the legislator, that is ensuring to the insured person the benefit under the insurance contract.

6.2 *Polish Method of Regulation*

Polish law is an example of jurisdiction conferring on the insured person the right to claim the payment of benefit from the insurer. Under Art. 808 § 3 of the Polish Civil Code (hereinafter: k.c.), within the framework of insurance for account of a third party, the insured person is entitled to claim the benefit due directly from the insurer, unless the parties agree otherwise in the agreement or in the General Terms and Conditions of Insurance.

In case of a group insurance contract with compulsory accession, it is the insured person that can claim the payment of benefit directly from the insurer, however, only if the contracting parties have not agreed otherwise. On the other hand, in group life insurance the party entitled to receive the sum insured in the event of the insured person's death is the beneficiary. In principle, according to Art. 831 § 1 k.c., the right to designate the beneficiary is vested in the policyholder. However, in the context of insurance contracts for account of a third party, designation of the beneficiary by the policyholder requires a prior consent from the insured person.

[111] See judgment of the BGH of 7 May 1975, IV ZR 209/73. NJW 1975, pp. 1273–1275.

[112] Judgment of the National Labor Court for Rheinland-Pfalz (LandesarbeitsgerichtRheinland-Pfa lz) of 18 August 2005, 1 Sa 171/05, citing prior case-law of the Supreme Labour Court.

Moreover, the contract or General Terms of Insurance may provide that this right can be exercised independently by the insured person (Art. 831 § 1^1k.c.).

The problem of asserting claims under the group insurance contract is particularly conspicuous in the context of *bancassurance* contracts. Here, the insurance contract is also intended to secure the bank against the risk of the borrower's insolvency. So defined purpose of concluding the insurance contract or acceding to the insurance contract requires that the insured person assign the receivable under the insurance contract or designate the bank as beneficiary. At the time of acceding to the group insurance, the insured person transfers, by way of assignment, the right to the benefit (in case of property insurance) or designates (consents to the designation of) the bank as beneficiary authorized to receive the benefit under the contract (in case of life insurance). As a result of such disposal of the insured person's right, in case of occurrence of the insured accident, the bank becomes the party entitled to seek payment of the insurance benefit in court proceedings. The rights of the insured person or his heirs to assert claims for payment of the insurance benefit are subject to far-reaching restriction.

The situation is unclear of an insured person, whose interest very often requires that the policyholder should exercise his right under the insurance contract, when the policyholder either delays or entirely abandons the exercise of his rights, especially when the policyholder and the insurer are members of the same capital group. In many situations, an arrangement made between the policyholder and the insurer according to which the party entitled to claim the benefit is the policyholder, and not the insured person, serves to deprive the insured person of the possibility to assert claims. Frequently, it is in the policyholder's interest that claims are made as rare as possible and cover the least possible amounts (especially when the insurer and the policyholder are related by shares or when they have concluded a contract under which the policyholder receives financial benefits if the claims made do not exceed a specific threshold – *no claims bonus*).

Similar problems arise in case of life insurance taken out by borrowers when the bank, under Art. 831 § 1 and § 2 k.c., is designated as party entitled to receive the insurance benefit in case of the borrower's death. It must be pointed out that attention was drawn in judicial practice to the fact that the insured person's heir, who is not authorized to claim payment of the sum insured, may sue the insurer for the ascertainment of a legal relationship (Art. 189 of the Code of Civil Procedure, hereinafter: k.p.c.).[113] Such position is correct. In the judgment of 9 September 2021, the Supreme Court as if responded to the expectations of insured

[113] Judgment of the Court of Appeal in Białystok of 22 February 2012, file reference I ACa 752/11; judgment of the Court of Appeal in Lublin of 7 October 2014, file reference I ACa 281/14, judgment of the Supreme Court of 12 September 2013, file reference IV CSK 91/13. Art. 189 of the Polish Code of Civil Procedure reads that "The plaintiff may request that the court ascertains the existence or non-existence of a legal relationship or right when the plaintiff has a legal interest in doing so."

persons,[114] however, despite giving precious guidelines, the Supreme court upheld the decision dismissing the claim. Assertion of claims by insured persons or their legal successors still requires certain procedural struggle. This is the case as the Supreme Court concluded that the ascertainment that, as a result of occurrence of an event subject to insurance coverage, the bank has a claim against the insurer does not directly affect the financial position of the insured person's heir vis-à-vis the bank, which position can only be changed by the payment of benefit by the insurer to the bank. However, such ascertainment, in a situation when the entitled bank does not assert claims against the insurer, allows to remove the legal uncertainty relating to the qualification of an event as insured accident and, accordingly, to an existing obligation of the insurer to pay the benefit and a corresponding claim held by the bank. The bank's further omission to assert the claim may be considered as legal basis for claims for damages if, as a result of the bank's omission to assert the claims, a financial detriment is suffered by the heirs of the insured person; this can be assessed in terms of the principles of social coexistence (Art. 5 k.c.[115]) if the bank, at the same time, asserts claims against the heirs for the repayment of the loan. Finally, an authoritative ascertainment that the insured accident has occurred may also incline the insurer to voluntarily pay the benefit. These circumstances should be considered sufficient to prove a legal interest in the understanding of Art. 189 k.p.c.

A question arises if this multi-stage model of asserting claims is efficient, sustainable and if it allows for the interests of both parties to the obligational relationship. An important signal given by the Supreme Court is that in a situation referred to in the discussed judgment, one should base the claim not on the legal regime of the insurance contract for account of a third party but on the regime of tortious liability. When assessing the solution adopted in art. 808 § 3 k.c., one should not lose sight of the fact that that claims sought within the framework of *bancassurance* relate to very important social questions, as they involve mortgage loan securities.

In Polish case-law, attention was justly drawn to the fact that it is not out of question to recognize a contractual provision as unfair contract term if the provision is compatible with the default statutory norm laid down in Art. 808 § 3 k.c. This legal norm is a part of the comprehensive regime of the insurance contract, which assumes that it is the policyholder and not the insured person that bears the burden of paying insurance premium. In the opinion of the Supreme Court, it must be considered if, in a situation when the insured person to whom special terms relating to consumers apply bears the economic burden of paying the insurance premium passed on by the policyholder to the insurer, the possibility under Art. 808 § 3 k.c. to exclude the insured person's right to seek the benefit directly from the insurer is of absolute nature or if, under certain circumstances, e.g., refusal by the policyholder

[114] Judgment of the Supreme Court of 9 September, file reference V CSKP 47/21, LEX no. 3231813.

[115] Art. 5 of the Polish Civil Code reads that "One cannot exercise one's right in a manner contradictory to its social and economic purpose or the principles of social coexistence. Such acting or refraining from acting by an entitled person is not deemed an exercise of that right and is not protected."

to assert the payment of benefit, a mechanism should be guaranteed enabling the insured person to assert the claim directly against the insurer. A contractual provision excluding the insured person's right to seek the payment of benefit from the insurer in case of the policyholder's refusal to exercise the same right leads, in the opinion of the Supreme Court, to a significant impediment in the obtainment of insurance coverage by the insured person.[116]

It cannot be concluded that the purpose of insurance contracts entered into in combination with the loan agreement is only to protect the bank against the debtor's insolvency. Undoubtedly, loan repayment insurance should secure, in the first place, the borrower (as economically weaker party), and in case of the borrower's death – his heirs. Therefore, imposition on the insured person or his legal successors of liabilities under the loan agreement inasmuch as they might be covered by the insurer can lead to the assessment of contractual clauses as contrary to good morals, grossly infringing on the insured person's or the heirs' interests (art. 358[1] § 1 k.c.). This conclusion is not affected by the view expressed in judicial practice that a legal successor of a deceased borrower covered by group life insurance under a contract concluded by the bank granting the loan and the defendant insurer under which the sum insured can be paid only at the request of the policyholder-bank has a legal interest in ascertaining, in accordance with Art. 189 k.p.c., that the borrower's death was an insured accident giving rise to the insurer's obligation to pay the benefit as provided for in the contract.[117]

Even a resolution favorable to the insured person or the insured person's legal successors in a case for the ascertainment that a given event was an insured accident does not yet mean that the insured person may successfully enforce the benefit due from the insurer. If the insurer fails to voluntarily pay the benefit, it is still only the party entitled to claim the benefit that could seek its payment in legal proceedings. In such situation, the insured person would have a claim for damages, within the framework of unjust enrichment, either against the party entitled to claim the payment of benefit under the insurance contract or against the insurance undertaking. Such complex, multi-stage legal method of enforcing the insurance benefit by the insured person significantly limits the possibility to obtain real insurance coverage and impedes the implementation of the right of access to the courts. The German model, as discussed above, is more favorable to the weaker party, more efficient and economically justified when it comes to procedural costs. The provisions of § 44 VVG and § 45 VVG allow to conclude that the relationship between the policyholder and the insured person involves the policyholder's right to claim the payment of benefit from the insurance undertaking and the policyholder's obligation to transfer to the insured person the benefit received from the insurance undertaking.[118] The

[116] See judgment of the Supreme Court of 12 September 2013, IV CSK 91/13, LEX No. 1413591.

[117] Judgment of the Court of Appeal in Białystok of 22 February 2013, I ACa 752/11, OSAB 2012, nr 1, poz. 19–24.

[118] Judgment of the BGH of 4 April 1973, IV ZR 130/71, "NeueJuristischeWochenschrift" 1973, pp. 1368–1369.

receivable and the substantive law claim for the payment of benefit under the insurance contract is vested in the insured person, and the formal right to dispose of the above exclusively in the policyholder. This right is exercised by the policyholder in his own name. On the other hand, the insured person has a claim against the policyholder for the transfer of the sum of the benefit paid by the insurance undertaking.[119] In the light of the above, it is clearly evident that, in the German system, the role of the policyholder is only that of an intermediary in satisfying receivables.[120]

7 The Premium in Group Insurance

7.1 Introductory Remarks

In French science, the obligation to pay the premium is quite often considered the element of the content of the legal relationship that allows to determine the legal status of a group insurance contract.[121] The establishment who and on what basis is the debtor obliged to pay the premium to the insurer is supposed to permit the determination if the insurance contract is concluded between the insurer and the group organizer, which is in line with the assumptions of the unitary conception, or between the insurer and the insured persons, according to the theoretical model of a so called dispersed insurance relationship.

A part of Polish academic authors also attempts to explain the legal relationship arising in the context of the group insurance contract by referring to the obligation to pay the premium. An opinion must be mentioned by W. Kamiński. The author points out that financing of the insurance premium by the insured person constitutes a transfer of means to the policyholder, who, under the provisions on the insurance contract for account of a third party, is obliged to pay the premium.[122] In the opinion of that researcher, under such conditions, it is possible to question the status of a bank as policyholder if the bank was released from debt without a valid legal cause (*causa*).[123] As a further consequence,"it canturn out that the insured person – as policyholder – is the party of an individual insurance contract concluded on the insured person's own account, and the «policyholder» [group organizer – M.F.] plays the role of an organizer of homogeneous legal relationships whose content is determined by the framework agreement, which is not the group insurance contract but a

[119] Judgment of the BGH of 27 May 1998, IV ZR 166/97, "NeueJuristischeWochenschrift" 1998, pp. 2537–2538.

[120] H. Sprau (2007), p. 1192.

[121] M. Bigot-Gonçalves (2009), p. 118.

[122] See art. 805 § 1 k.c.i art. 808 § 2 k.c.

[123] W. Kamieński (2012), p. 167.

contract for cumulative insurance."[124] It is symptomatic that the author's comments relate to a construction that, as a part of this study, is referred to as group insurance contract with voluntary accession.

7.2 *The Content of the Obligation to Pay the Premium*

The analysis of that question in the context of French law requires a brief presentation of the solutions found in individual insurance contracts. Under Art. L. 113-2 item 1 CA, the obligation to pay the premium is imposed on the insured party. However, this provision has a particularly unfortunate wording. In literature of the subject, it is emphasized that the use of the term "insured party" is an example of the legislator's inadvertence. The legislator limited itself to adopting a legal regime only for the least complex subjective configuration of the insurance contract in which the insured party is at the same time the policyholder. In literature, it is argued that the provision of Art. L. 113-2 item 1 CA should be interpreted so that the addressee of the obligation to pay the premium is always the "policyholder" (*souscripteur, preneurd'assurance*).[125] M. Bigot-Gonçalves points out that the line of interpretation suggested above is also confirmed by the conclusions from systemic interpretation of the Insurance Code. In that author's opinion, a meaningful example can be found in the provision of Art. L. 112-1(3) CA, under which, in insurance contracts for account of an unspecified person, the obligation of paying the premium is imposed on the policyholder.[126] Aside from the accurate opinion about the need to depart from the literal meaning of Art. L. 113-2 item 1 CA, an argument based on systemic interpretation does not seem convincing. Bearing in mind that in the contracts referred to in Art. L. 112-1(2) CA, the insured person is specified at the time when the insurance accident occurs, it would not be possible to impose on that party the obligation to pay the premium in a period preceding the materialization of risk. In the light of such limitations, the party obliged to pay the premium must be the policyholder.

On the other hand, we have to do with a certain variation in case of life insurance contracts. Under Art. L. 132-20 (1) CA, the party granting insurance protection does not have the right to claim payment of the premium. Asa consequence, the insurer is not in a position to seek such payment before the court. The sanction for untimely payment of the premium, however, may be termination of the contract by a declaration of intent made by the insurer (Art. L. 132-20 (2) CA).

In French science, no consistent position has so far been worked out when it comes to the determination of the party obliged to pay the premium to the insurer

[124] Ibid., pp. 167–168.

[125] Y. Lambert-Faivre, L. Leveneur (2011), p. 326.

[126] M. Bigot-Gonçalves (2009), p. 119.

under group insurance contracts. Representatives of legal science draw attention to the fact that analysis of the literal wording of the provisions of Book I Title IV CA is insufficient to formulate unambiguous conclusions in this regard.[127]

Under Art. L. 141-2 CA, the amounts that the insured party is obliged to pay to the policyholder under the insurance contract should be calculated independently from other amounts the insured party is obliged to pay to the group organizer under another contract. This provision excludes the group organizer's possibility to credit the transferred means towards a debt that is unrelated to the concluded insurance contract. On the other hand, under Art. L. 141-3(1) CA, the group organizer may not deprive the insured party of the benefits arising from the insurance contract otherwise than in a situation of termination of the non-insurance relationship between the group organizer and the insured party or failure of the latter to pay the premium.

Apparently, it seems that those rules provide for the existence of the insured party's obligation to pay the premium. They refer to "amounts that the insured party is obliged to pay to the policyholder [group organizer – M.F.] by virtue of the insurance contract" (art. L. 141-2 CA) and to the insured party's failure to pay the premium (Art. L. 141-3 CA).

However, an analysis of those provisions leads to the conclusion that they do not relate at all to the relation between the insured party and the insurer. Instead, they refer to the relation between a member of the group and the group's organizer. Following the wording of Art. L. 141-2 CA and Art. L. 141-3 CA, two mutually exclusive hypotheses can be formulated. According to the former, a member of the group is the debtor on account of the payment of premium to the insurer. The other proposal assumes, on the other hand, that a member of the group only incurs the economic burden of the insurance, and the debtor in relation to the insurer is the group's organizer.

An argument in support of the first hypothesis can be derived from the wording of Art. L. 141-6 CA. Under that provision, the policyholder is, in principle, considered to be the insurer's representative "in relations with the acceding party, the insured party and the beneficiary." The obligation of the acceding party to pay the premium is performed, so to say, "through" the policyholder, who acts solely as representative of the insurer.

The second proposal is supported by the above-mentioned Art. L. 141-3 CA. This norm provides for a right to deprive the insured party of the protection under the group insurance contract. This right is not vested in the insurer but in the group organizer. Since the latter decides about the termination of insurance coverage, such entitlement should be awarded to the group organizer as creditor who, at his or her discretion, may sanction improper performance of the obligation by the debtor (insured party).

It must be considered if a different interpretation of the provision under Art. L. 141-3 CA is also acceptable. One can defend the opinion that Art. L. 141-3 CA

---

[127] L. Mayaux(2007), p. 716.

is intended to protect the interests of the group organizer. In the lack the norm under Art. L. 141-3 CA, temporary difficulties with the payment of premium by the insured party would entitle the insurer to deprive the insured party of insurance coverage. In certain situations, in life, the organizer of the insurance may be interested in continual duration of the insurance coverage even though the insured party has stopped paying the insurance premium. Such distribution of interests is characteristic of group insurance contracts of borrowers (*bancassurance*).[128] In the light of the above, one can defend the view that the provision of Art. L. 141-3 CA deprives the insurer of the right to refuse insurance coverage to the insured party even though the insurer is the creditor entitled to claim payment of the premium from the insured member of the group.

It seems, however, that such interpretation of Art. L. 141-3 CA is not legitimate. Even in the lack of that provision, the organizer could prevent the termination of insurance coverage by paying the premium to the insurer as a third party. Under Art. 1236 (1) CC, a provision may be rendered, in lieu of the debtor, by any person having an interest in doing so (*toutepersonne qui y estintéressée*), such as co-debtor or guarantor. For example, a tenant paying the premium instead of the landlord can avoid termination of the insurance coverage in relation to the flat occupied by the tenant. A similar effect will be produced by the payment of premium by a mortgagee, who, by doing so, releases from debt the owner of the mortgaged property.[129] The interest in paying the premium in lieu of the debtor is identified with an aspiration to preserve a certain asset. As a result, it seems that the interest of a bank in the maintenance of the insurance protection within the framework of *bancassurance* is sufficient to render the provision with the effect of releasing the group's member. At this point it must be noted that, under Art. 1236 (2) CC, a provision may be rendered even by a third party other than a person having an interest in the understanding of paragraph (1)as long as such third-party acts on behalf of the debtor and with the intention to release the debtor from the obligation to render to the creditor.

A clear answer to the question formulated above has not been so far provided by judicial practice. In case-law, for a relatively long time, the dominant opinion was that the party considered the debtor obliged to pay the premium to the insurer was the group organizer.[130] However, the judgment of the Cassation Court of 7 June 1989[131] started a trend in case-law according to which the discussed obligation is imposed on the persons who acceded to the insurance contract.[132] The expression of consent to the emergence of insurance coverage is the source of the obligation to pay the premium by such acceding persons. Analysis of the written justification of the judgment leads to the conclusion that the adoption of that view was supported,

[128] N. Lebond, (2010), p. 11.

[129] V. Nicolas (2002), p. 636, and the case-law cited therein.

[130] L. Mayaux(2007), pp. 718–719.

[131] Cass., 1ère civ., 7 juin 1989, pourvoi n° 87-14. 648.

[132] See also G. Venandet, F. Jacob, X. Henry, A. Tisserand-Martin, G. Wiederkehr (2011), p. 1274.

in the first place, by the intention to secure the interests of the members of the insured persons' group. Imposition of the obligation to pay the premium on the organizer gives rise to a situation in which the insured parties can be deprived of insurance protection irrespective of their intention and knowledge when the group organizer stops paying the amounts due to the insurer.

However, the French Cassation Court was relatively inconsequent and, in its later decisions, the Court departed from that view. In its decision of 13 November 1996, in a factual situation relating to a group insurance contract, the Cassation Court expressed an opinion that the debtor obliged to pay the premium to the insurer is the group organizer.[133]

7.3 *Voluntary and Compulsory Group Insurance*

Certain authors propose to assume that the nature of the relationship arising under group insurance depends on whether the accession to the insurance is voluntary or compulsory.[134] In insurance with compulsory accession, in whose case one can speak about an insurance contract *sensu stricto* only between the insurer and the group organizer (policyholder), the obligation to pay the premium may be imposed only on the latter. The contract between the insurer and the organizer is the only bilateral legal act established in the context of the group insurance relationship. Therefore, this contract should include all the material components of an insurance contract. One of such material components is the obligation to pay the premium. Its addressee can only be the group organizer since it is the group organizer, and not the group's members, that is a party to the insurance contract.

On the other hand, in insurance with voluntary accession, the obligation to pay the premium is imposed on the member of the group. The source of that obligation is the insurance contract between the group's member and the insurer,[135] concluded at the time of receipt of the insurance declaration by the insurer. In the absence of clear norms in Book I Title IV CA, the obligation to pay the premium is, in principle, governed by the general provisions on individual insurance contracts. Also, special rules must be followed laying down the terms of paying the premium in life insurance contracts. It must be recalled that in case of life insurance contracts, Art. L. 132-20 (1) CA applies, under which the insurer may not claim payment of the insurance premium. The admissibility to apply that provision can raise doubts in a situation when, within the framework of one group insurance, the insurance coverage relates both to the risk of death of the insured person and the risk pertaining, for example, to loss of employment. Literal interpretation of those provisions leads to

133 Cass. 1ère civ., 13 novembre 1996, RGDA 1997, p. 221.

134 L. Mayaux(2007), pp. 718–719.

135 Ibid.

the conclusion that, in such situations, the insurer could seek, by legal proceedings, payment of the part of the premium for the insurance relating to loss of employment. However, this conception was rejected in judicial practice. As a part of one insurance contract, it is inadmissible to decompose the obligation so as to single out particular risks and apply appropriate provisions to each of them separately. As a result, the insurer may not claim only the part of the premium corresponding to the insurance contract other than life insurance. In the light of case-law, the insurer, in such situations, has the right to claim full premium, including the life insurance component.[136]

In individual insurance, failure to pay the premium entitles the insurer to refuse insurance protection. This right arises after the expiry of thirty from the beginning of the debtor's delay. The insurer may terminate the insurance contract after the following ten days from the end of the above-mentioned thirty-day period (Art. L. 113-3 ust. 3 CA).

On the other hand, in group insurance, the group organizer may not deprive the insured party of the right to take advantage of the coverage under the insurance contractunless the non-insurance relationship has been broken between the two or the insured party failed to pay the premium (Art. L. 141-3 (1) CA). However, the organizer may sanction delay in the payment of premium and refuse protection to the acceding party under the insurance contract. The organizer, however, must first exhaust the procedure laid down in Art. L. 141-3 (2)and (3) CA. After ten days from the expiry of the deadline to pay the premium, the organizer may send a letter to the insured party notifying the latter about the predicted date of termination of the insurance coverage if the premium is still not paid (Art. 141-3 (2), second sentence, CA).[137] Such consequence can take place at the earliest after fourteen days from the date of addressing to ma group member the letter informing about the delay in the payment of the premium (Art. 141-3 (2), first sentence, CA). The legislator does not require, however, that the organizer first send a call for payment of the overdue premiums and only then, upon expiry of the deadline set in that call for payment, send to the member of the group a declaration of termination of the insurance coverage.[138] It is sufficient that the organizer addresses to the group's member a call for payment in which the member is warned about the ending date of the insurance coverage.[139]

In the light of the above, under the Insurance Code, there are two independent provisions that, *de legelata,* allow to sanction improper performance of the obligation to pay the premium, respectively on the initiative of the insurer (Art. L. 113-3 CA) and the policyholder (Art. L. 141-3 CA). Unfortunately, the legislator did not explain the mutual relation between those provisions.

---

[136] J. Landel (1993), p. 20,and the case-law cited therein.

[137] J.C. Ponge (2010), p. 56.

[138] Cass 1ère civ., 12 oct. 2004, no 02-12564, RCEA 2005, comm. 41.

[139] J.C. Ponge (2010), p. 56.

Bearing in mind the scheme of the Insurance Code, it seems that the provision of Art. L. 141-3 CA, situated in Book I Title IV CA and relating to group insurance contracts, is *lex specialis* vis-à-vis Art. L. 113-3 CA, situated among general provisions of Book I Title I.

This interpretation is also supported by the comparison of the normative content of the provisions of Art. L. 141-3 and Art. L. 113-3 CA. The provision of Art. L. 141-3 CA is based on Art. L. 113-3 and Art. L. 132-20 CA,[140] specifying the rights of the insurer in case of untimely payment of premium. It is hard to believe that the intention of the legislator was to multiply the number of parties granted the right to deprive group's members of the protection under the insurance contract.

In the context of the differences discussed above between voluntary and compulsory accession to insurance, it should be considered if the structural differences between the two affect the consequences of the untimely payment of premium.

The provision of Art. L. 141-3 CA undoubtedly corresponds to contracts with compulsory accession. Insured persons are not parties to a separate contract with the insurance company. The insurer may claim the payment of premium directly from the group organizer (policyholder). As a result, it is the latter that should decide whom to deprive of insurance protection, as the party obliged to pay the premium.

Much more difficulties in this context are caused by insurance with voluntary accession. In this case, the group organizer is only a party to the framework agreement concluded with the insurer. On the contrary, the group organizer is not a party to the contracts between the group members and the insurer. Therefore, the group organizer is not in a position to terminate those contracts by unilateral declaration of intent. However, the provision of Art. L. 141-1 (1) CA gives the group organizer a special right to deprive a particular person of the benefits under the insurance contract, but only if such person defaults to pay the premium.[141]

This solution may give rise to certain doubts. Since Art. L. 141-3 CA is a *lex specialis* to art. L. 113-1 CA, also in the context of insurance with voluntary accession, the insurer may not refuse coverage to a group member even when the insurer does not receive the premium due. In the opinion of certain authors, the existence of a special norm under Art. L. 141-3 CA does not deprive the insurer, in absolute terms, of the right to sanction delays in the payment of premium. Proponents of that opinion point out that in such situations the insurer may take advantage of the remedy laid down in Art. 1184 CC.[142] Under that provision, a party vis-a-vis whom a contract partner non-performs an obligation may terminate the contract if the contract is reciprocal. This provision enables the insurer to terminate the contract even where it is impossible to apply Art. L. 113-3 CA. It allows to terminate the contract in a situation of an agreement between the group organizer and the group's member to withhold the payment of premium. In the absence of Art. 1184 CC, the insurer

---

[140] L. Mayaux(2007), p. 724.

[141] H. Groutel, (1990), p. 8.

[142] M. Bigot-Gonçalves (2009), p. 224.

would be obligated to comply with the contractual provisions until the group organizer exercises the right provided for under Art. L. 141-3 CA.

8 Expiration of the Group Insurance Relationship

Expiry of the legal relationships arising in the context of group insurance can be a consequence of many legal events, which means that their exhaustive discussion reaches beyond the scope of this study. Bearing in mind the specific subjective configuration within the framework of in group insurance, it does not seem that the legal relationships between particular parties are to terminate at the same time.[143] This does not seem, however, that such legal relationships are independent from one another, which will be discussed below in more detail.

When analyzing the causes of expiration of an insurance contract, one should follow the division adopted in the literature of the subject into insurance contracts with compulsory accession and insurance contracts with voluntary accession. Those insurance types show far-reaching differences in terms of their structure. In insurance with compulsory accession, the insurance contract *sensu stricto* is concluded between the group organizer (policyholder) and the insurer. The grounds for its termination are specified in those provisions of insurance law[144] that apply to individual insurance contracts. On the other hand, as far as contracts with voluntary accession are concerned, the group organizer and the insurer are bound by a framework agreement that only creates the technical and organizational conditions for concluding individual insurance contracts with particular members of the group. The organizing agreement is not an insurance contract in the strict sense of the word. This is because the organizing agreement does not contain the material elements of the insurance contract. The grounds for its termination are laid down, in principle, in the general provisions of the law of obligations. The provisions of insurance law will apply in this context only exceptionally, where the legislator has provided for specific rules on the contracts organizing group insurance. The insurance regime governs, however, to a full degree the relationships between the insurer and individual group members (policyholders).

The above assumptions can be analyzed considering several examples discussed in the context of French law. The insurance contract between a group member and the insurer within the framework of voluntary insurance expires after a certain term for which the contract was concluded. As a rule, the provisions pf insurance law do not provide for any specific restrictions in this regard. For example, among the provisions of Book I Title IV of the French CA, there are no rules arbitrarily determining a term for which a group insurance contract may be concluded. Therefore,

[143] J. Bigot (1998), p. 605.

[144] For more on the French legal regime, see P.G. Marly (2013), p. 284.

the Relevant legal regime should be sought among the general provisions situated outside Book I Title IV CA. Under the provision of Art. L. 113-12 (1) CA, the insurance contract is concluded for a term specified in the policy. This means that the parties may freely specify the duration of the insurance relationship. Importantly enough, in group forms of insurance, this will be determined already in the framework agreement. This arrangement will translate into the substance of individual insurance contracts, concluded subsequently by the group members who decide to accede to the insurance. These remarks should be referred also to the contract between the group organizer (policyholder) and the insurer within the framework of insurance with compulsory accession. This observation remains valid also with regard to framework agreements between the group organizer and the insurer in insurance schemes with voluntary accession, with the proviso that the relevant legal regime will be the general provisions of the law of obligations, and not the provisions on the insurance contract.

Subject to certain restrictions, an insurance relationship may terminate upon notice given by one of the parties. Remaining within the realm of the French legislation, it should be noted that according to Art. L. 113-12 (1) CA, the terms of terminating the contract, just as the duration of insurance, are laid down in the policy. Paragraph (2) of that provision stipulates for the insured person a right to terminate the contract at the end of every subsequent year of the insurance period. The insured person's declaration must be addressed to the insurer at the latest two months ahead of the end of the yearly term of insurance coverage. This right is also vested in the insurer, who must also comply with the deadlines set out in Art. L. 113-12 (2) CA. The provision discussed above applies to a contract between the group organizer (policyholder) and the insurer within the framework of insurance with compulsory accession as well as insurance contracts concluded between members of the group and the insurer within the framework of insurance with voluntary accession.[145]

An insurance relationship may expire as a result of secession by an insured party from the insurance when the insured party does not agree to an amendment of the insurance terms (Art. L. 141-4 (3) CA).

[145] Analogous provisions are contained also in other statutes, regulating the rights and obligations of parties to collective insurance other than group insurance under Art. L. 141-1 CA. According to Art. L. 221-10 (1)of the Mutual Society Code, the insured party may terminate the contract at the latest two months ahead of the end of the insurance term. Failure to comply with this deadline will lead to extension of the insurance period. However, this provision does not apply to insurance with compulsory accession. Under Art. 5 of the Act No. 89-1009 of 31 December 1989 (loiEvin),the insurance contract should specify the period of notice as well as the time preceding the end of insurance coverage when the insured party is obliged to notify his or her intention to withdraw from the insurance on pain of renewal of the contract. The above-mentioned provisions are mandatory and may not be superseded by the parties' agreement. In the context of the currently applicable legislative framework, it is therefore inadmissible to shorten the deadlines on which the effective exercise of the right to terminate the contract depends. Cass. 2è civ., 15 septembre 2011, n° 10-23837.

For example in Turkish law, under Art. 1496 (4) TTK, loss of the status of a group member is considered an event leading, as a rule, to the expiry of the insurance coverage.[146]

The relationship between membership in the group and existence of insurance protection was also recognized by the French legislator. One of the few provisions of Book I Title IV of the Insurance Code that relates to the question of expiry of insurance coverage under the group insurance contract is Art. L. 141-3 (1) CA. According to that provision, the organizer may not deprive a group member of the benefits under the group insurance unless the member of the group failed to pay the premium or the tie was broken between the member of the group and the group's organizer. This provision distinguishes two situations in which the insured party may be deprived of insurance coverage.

The first of the two correlates the expiry of insurance protection to violation of the obligation to pay the premium. The contract may be terminated only after exhausting of the procedure under Art. L. 141-3 (2)and (3) CA. The provision of Art. L. 141-3 CA is mandatory insofar as it sets out the deadlines that must be complied with to effectively exercise the right. It is inadmissible to shorten those periods under a legal act.[147] It must be emphasized that the right to refuse the benefits under the insurance contract was reserved to the group organizer and not the insurer.

As far as the second situation covered by Art. L. 141-3 CA is concerned, the French legislator refers to the question of cessation of the tie between the group organizer and the group's members. In this case, it is not necessary to exhaust the procedure laid down under Art. L. 141-3 (2)and (3) CA.[148] However, the provision of Art. L. 141-3 (1) CA was rather unfortunately worded as far as it specifies the consequences of cessation of the non-insurance relationship between the group organizer and the insured party. Literal interpretation of that rule suggests that in case of cessation of the tie between the interested parties, the group organizer may decide about discontinuing the insurance coverage in the same way as in the event of untimely payment of the insurance premium. However, such interpretation does not reflect the normative contents of Art. L. 141-1 (2) CA, under which a precondition to accession to the insurance is an existing tie between the group organizer and the group's members. Undoubtedly, the tie must hold at the

[146] Under Art. 1496 (4) of the Turkish Commercial Code of 2012: "In the event of loss of the status of a group member during the period of insurance, insurance coverage afforded as a part of group insurance may be continued as a part of individual insurance by the policyholder, the insured person or the beneficiary."

[147] It must be noted that only under the above-mentioned Regulation of 30 January 2009, the provisions of Book I Title IV CA became iuriscogentis. In a period preceding the entry into force of that Regulation, an opinion was expressed in case-law about the admissibility to depart from the literal meaning of Art. L. 141-3 CA. In a decision of 10 July 2008, the Cassation Court held in favor of the admissibility to specify, by mutual agreement of the parties, reasons for terminating the insurance coverage other than under Art. L. 141-3 CA. Seethe decision of 10 July 2008, Cass., 2e ch. civile, 10 juillet 2008, n° 06-11397.

[148] Cass. 2e civ., 8 juillet 2010, n° de pourvoi: 09-67396.

time of accession to the insurance although its existence does not have to precede such accession in time.[149] More doubts are raised, however, by the question if the cessation of the tie already after an effective accession to the insurance gives rise to a situation in which the person so far covered by the insurance, by operation of law, may no longer take advantage of the rights under the insurance contract, or if that consequence arises only as a result of certain acts performed by the group's organizer. Adoption of the latter proposal would be undoubtedly more favorable to the group's members, who would not be exposed to unexpected expiry of the insurance coverage in case of abrupt discontinuation of the tie with the insurance operator. Nevertheless, uncritical acceptance of that opinion does not seem reconcilable with the nature of group insurance. A prerequisite for acceding to a group insurance contract is the existence of a non-insurance relationship between the person acceding to the insurance and the group organizer (art. L. 141-1 (2) CA). This means that there is no justification for further persistence of the insurance coverage in a situation when the underlying relationship ceases to exist. In reference to the conception of "initial incapacity to be the insured party," proposed in the context of situations of non-compliance with the criteria of membership in the group, at this point, the discussed condition should be defined as posterior loss of the capacity to be insured.

If the non-insurance relation between the group organizer and the group's member arises from a legal relationship, its existence will be decided by the provisions governing the conclusion, duration and termination of that relationship. If the group of the insured parties comprises persons employed by the group organizer under an employment contract, expiry of the employment contract will lead, at the same time, to the cessation of the insurance coverage. However, the employee benefits from the insurance protection during the period of notice. This observation leads to the conclusion that a member of the insured persons' group may withdraw from the insurance not only as a part of the procedure laid down in the Insurance Code but also as a consequence of termination of the underlying legal relationship that allowed him or her to accede to the insurance.[150]

The impact of the non-insurance relation between the insured person and the group organizer on the relationship arising under the group insurance contract can be additionally considered from the point of view of their mutual interrelation.

The belief about the need to respect the relation between legal relationships is well-established in French case-law. This conception is based on a conviction that the existence of a legal relationship may depend on another contractual obligation if there is a strict connection between the two. This belief is related, among others, to loan agreements concluded for the purpose of financing a specific business venture. In French literature, it was proposed to use the term 'bundle of contracts' (*groupe*

[149] In the event of insurance with compulsory accession, the establishment of insurance coverage and the establishment of the tie generally coincide in time.
[150] V. Bourdon (2002) I, p. 340.

des contrats)[151] or 'interdependent contracts' (*contratsinterdépendants*)[152] in reference to the principal contract and the loan agreement concluded for the purpose of implementing a certain business venture (subsidiary contract). If the loan obligation is incurred with the intention to finance a purchase of an immovable property under a contract affected by invalidity or terminated subsequently by one of the parties, the loan agreement shares the fate of the contract for sale.[153] The subsidiary contract will expire or will be invalid *ex tunc*. This consequence, however, does not depend on a prior agreement between the seller or the buyer (borrower) with the lender. In more recent decisions, the judicial practice supports the contract's ineffectiveness[154] regardless of whether the principal contract has been terminated by one of the parties or affected by the sanction of invalidity.[155] The above concept was referred to by the Cassation Court in the judgment of 4 April 2006.[156] This decision was delivered in the following factual situation. A company managing a military hospital concluded a contract for servicing the heating installation with another company incorporated under the laws of France, and a contract with a transmission company under which gas power was supplied to the hospital. The parties agreed that the company managing the hospital may not obtain supply from another enterprise. As a result of gaining access to the urban heating network, the managing company terminated the contract for the servicing of the hospital's installation. At the same time, the company requested termination of the contract for the supply of energy, to which the transmission company did not agree. The Cassation Court concluded that termination of the contract for the servicing of heating installation led to ineffectiveness of the supply agreement. In justification of this opinion, it was argued that both contracts referred to the same commercial transaction and constituted an indivisible whole (*ensemble contractuel indivisible*). The Cassation Court clearly pointed out that the contract for servicing the installation was an exclusive cause (*seule cause*) of the supply agreement.

Analysis of the case-law presented above leads to the conclusion that a legally relevant correlation between two legal relationships is decided by the fact that the two relationships serve the same economic purpose, which cannot be achieved in the event of termination of the principal agreement. In such case, there is no justification for further subsistence of the subsidiary contract.

---

[151] S. Bros (2010), p. 45.

[152] S. Bros (2009), p. 960.

[153] Cass. 1èreciv., 1 décembre 1993, JCP 1994 II 22325.

[154] As opposed to invalidity of a contract, under the French law, ineffectiveness gives rise to an ex nunc effect. Nonetheless, in the judgment of 5 July 2007, the Cassation Court held in favor of a retroactive effect of the ineffectiveness of a contract subsidiary to the principal contract. Cass. Com., 5 juin 2007, n°04-20380, JCP 2007, II, 10184. For more on the differences between ineffectiveness and invalidity under French law, see Y. Buffelan-Lanore, Essai sur la notion de caducité des actesjuridiquesen droit civil, Paris 1963.

[155] Cass. Com., 5 juin 2007, n° 04-20380, JCP 2007, II, 10184.

[156] Cass. 1ère civ., 04 avril 2006, pourvoi n° 02-18277, Bull. civ. 2006 I N° 190, p. 166.

However, this criterion is insufficient. In literature of the subject, the dominant view is that the mutual correlation is predestined by the will of the parties, which cannot be presumed.[157] In the light of the above, the parties may decide to disconnect the contractual obligations even if they pursue the same economic purpose.[158]

It must be noted that French courts, for a relatively long time, referred sceptically to the concept of bundle of contracts for the purposes of resolving disputes arising out of insurance contracts. At the end of the day, this conception was developed, first of all, for the sake of assessing the influence of the loan agreement on the persistence of an insurance contract of the *bancassurance* type.

As late as in the judgment of 18 January 2000, following well-established case-law, the Cassation Court clearly held in favor of independence of the loan agreement and the insurance (*bancassurance*) contract, pointing out that the insured party may take advantage of the insurance coverage even despite accelerated maturity of the loan obligation.[159] On the other hand, already in the judgment of 26 April 2000, the Cassation Court expressed an opinion that an insurance contract shares the fate of the loan agreement if the borrower and the lender provided so in the concluded agreement.[160] Insurance coverage is discontinued without the need to terminate the contract or take any other steps by the interested parties. An analogous position was taken by the Cassation Court in the judgment of 10 July 2008.[161]

9 The Consequences of Expiry of the Group Insurance Relationship

Although the question was not subject to broader discussion in Polish literature, much attention was paid to it in French literature of the subject. Among the few provisions on the consequences of terminating an insurance contract, attention should be drawn to the norm under Art. L. 141-3 (4) CA. Under that provision, exclusion of the insured party from the group of persons covered by the group insurance contract does not deprive the insured party of the rights he or she acquired in consideration of the previously paid premiums. On the linguistic level, this provision does not correlate the end of the insurer's liability with the moment of depriving the insured party of insurance protection by the policyholder's acts. On the other hand, the norm under Art. L. 141-3 (4) CA points to a

[157] S. Bros (2009), p. 961.

[158] Cass Comm., 15 février 2000, Bull civ. IV, n° 29.

[159] Cass. 1ère civ., 18 janvier 2000, RGDA 2000, p. 159.

[160] Cass. 1ère civ., 26 avril 2000, RGDA 2000, p. 891.

[161] Cass. 1ère civ., 10 juillet 2008, n° pourvoi 07-17932.

close connection between the duration of insurance coverage and the payment of premium. Nonetheless, most opinions expressed in judicial practice and literature disregard such nuances. By way of interpretation of Art. L. 141-3 (4) CA, a principle was formulated allowing to resolve conflicts in relation to the right to receive the benefit from the insurer depending on whether the risk materialized before or after the expiry of the insurance relationship. Bearing in mind that most group insurance schemes *sensu stricto* involve risks of personal nature, it is quite widespread that the event giving rise to the insurer's liability takes place already in the insurance period, however, its consequences affect the insured party also after the end of that period. Termination of the insurance contract after the materialization of the agreed risk does not release the insurer from the obligation to render the benefit to the entitled party.[162] It is inadmissible to include in the insurance contract a clause departing from that rule. Such contractual provisions are considered by the courts to be "non-stipulated."[163] On the other hand, the insured party may not hope to obtain a benefit provided for in the contract if the risk materialized already after the expiry of the insurance relationship,[164] unless an exception to that rule is provided under the insurance contract.

Considering the similarities between the expiry of a contract and amendment to its provisions in the period of insurance protection, a proposal might seem intellectually tempting to apply by analogy the provision of Art. L. 141-4 CA, regarding the procedure of amending the terms of coverage in group insurance, to assess the consequences of expiry of the insurance contract. However, this view was categorically rejected by the French Cassation Court.[165] The silence of the legislator and the impossibility to adopt a universal principle according to which the assessment of the consequences of termination of an insurance contract is made by analogy to Art. L. 141-4 CA inclined the courts and academic authors to formulate several rules deriving from the very nature of group insurance, and, as such, those rules may also apply in the Polish jurisdiction.

According to a well-established opinion in French case-law, expiry of a contract between the group organizer and the insurer entails termination of the legal relationships between the members of the insured persons' group and the insurance company.[166] This principle applies to all group insurance contracts, irrespective of whether the accession to the insurance is compulsory or voluntary.[167] However, in literature of the subject, attention was drawn to the fact that

[162] P.G. Marly (2013), p. 291; Cass. 2e civ., 8 mars 2006, JurisData n° 2006-032805; Bull. civ. 2006, II, n° 65; Resp. civ. et assur. 2006, comm. 172.

[163] The decision of Cour de Cassation Chambre civile 1 of 13 June 1995, N° de pourvoi: 92-16035.

[164] V. Nicolas (2002), p. 913; P.G. Marly (2013), p. 291.

[165] The decision of 18 June 2002, Cour de cassation chambre civile 1, N° de pourvoi: 01-00050.

[166] G. Venandet, F. Jacob, X. Henry, A. Tisserand-Martin, G. Wiederkehr, (2011), p. 1436.

[167] C. Larroumet (2007), p. 982.

uncritical acceptance of that view with regard to the insurance with compulsory accession may give rise to doubts, considering the restrictions relating to the construction of rendering performance to a third party. According to the principle expressed under Art. 1121 CC, a party reserving a benefit to a third party loses the possibility to cancel the reservation made for account of a third party when the third party declares an intention to take advantage of the reservation.[168] Taking the view that the expiry of the contract between the group organizer and the insurer leads to the expiry of the relationship between the insured party and the insurer, one should accept, at the same time, that the policyholder may indirectly cancel the reservation made for account of the insured person. However, the opinion dominant in literature is that in the light of the categorical wording of Art. 1121 of the French Civil Code, any attempts at indirect cancellation of the reservation made for account of a third party must always be approached as attempts to circumvent the law.[169] Seeking to remove this contradiction, certain authors assume that in the insurance with compulsory accession, the insured party consents to being covered by insurance protection only during the term of the insurance contract.[170] In other words, the duration of insurance coverage is made dependent on the existence of the contract between the policyholder and the insurance company.

Prima facie, these observations lead to a conclusion that the insurance model with voluntary accession protects the insured parties to a lesser degree than insurance with compulsory accession. The grounds for termination of the framework agreement in the insurance with voluntary accession are laid down in the provisions of the Civil Code. On the other hand, within the framework of insurance with compulsory accession, the contract between the organizer (policyholder) and the insurer may, in principle, expire only under and on the terms laid down in the provisions of the Insurance Code. The provisions of insurance law are characterized by a tendency to protect the insured parties and policyholders, whereas the general provisions of civil law are based on the assumption of equivalent position of the parties to an obligational relationship. From the perspective of a professional trading participant, it is less problematic to terminate a contract regulated by the general provisions of the law of obligations than a contract governed by the provisions oriented towards protecting the "weaker party" of the insurance contract. However, this view is not entirely convincing. It must not be forgotten that the mere fact of terminating the group insurance contract does not mean the end of insurance coverage. As a consequence, the level of protecting the interests of the interested (insured) parties must be assessed taking into account if a given construction allows to continue insurance in spite of the expiry of the originally concluded contract.

---

[168] See. 1121 CC.

[169] F. Terré, P. Simler, Y. Lequette (2005), pp. 526–527.

[170] M. Bigot-Gonçalves (2009), p. 274.

10 Continuation of the Insurance Contract

In Polish literature, it is indicated that the standard within the framework of group life insurance is so called individual continuation of insurance coverage.[171] This refers to a possibility of further use of the insurance coverage after losing the status of member of the insured persons' group. This right is exercised by concluding an individual insurance contract in which the role of policyholder is assumed by a person being so far an insured party.[172]

Under Polish law, such right may arise only under the provisions of the group insurance contract. Stipulation of an option to continue insurance coverage should be accompanied bya contractual obligation to notify the insured parties about the option and provisions governing the method of its exercise.[173]

This observation reveals essential drawbacks of the solely contractual status of the right to individually continue insurance coverage. The group organizer together with the insurer have full discretion in defining the discussed right. A consequence of the merely contractual nature of that right and the correlated obligations of the group organizer are doubts relating to the existence of liability for damages for the breach of the obligations, not to mention the practical difficulties with effective enforcement of such claims in court.[174]

An answer to the shortcomings of the solely contractual right to individually continue insurance protection would be to grant the same right within a normative framework. Such mechanism must, on the one hand, ensure the desired protection level to the insured parties and, on the other hand, prevent a practice of acceding to the insurance for the sole purpose of obtaining coverage on preferential terms, which is then continued as a part of individual insurance. In this context, questions arise about the method of implementing the risk assessment at the time of establishing individual insurance and about the terms of calculating the insurance premium.

The intention to regulate the continuation of insurance under the draft prepared by the Civil Law Codification Commission attached to the Minister of Justice is demonstrated by the wording of Art. 834^{12} § 2 of the Draft CC. ("In the event of leaving the group by the insured party, the insured party's obligations shall be extinguished.") The cited provision refers only to the obligations of the insured person, and not to his or her rights. It seems, however, that such formulation was unintentional. At the same time, this general rule is anything but sufficient.

In foreign literature and case-law, the discussed legal construction is subject to much interest. For example, in the context of French law, the concept of so called individual continuation of insurance was developed despite only fragmentary legal

[171] Ibid.,p. 113.

[172] In German law, such contractual clause is referred to as 'continuation clause' (Fortsetzungsklausel). For more, see F. Herdter, (2010), pp. 174–176.

[173] Ibid., p. 114.

[174] Ibid., pp. 115–116.

regime of the question. The possibility of further insurance coverage despite termination of the contract between the insurer and the policyholder was mentioned by the French legislator in Art. L. 141-6 (1), second sentence, CA. Under that provision, in case of termination of the legal existence of the group organizer or the group organizer's liquidation, the group insurance contract is transformed into individual insurance contracts between particular members of the group and the insurer.

In French literature, attention is drawn to a relatively narrow scope of application of that provision. A part of authors assumes that Art. L. 141-6 (1), second sentence, CA relates only to group insurance contracts with voluntary accession.[175] This is an insurance formula under which, beside the framework agreement between the group organizer and the insurer, there are as many insurance contracts as insured parties. The provision of Art. L. 141-6 (1), second sentence, CA allows for further persistence of such insurance contracts despite termination of the framework agreement. On the other hand, this construction does not match the theoretical model of the insurance contract with compulsory accession, which can be accounted for by the unitary conception.

Irrespective of the discussed doubts, it must be emphasized that the provision of Art. L. 141-6 (1), second sentence, CA may apply only when the cause of expiry of the framework agreement is the termination of legal existence of the group organizer. Such situations, however, are rare. Much more often, expiration of the group insurance contract, effective for all insured parties, is a consequence of the contract's termination by the organizer or the insurer.

In literature, much attention has been paid to the pursuit of a legal construction that would allow to secure the insured parties against being deprived of the benefits under the insurance in the event of expiry of the contract between the group organizer and the insurer. One of the proposals was based on the belief that in such situations, one can resort to the construction of assignment of rights and obligations.[176] Another opinion presented in the literature is that the change of the insurer is possible due to a transfer of the insurance portfolio to another insurer.[177] Proponents of those conceptions, however, seem not to notice that the need to secure the interests of the acceding persons becomes apparent already after the termination of the insurance contract. At that time, there are no longer any rights and obligations that could be transferred to another insurance company.

Seeking to eliminate this contradiction, certain French academic authors support an opinion that continuation of group insurance under an individual insurance contract is an example of modification of rights and obligations during the insurance period,[178] referred to in Art. L. 141-4 CA.[179] The last of the discussed concepts has

---

[175] M. Bigot-Gonçalves (2009), p. 285.

[176] V. Bourdon (2002) II,p. 440.

[177] Ibid., p. 450.

[178] L. Mayaux (1998), p. 117.

[179] Under Art. L. 141-4 CA, the policyholder (group organiser) is obliged to notify the insured parties about amendments to their rights and obligations at least three months ahead of the entry into force of such amendments. It is the policyholder (group organiser) that incurs the burden of proving that the insured person was duly notified about the amendment. However, the insured party

been accepted in judicial practice. In the judgment of 18 June 2002,[180] attention was drawn to the fact that such modification does not require consent from persons who already acceded to the insurance as long as the policyholder was granted the right to conclude a contract with another insurer.[181] Even in the lack of such agreement, the case-law points to a possibility of expressing such consent by the parties covered by the insurance, even implicitly.[182] It seems that, on each such occasion, all circumstances of the case should be taken into account as well as legitimate interest of the members of the insured persons' group, who should not be exposed to unexpected loss of insurance coverage.

Also, the case-law takes a similar approach, pointing to a possibility of individual continuation of insurance coverage after losing the status of group member by a particular insured party.

In the decision of the Cassation Court of 5 January 1977,[183] the Court presented an opinion that an ex-employee who, in the term of employment, acceded to group insurance, may take advantage of the insurance protection after the termination of the employment relationship if he or she was paying the premium up to the date when the risk materialized. An analysis of the justification of this ruling leads to the conclusion that further persistence of the insurance coverage depends on the behavior of the group organizer, the insured party and the insurer already after the expiry of the non-insurance relation (employment relationship) between the insured person and the group organizer. If the insurer accepts the premium paid, and the organizer does not take steps that would point to the organizer's intention to terminate the insurance, the member of the group still takes advantage of the insurance coverage. However, one can but agree with the authors indicating that in such situation the insurance coverage arises under an individual insurance contract concluded implicitly after the termination of the group insurance.[184]

In the judgment of 31 March 1981, the Cassation Court expressed an opinion that an employee who, as a result of the employer's omission, lost the status of an insured person should be treated as though being subject to insurance coverage if the premium due under the concluded insurance contract was paid.[185] In the justification of the judgment, attention was drawn to the fact that an omission by the group's organizer may not lead to negative consequences for the insured party if the omission took place without the insured party's intention or fault. This solution relieves the insured party from the obligation to examine if the group organizer duly

may leave the insured persons'group if he or she does not consent to the amendments. Nevertheless, the insured party may not exercise that right if, in the light of the non-insurance relationship between the insured party and the policyholder,accession to the insurance is compulsory.

180 Civ. 1ère civ., 18 juin 2002, no. 01-00-050, Bull. Civ. 1. No 167.

181 M. Bigot-Gonçalves (2009), p. 280.

182 P.G. Marly (2013), p. 291.

183 Cass. 1ère civ., 5 janvier 1977, 75-12.098.

184 L. Mayaux(2007), p. 707.

185 Cour de Cassation Chambre sociale, 31 mars 1981, N° de pourvoi: 79-17101.

performs the organizer's duties as long as the insured party takes care to timely pay the insurance premium.[186] Also in this situation, the construction should be used of continuing insurance coverage as a result of concluding (even implicitly) another individual insurance contract, instead of seeking justification for further subsistence of the insurance coverage in the group insurance contract.

The French solution might be a manifestation of the rightful belief that the insured party should not be exposed to unexpected loss of insurance coverage, however, it is not conducive to legal certainty and predictability of court decisions. It should be noted at this point that the tendency to justify further subsistence of insurance protection can be identified, first of all, in matters relating to employee group insurance contracts.

On the other hand, the German legislator decided to introduce explicit normative grounds for the right to continue insurance coverage. This right is vested only in such insured parties that acceded to the insurance of risks relating to their health. It must be noted that the provisions are semi-mandatory. Modification of the solutions discussed below can take place only to the benefit of the policyholder or the insured party (§ 208 VVG).

For the purposes of group insurance, the above-mentioned provision of § 206 (4) VVG modifies the terms of terminating the insurance contract by the insurer. The insurer may terminate the group insurance as long as the insured parties are in a position to use insurance protection under an individual insurance contract.

On the other hand, § 207 VVG provides for the right to continue insurance coverage despite expiry of the group insurance contract for reasons relating to the group's organizer. At the beginning of this provision, the German legislator reminds that the death of the group organizer (policyholder) leads to expiration of the insurance contract (§ 207 (1) VVG). However, the insured parties may apply for continual insurance by assuming the role of the policyholder within two months from the death of the previous policyholder (§ 207 (1) VVG).

This solution applies as appropriate if the group organizer terminates the insurance contract in relation to all or certain insured parties (§ 207 (2), first sentence, VVG). Termination of the insurance vis-à-vis a particular insured party is affected only as long as the insured party learns about the termination notice given by the insurance operator (§ 207 (2), second sentence, VVG).

If the termination relates to a group insurance contract and the new organizer has not been indicated, the members of the group will have the right to take advantage of insurance coverage as a part of individual insurance (third sentence). This right is extinguished after two months from the date when the insured party learned about the possibility to continue the insurance coverage (fourth sentence).

[186] This conception must be distinguished from situations in which the policyholder incurs liability for a "loss of chance of insurance." This construction applies to factual situations in which the insured party did not receive a benefit from the insurer because of maladjustment of the insurance to the insured party's personal conditions and characteristics. Consequences of such malpractice are borne by the policyholder, who is obliged to redress the damage caused to the acceding party.

Individual continuation of insurance protection was also regulated in the Austrian Act on the insurance contract as a special right of the insured parties within the framework of insurance against health-related risks.[187]

If a party insured as a part of group insurance leaves the insured persons' group, e.g., as a result of termination by the insurer or retirement, or if the entire group insurance contract is terminated, the party insured within the framework of group insurance is entitled to declare that further coverage is to be provided under an individual insurance. In such situations, such terms and tariffs will apply as applicable to individual insurance. Continuation of the insurance does not require a repeated risk assessment if the insured party could have been insured within the framework of individual insurance on the date of acceding to the group insurance (§ 178m (1), first sentence). The premium for the purposes of individual insurance is determined according to the insured party's age as at the time of acceding to the group insurance (§ 178m (3)).

As under the German legislative framework, in the Austrian law, the right to individual continuation of the insurance expires over time. A request to continue the insurance must be made by the insured party within one month from the loss of the status of member of the group or termination of the group insurance contract (§ 178m (2), first sentence).

The insurer must notify the insured parties about the right to individually continue the insurance (§ 178m (1), second sentence). If the insurer has not informed the insured parties about the possibility to continue the insurance, then the deadline does not begin to run (second sentence). Moreover, at the time of accession to the group insurance, the insurer is obliged to expressly notify every party insured as a part of the group insurance under what terms the insured party's coverage is terminated and what the consequences are, in terms of the premium amount, of individual continuation of the insurance (§ 178m (6)).

The right of individual continuation is not vested in an insured party who lost the status of the group's member as a result of termination of the insurance relationship by the insurer for breach by the group's member of the obligations laid down in the insurance contract (§ 178m (4)).

Changes to the composition of the insured persons' group may affect the amount of insurance premium. In particular, this relates to a change of the average age of the insured parties (§ 178m (5)).

The right to continue insurance was also regulated in the provisions of the Turkish Commercial Code of 2012. However, it must be noted that, under that Code, the concept of group insurance is referred only to life insurance, being one of the types of personal insurance. Therefore, the right to continue insurance coverage is a special privilege of parties insured within the framework of life insurance.

[187] The Austrian Act on the insurance contract of 2 December 1958,Bundesgesetzvom 2. Dezember 1958 über den Versicherungsvertrag (Versicherungsvertragsgesetz – VersVG), StF: BGBl. Nr. 2/1959, tj.: BGBl I No. 34/2015.

Art. 1496 (4) TTK provides that: "In the event of losing the status of the group's member in the period of insurance, the insurance coverage provided as a part of group insurance may be continued under individual insurance by the policyholder, the insured party or the beneficiary. Continuation of the insurance by the insured party or the beneficiary is possible as long as they assume the role of the policyholder." In the third sentence of the discussed provision, it is stipulated that such persons (the insured party or the beneficiary) are then jointly and severally liable together with the previous policyholder for any overdue premiums. It must be noted that the Turkish legislator provided for a possibility of further provision of the insurance coverage in an unchanged subjective configuration. The group organizer may act as policyholder concluding an individual insurance contract for account of a particular member of the group.

11 Instead of Conclusions: Solutions Offered in European Model Law

A special manifestation of the tendency for the unification of international contract law are the model rules on the insurance contract, better known as the Principles of European Insurance Contract Law (PEICL), developed by the members of the Project Group on a Restatement of European Insurance Contract Law.[188] As a part of the project, which initially was a typically academic undertaking, an effort was made to create uniform rules on the insurance contract which would make a set of solutions positively evaluated by the representatives of legal science and market participants. It was intended to reach that objective taking into account the conclusions following from comparative law analysis. Because of the supranational character of the prepared rules, precedence in interpretation of its provisions was afforded to the conception of autonomous construction.[189]

In 2016, the full text of the PEICL was published together with commentary.[190] The original version of the PEICL did not contain the provisions on group insurance.[191]

As the works progressed, the authors of the PEICL eventually decided to introduce a definition of the group insurance contract which – beside the definition of "insurance contract," "damage insurance" and "fixed-sum insurance" – was covered by the provision of Art. 1:201, in paragraph (7)of that provision. It was concluded that group insurance contracts are based on the agreement between the

[188] M. Lakhan, H. Heiss (2012), pp. 1–11.

[189] D. Fuchs (2010), p. 132; id., Status ubezpieczonego według rozporządzenia Rady (WE) nr 44/2001 – wnioski de lege ferenda dla prawodawcy polskiego, EPS 2012, No. 5, p. 27.

[190] J. Basedow, J. Birds, M. Clarke, H. Cousy, H. Heiss, L. Loacker (2016).

[191] Ch. Armbruester (2013), p. 150.

insurer and the group organizer concluded for the benefit of the insured parties who have a common connection with the organizer and meet the requirements set forth in such agreement. So determined circle of the insured parties is referred to as "group". At the same time, the definition expressly mentions the possibility of obtaining protection by members of the insured party's family under the group insurance contract.

Researchers from the Restatement Group opted as well for sanctioning the distinction between insurance with compulsory accession (*accessory group insurance*) and insurance with voluntary accession (*elective group insurance*). The first of these concepts is defined as group insurance in which the existence of insurance protection is a consequence of belonging to a given group. The insured party may not withdraw from the insurance coverage. The second category, on the other hand, refers to situations in which accession to a group insurance is a consequence of submitting to the insurer a notice of intention to join the circle of insured parties or absence of refusal to accede to the insurance.[192]

In the provision of Art. 1:201 PEICL, containing a dictionary of terms used in the PEICL, the authors additionally introduced definitions of the group insurance contract (Art. 1:201 item 7), group insurance with compulsory accession (*accessory group insurance*) (Art. 1:201 item 8) and group insurance with voluntary accession (*elective group insurance*) (Art. 1:201 item 9).

At the same time, the authors of the PEICL decided to refer to the person entering the group insurance contract with the insurer as "group organizer." This term applies regardless of the compulsory or voluntary nature of accession to the group insurance contract. However, the authors did not decide to define that concept under Art. 1:202, which determines the meaning of such terms as "insured" (Art. 1:202 item 1) or "insurance agent" (Art. 1:202 item 5). It must be noted that the authors of the instrument use of the term "group organizer" inconsistently. As a part of the provisions on group insurance contracts, they also make references to the "policyholder" (Art. 18:204 item 2). It seems, however, that the distinction is unintentional and the terms "group organizer" and "policyholder" can be used interchangeably for the purposes of the discussed rules.

There are important structural differences between insurance contracts with compulsory accession and insurance contracts with voluntary accession. An insurance contract with compulsory accession (*accessory group insurance*) is an insurance contract *sensu stricto*. On its basis individual insured persons obtain insurance coverage. However, direct application of the PEICL provisions could give rise to multiple doubts bearing in mind the specific nature of group insurance. It seems that such doubts are shared by the authors of the PEICL. According to the principle expressed in Art. 18:201 PEICL, where necessary, the PEICL, shall be applied to accessory group insurance *mutatis mutandis*.

The authors of the PEICL have also noticed threats relating to the double status of the group organizer in relation to particular members of the group, as voiced in

[192] M. Fras, (2020), pp. 179–231.

Art. 18:102 (1). This provision imposes on the group organizer (policyholder) an obligation to act dutifully and in good faith taking account of the legitimate interests of the group member when negotiating and performing the contract. This principle applies both to insurance with voluntary accession and to insurance with compulsory accession. The norm under Art. 18:102 (1) was placed in Part 6 Section 1 of the draft, containing the general provisions on group insurance. It should be concluded that the obligation set out in Art. 18:102 (1) PEICL refers predominantly to the activities undertaken by the group organizer as a part of the relationships between the group organizer and particular members of the group.

The principle laid down under Art. 18:102 (1) PEICL shows a far-reaching similarity to the solution adopted as a part of the Community regime of commercial agent under Directive 86/653.[193] Under Art. 3 of the Directive, in performing his activities on behalf of his principal, a commercial agent must look after the principal's interests and act dutifully and in good faith.[194] An analysis of the remaining provisions of the draft prepared by the researchers from the Restatement Group reveals further similarities between their proposal and the solutions adopted in the above-mentioned Directive. The agent's duty to act dutifully and in good faith was made specific in Art. 3 (2) of the Directive. Under this provision, in particular, a commercial agent is obliged to communicate to his principal all the necessary information available to him (Art. 3 (2) letter (b) of the Directive). An analogous solution has been adopted in Art. 18:102 (2) PEICL, under which the group organizer shall forward any relevant notices issued by the insurer to the group members and inform them about any amendments to the contract.

As a part of another section, the authors introduced the provisions on group insurance contracts with voluntary accession (*elective group insurance*). At the same time, the authors accentuated the special type of relationship between the insurer and an individual insured person that can be observed in this type of contracts. As opposed to contracts with compulsory accession, in this case the insurance contract *sensu stricto* is concluded only between the insurer and the insured person. The group organizer, on the other hand, is a party to the framework agreement concluded with the insurer (Art. 18:301 (1) PEICL). Group insurance with voluntary accession makes up a specific legal construction, being a combination of individual insurance with a special type of framework agreement between the insurer and the group organizer (Art. 18:301 PEICL). However, the question of applicability of the PEICL to the insurance contracts concluded between the insurer and individual insured parties is resolved by the parties to the framework agreement. The framework agreement, as such, is not an insurance contract. As a consequence, it should not be subject to the provisions of the PEICL. However, categorical application of this solution might lead to a situation in which insurance contracts are governed

[193] Council Directive 86/653/EEC of 18 December 1986 on the coordination of the laws of the Member States relating to self-employed commercial agents (86/653/EEC) (OJ L 382, 31.12.1986, p. 17).

[194] E. Rott-Pietrzyk (2006), p. 32

by the PEICL provisions, whereas the law applicable to the framework agreement is inadequate to the requirements of the construction laid down under Art. 18:301 PEICL. Recognizing a possibility of discrepancy in that regard between the insurance contracts and the framework agreement, the researchers from the Restatement Group decided that the requirement under Art. 18:102 (1) PEICL to act dutifully and in good faith when considering the interests of the group members applies also to the agreement entered into by the group organizer (Art. 18:301 (2)).

The above observations arouse doubts whether Art. 11:103 PEICL applies to the group insurance contract with voluntary accession. It should be reminded that the provision in question is intended to individualize civil law sanctions for improper performance of the duties imposed on the insured person. The provision introduces a principle according to which a breach of duty under the insurance contract by one insured person does not adversely affect the rights of the other persons insured under the same insurance contract. The group insurance contract with voluntary accession is not an example of insuring several insured persons "under the same insurance contract." At most, one can speak of a bundle of individual insurance contracts that have been concluded thanks to a single agreement organizing the insurance.

An issue vividly discussed by the members of the Restatement Group was the question of disclosure obligations the proposed instrument was to impose on the insurer and the policyholder.

As far as individual insurance is concerned, the question of disclosure obligation is governed by the provisions of Art. 2:202 PEICL. Under the provision of Art. 2:202 (1) PEICL, when concluding the contract, the insurer shall warn the applicant of any inconsistencies between the cover offered and the applicant's requirements of which the insurer is or ought to be aware, taking into consideration the circumstances and mode of contracting and, in particular, whether the applicant was assisted by an independent intermediary. In the light of the above, the addressee of disclosure obligations at the contracting stage is the insurer. The provision of Art. 2:202 (2) PEICL provides for sanctions for non-performance or improper performance of the discussed obligations. Beside the right, conferred on the policyholder under Art. 2:202 (2) letter (b) PEICL, to terminate the contract, the provision of Art. 2:202 (2) letter (a) PEICL obliges the insurer to pay the benefit to the policyholder also in respect of "all losses resulting from the breach of this duty to warn unless the insurer acted without fault."

However, this construction is incompatible with group insurance. First, the policyholder does not pay the insurance benefit to the insured persons. Doubs arise in the context of the attempts to adopt, for the purposes of disputes relating to group insurance, such interpretation of Art. 2:202 (2) letter (a) PEICL so as to obligate the policyholder to indemnify the insured person against the difference between the benefit that could have been received and the benefit actually paid by the insurer. An analogous construction introduced by the French judiciary is a source of numerous interpretative doubts and may discourage policyholders from entering into contracts for account of persons interested in the accession to group insurance. The provision of Art. 2:202 PEICL, following the solutions adopted by national legislators, is an expression of the belief that the policyholder is the weaker party of the insurance contract, who concludes the contract on the terms authoritatively imposed by the insurer. However, the situation looks different in the context of group insurance, in which case the role of policyholder is assumed by a party having at its disposal the support of specialists, with the involvement of whom the terms of insurance are negotiated. In the light of Art. 2:202 (1) PEICL, the insurer should adjust the form and contents of the information to the policyholder "taking into consideration the circumstances and mode of contracting and, in particular, whether the applicant was assisted by an independent intermediary." When these criteria are applied to the policyholder in group insurance arrangements, it can be concluded with some caution that the insurer is exempt at all from disclosure obligations to the policyholder.

Within the framework of the PEICL, the authors decided to define the scope of the disclosure obligation according to the type of insurance contract. An exception in this regard is the above-mentioned provision of Art. 18:102 (2) PEICL. In group insurance with voluntary and compulsory accession, the group organizer is obliged to forward to the group members any notices issued by the insurer which are relevant from their point of view, and to inform them about any amendments to the contract (Art. 18:102 (2)).

The principle of acting dutifully, in good faith and taking account of the interests of group members applies to the assessment of any activities undertaken by the policyholder. Therefore, it seems that it should serve as a specific directive of interpretation allowing to specify how the disclosure obligation should be discharged when it is insufficient to merely read the provisions of the PEICL for the assessment of a particular case.

In case of insurance with compulsory accession, the group organizer is obliged to provide information relating to the insurance without undue delay to a person acceding to the group (Art. 18:202 (1)). The scope of this obligation covers information about the existence of the insurance contract, the extent of cover, about any precautionary measures and any other requirements for preserving cover, and the claims procedure (Art. 18:202 (1) letters (a)–(d)). This catalog is exhaustive. However, there are no obstacles for the group organizer to provide a wider range of information to the acceding person. In the process, the group organizer should take care to document the fact of informing the interested party about the terms of insurance. It is the group organizer that bears the burden of proof in this regard (Art. 18:202 (2)). In the lack of any special provisions, violation of that obligation must be assessed in terms of improper performance of the contract. PEICL does not contain any provisions in that regard. Consequently, provisions defining the regime of liability *ex contractu* come to the fore as a part of the law applicable to the contract.

In the light of literal interpretation of particular provisions of the PEICL, the solution provided under Art. 18:202 does not refer to an amendment of contract terms during the period of insurance coverage. If a modification of the insurance terms is introduced already after the establishment of insurance coverage, the group organizer is obliged to notify the group members about any modifications introduced to the contractual clauses (Art. 18:102 (2)). Considering the scheme of the PEICL adopted by the authors of the instrument, the provision of Art. 18:102 applies to both types of group insurance. However, in case of insurance with voluntary accession, any amendment to the terms of insurance requires exhaustion of the procedure provided for individual insurance contracts. This principle relates both to situations when a modification of the insurance terms is introduced as a part of the relationship between the insured person and the insurer and when it is a consequence of an amendment to the framework agreement. In this way, the group organizer and the insurer are not allowed to amend the terms of insurance coverage *ex post*, somehow bypassing the insured persons.

The direction of works on the legal regime of group insurance under the PEICL allows to conclude that the authors of the instrument decided to clearly specify the consequences of exercise by the insurer of the insurer's right to terminate the insurance contract. In the context of specific national legislative frameworks, there have been doubts relating to the establishment if the notice of termination given by the insurer leads to termination of the insurance contract effective vis-à-vis all insured persons or only vis-à-vis particular persons covered by the insurance protection.

In case of insurance with obligatory accession, the authors of the PEICL clearly resolved that matter by adopting a solution affording fuller protection to the interests of the group members. If the insurance contract provides a sanction for a breach by the insured person of the precautionary measures in the form of the insurer's right to terminate the contract, the notice of termination given by the insurer is effective only vis-à-vis the group member whose act or omission could cause a damage (Art. 18:203 (2)). Similar conclusion should be drawn in the context of disposal of the object of insurance by one of the group members (Art. 18:203 (3)). The insurance contract is terminated only vis-à-vis that person. In the light of the general principles of the PEICL, this rule will not apply when the change of the entitled party is a consequence of inheritance ("transfer of title by inheritance") or when otherwise agreed in the insurance contract (Art. 12:102 (3)). In consequence, the authors of the PEICL adopted a solution according to which a transfer of title to the insured object, as a rule, implies the need to establish a new insurance law relationship with the transferee.

Within the framework of the PEICL, a need has been identified for a solution allowing to continue insurance under an individual contract when the interested party loses the status of the group's member and, in the same way, can no longer enjoy the coverage under the group insurance. Those assumptions were put in practice only for the purposes of drafting the provisions on life insurance. In case of life insurance contracts, the accession to which is compulsory (*accessory group life insurance*), a special regime was introduced defining the date of expiry of the contract. Insurance coverage expires after 3 months from the contract's termination or loss by the insured person of the membership status in the group, or at the date when the period of insurance ends as provided in the contract if that date falls before the end of the 3-month protective period. Then, the group member is in a position to conclude a new insurance contract without the need for a repeated risk assessment (Art. 18:204 (1)). The policyholder is obliged to inform the group member about the possibility to continue the insurance under an individual contract. In group life insurance contracts, the premium is calculated on the basis of the insured person's individual qualities as on the date of the insured person's accession to the group

(Art. 18:204 (3)). On the other hand, in the context of insurance with voluntary accession, expiry of the framework agreement or loss of the membership status in the group does not affect the individual insurance contract between the insured person and the insurer (Art. 18:303).

It is necessary to track down the reasons behind the popularity of group insurance contracts with a view to identifying the nature of that insurance product and its legal construction. Group insurance is not a simple aggregate of individual insurance contracts. It belongs to a wider category of collective insurance. The essence of group insurance is that it may cover multiple persons belonging to a group identified according to specific criteria, though not necessarily all such persons, and the premium does not have to be paid by the policyholder, so that one contract gives rise to a number of insurance relationships. The differences between group insurance contracts and individual insurance contracts are:

- economic purpose,
- insurable interest (who is interested in insurance protection), which may be very diversified and, consequently, may refer to interests of the policyholder, the insured party and the policy holder, or the insured party,
- sometimes, the sole reason for the conclusion of a group insurance contract is organizational facility,
- type of the benefit rendered to the person covered by insurance protection,
- method of calculating the risk, depending on whether it takes into account individual characteristics of a specific person or features of an abstract group member.[195]

No definition of group insurance exists at any international level. Even when ruling on group insurance, the Court of Justice of the European Union (CJEU) refrained from providing any definition. It causes a lot of problems in private international law.[196]

Normative goals which should be regulated are:definition of group insurance contract, information duties of group organizer, asserting claims under the group insurance contract, based on the construction of Insurance contract for account of a third party; the content of the obligation to pay the premium, termination of group insurance contract by the Insurer and right to continue cover

References

Armbruester, Ch. (2013). PEICL – The Project of a European Insurance Contract Law, *Connecticut Insurance Law Journal*, vol. 20, p. 54.

Baars, G., & Sennett, N. (1993). *The Fundamentals of Group Insurance*, Zurich.

Basedow, J., Birds, J., Clarke, M., Cousy, H., Heiss, H., & Loacker, L. (2016). *Principles of European Insurance Contract Law (PEICL)*, 2nd Expanded Edition, Köln.

[195] M. Fras,(2020), pp. 179–231.

[196] M. Fras (2019)

Berdot, F. (1980). L'assurance de groupe, RGAT, p. 11.
Bigot-Gonçalves, M. (2009). *Les assurances de groupe*, Aix-en-Provence.
Bigot, J. (1998). La cessation du contratd'assurance collective, Colloque AIDA, RGDA, p.605.
Bosredon, M. (1990). *Histoire des assurances sur la vie, origines, développementsen France*, Bordeaux.
Bourdon, V. (2002). I, Des difficultés pour une association souscriptrice à changer d'assureur, RGDA, pp. 340–440.
Bourdon, V. (2002). II, La distribution de l'assurance par les associations.
Braun, H. (1925). *Geschichte der Lebensversicherung und der Lebensversicherungstechnik*, Nürnberg.
Bros, S. (2010). Le créditaffecté: entre groupe de contrats et opérationjuridique à trois personnes (in:) S. Bros, B. Mallet-Bricout (ed.), *Liber amicorum Christian Larroumet*, p. 60, Paris.
Bros, S. (2009). Les contratsinterdépendants: actualité et perspectives, RD, no. 14, p. 45.
Buffelan-Lanore, Y. (1963). *Essai sur la notion de caducité des actesjuridiquesendroit civil*, Paris.
Bzdyń, A. (2011). Ubezpieczenia grupowe we francuskim "code des assurances" (in:) E. Kowalewski (ed.), *Ubezpieczenia grupowe na życie a prawo zamówień publicznych*, Toruń.
Chagny, M., & Perdrix, L. (2012). *Droit des assurances*, Paris.
Chandler, D. K. (1997). *The Group Life Insurance Handbook*, Cincinnati.
Clark, K.L. (2012). The Group Insurance Marketplace (in:) W.F. Bluhm (ed.), *Group Insurance*, Winsted.
Comiti, V. P. (1985). Histoire des assurances sur la vie à la fin du XIXesiècle et audébut du XXesiècle, *Histoire des sciencesmèdicales*, t. 19, vol. 2, pp. 124–125.
Courtieu, G. (1999). Un suicide raté ou le législateur se tire une balle dans le pied, *Gazette du Palais*, 8–9, p. 2, janvier.
Cornu, G. (2001). *Vocabulaire juridique*, Paris.
Fabre A., Lefresne F., & Tuchszirer C. (2008). L'accord du 11 janvier 2008 sur la modernisation du marché du travail. *Une tentative d'évaluation,* p. 8, *Revue de l'OFCE.*
Fauque, M. (1971). *Les assurances*, Paris.
Field, I. M. (2012). *Employee group property and liability insurance*, Portland.
Fischer, A., & Lübcke, T. (2022). Ende oderNeuanfangimGruppenversicherungsmarkt? ZugleichAnmerkungzumUrteil des EuGH v. 29.9.2022 – C-633/20, *Versicherungsrecht (VersR) Zeitschrift für Versicherungsrecht, Haftungs – und Schadensrecht* (23/2022), p. 1480.
Fuchs, D. (2010). InsuranceRestatement jako europejski instrument opcjonalny służący regulacji umów ubezpieczenia, *RU* 2010, p. 132.
Fras, M. (2019). The Group Insurance Contract in Private International Law. *"Netherlands International Law Review"*, pp. 507–535. https://rebus.us.edu.pl/bitstream/20.500.12128/11663/1/Fras_The_group_insurance_contract.pdf (last accessed: 27 June 2024).
Fras, M. (2020). The European Context of the Group Insurance Contract. *Problemy Prawa Prywatnego Międzynarodowego*, 27, pp. 179–227. https://journals.us.edu.pl/index.php/PPPM/article/view/10538 (last accessed: 27 June 2024).
Fras, M., & Zgonina, O. (2023). *ECLI:EU:C:2022:733, ECJ – Group organizer as a distributor by terms of IDD. Commentary Judgement of the Court (First Chamber) of 29 september 2022 in case C-633/20, Bundesverband der Verbraucherzentralen und Verbraucherverbände – VerbraucherzentraleBundesverband eV v.* TC Medical Air Ambulance Agency GmbH, WiadomościUbezpieczeniowe nr 1, https://piu.org.pl/wp-content/uploads/2023/05/WU-2023-01_06_Fras.pdf (last accessed: 27 June 2024).
Gogueld'Allondans, A. (2000). *Les fonds de pension en France. Vers un nouveaumode de régulation des retraites?*, Paris.
Grau, J. B., Chiner, N. L., & Iglesia, J. O. (2014). *Insurancelaw in Spain*, Wolters Kluwer.
Groutel, H. (1990). La réforme du Code des assurances, *RCEA*, n° 3, p. 8.
Handschke, J., Kęszycka, B., & Kowalewski, E. (2007), Problematyka grupowych ubezpieczeń na życie w świetle znowelizowanych przepisów k.c. o umowie ubezpieczenia. Spór o intencjeustawodawcy, WiadomościUbezpieczeniowe, No. 7–8.

Heiss, H. (2012). Proportionality in the new German insurance contract act 2008, *Erasmus Law Review*, vol. 5, p. 105.
Herdter, F. (2010). *Der Gruppenversicherungsvertrag: Grundlagen und ausgewählteProblemfelder*, Karlsruhe.
Herrick, J. M. (2005). *Stuart P.H., Encyclopedia of Social Welfare History in North America*, Thousand Oaks.
Hémard, J. (1924). *Théorie et pratique des assurances terrestres*, t. 1, Paris.
Hjalmarsson, J. (2008). The Swedish Insurance Contract Act 2005 – an overview, *Nordisk forsikringstidsskrift*, pp. 91–92.
Jerry, R.H., & Richmond, D.R. (2012). *Understanding Insurance Law*, New Providence.
Kamieński, W. (2012). Glosa do wyroku Sądu Apelacyjnego w Warszawie z dnia 14 maja 2010 r., dotyczącego wysokości opłaty likwidacyjnej, Rozprawy Ubezpieczeniowe, nr 2, z. 13.
Kropka, M. (2007). Prawo właściwe dla umowy ubezpieczenia następstw nieszczęśliwych wypadków. Glosa do wyroku Sądu Najwyższego z dnia 3 lutego 2006 r., II PK 152/05, PPPM, t. 2.
Kurzendörfer, V. (2000). *Einführung in die Lebensversicherung*, Karlsruhe.
Lakhan, M. & Heiss, H. (2010). An Optional Instrument for European Insurance Contract Law,*Utrecht Journal of International and European Law*, vol. 71, part 27 , p. 170.
Lambert-Faivre, Y. (2011). *Leveneur L., Droit des assurances*, Paris.
Landel, J. (1993). L'assurance de groupe à la lumière de la jurisprudencerécente, RGAT.
Larroumet, C. (2007). *Les obligations, Le contrat, 2e partie, Effets*, 6e éd., Paris.
Lebond, N. (2010). Réflexions sur la nature juridique des assurances du crédit: assurance-emprunteurs et assurance-crédit, *Gazette du Palais*, n° 25, pp. 190–191.
Loacker, L.D. (2015). *InformedInsuranceChoice?: The Insurers Pre-Contractual Information Duties in General Consumer Insurance*, Cheltenham.
Łazowski, J. (1998). *Wstęp do nauki o ubezpieczeniach*, Sopot.
Łyskawa, K. (2007). *Grupowe ubezpieczenia na życie z funduszem kapitałowym w systemie zabezpieczenia emerytalnego w Polsce*, Warszawa.
Marly, P. G. (2013). *Droit des assurances*, Paris.
Marques, N. (2000). Le monopole de la Sécuritésociale face à l'histoire des premières protections sociales, *Journal des Economistes et des études humaine*, vol. X, no. 2, p. 57.
Mayaux, L. (2007). (in:) J. Bigot (ed.), *Traité de Droit des assurances. Tome 4. Les assurances de personnes*, Paris.
Mayaux, L. (1998). note sous Cass. civ. 1ère, 9 déc 1997, RGDA.
Milcamps, M. (1956). Le décret du 24 Janvier 1956 et l'assurance de groupe, RGAT.
Nicolas, V. (1996). *Essai d'une nouvelle analyseducontratd'assurance*, Paris.
Nicolas, V. (2002). (in:) J. Bigot (ed.), *Traité de Droit des assurances*. Tome 4, pp. 620–790, Paris.
Ponge, J. C. (2010). *Les sanctions en droit des assurances*, Paris.
Prölls, J. (2004). in: *Versicherungsvertragsgesetz*. Hrsg. J. Prölls, A. Martin. Munchen.
Rajcher, W. K. (1951). *Społeczno-historycznetypyubezpieczeń*, Warszawa.
Rigaud, D., Baron, P., & Pignaud, X. (2009). Le prévoyance collective des salariés et la loi Evin, *Droit social*, no 4, p. 465.
Rott-Pietrzyk, E. (2006). *Agent handlowy – regulacje polskie i europejskie*, Warszawa.
Roueil, E. (1998). *Essai sur le contratd'assurancecollective*, Orléan.
Routel, E. (2001). *La prévoyance dans l'entreprise*, Paris.
Serwach, M., & Kliszcz, J. (2010). Grupowe ubezpieczenie na życie w świetle prawa, doktryny i praktyki ubezpieczeniowej, *Prawo Asekuracyjne*, No. 2, p. 33.
Schickinger, W. F. (1988). Gruppenversicherung, insbesondereGruppenlebensversicherung (in:) D. Farny, E. Helten, P. Koch, R. Schmidt (ed.), *Handwörterbuch der Versicherung*, Karlsruhe.
Sargos, G. (2012). *Le contratd'assurance de personnes et sestroisprincipauxcodes: analysecomparative et prospective*, Paris.
Sprau, H. (2007). in: *PalandtKommentarzumBugerlichenGesetzbuch*, p. 1192. Munchen.
Szczepańska, M. (2008). *Ubezpieczeniana życie. Aspekty prawne*, Warszawa.
TTK – (TürkTicaretKanunu, 13.1.2011, No.: 6102, ResmiGazete 14.2.2011, No. 27846).
Terré, F., Simler P., & LequetteY. (2005). *Droitcivil – Lesobligations*, Paris.

Wieser, A. (2006). *Gruppenversicherungen*, Wien.
Venandet, G. (2011). Jacob F., Henry X., Tisserand-Martin A., Wiederkehr G., *Code civil*, Paris.
Voigt, J. (1942). *L'assurancegroupe, régime de prévoyance des cadres et techniciens*, Paris.

Legal and Economic Aspects of Co-Opetition Among Insurance Brokers: The Polish Case

Marcin Kawiński and Michał P. Ziemiak

1 Introductory Remarks

Co-opetition, a situation with simultaneous collaboration and competition, was coined by (Brandenburger & Nalebuff, 1996) and has gained significant interest in management science and come with diverse definitions(Koszarna, 2022). In this article, the authors use a narrow approach, hence the collaboration of competitors (Bengtsson & Kock, 1999). However, there are still plenty of options available. For example, this strategy could be planned within the company (Czakon, 2018) or forced by outside factors such as the client (Wiener & Saunders, 2014). It brings competitors of the same size (Gnyawali & Park, 2011) or the opposite (Hora i in., 2018). Finally, it is an intentional strategy (Luo, 2007) or an ad hoc solution (Pattinson i in., 2018).

The insurance market is one of the potential choices when exemplifying co-opetition, the UK and Germany are worth mentioning in this regard. This unique form of collaboration among competitors could have specific aims (Gnyawali i in., 2006):

- Sharing technology and resources (data sharing, joint ventures)
- Market expansion (collaborative marketing, cross-selling)
- Regulatory compliance (best practices sharing)
- Innovation and R&D (joint research initiative)
- Risk pooling (reinsurance collaboration)
- Customer experience improvement (collaborative platforms)

M. Kawiński
Department of Social Insurance, Warsaw School of Economics, Poland
ORCID: 0000-0003-4706-9171
e-mail: mkawin@sgh.waw.pl

M. P. Ziemiak
Department of Insurance and Medical Law, Nicolaus Copernicus University, Toruń Poland, Financial Ombudsman of the Republic of Poland
ORCID: 0000-0001-8543-9458
e-mail: mpz@umk.pl

P. Marano (ed.), *Emerging Legal Frontiers in Insurance*,
AIDA Europe Research Series on Insurance Law and Regulation,
https://doi.org/10.1007/978-3-032-09716-3_7

While co-opetition in the insurance market offers significant benefits, it also presents its own set of challenges. These include trust issues, complex relationships, and intellectual property concerns.

Most examples of co-opetition in the insurance market are among insurers, especially within coinsurance or consortia, to cover specific risks. It is crucial to understand the European legal framework, particularly the Insurance Block Exemption Regulation and its expiration on 31 March 2017. This regulation allowed relatively broad collaboration, typically considered an anti-competition practice. However, the Horizontal Block Exemption Regulations have allowed the joint creation and distribution of compilations, tables, and studies within research and development agreements, an important aspect to consider.

However, co-opetition is not limited to insurance companies. Intermediaries also take advantage of this opportunity. In this article, the authors analyze insurance brokers. As the legal framework mostly depends on local legislation, the authors chose Poland as the major field of interest. Poland is also an example of a significant and developing insurance market.

Insurance brokers are next to insurance agents (including agents offering additional insurance) and are at the core of the Polish insurance intermediaries market. Polish Insurance Distribution Act of December 15, 2017 (Insurance Distribution Act – IDA) defines insurance mediation as the performance of insurance distribution or reinsurance distribution by insurance intermediaries. The total number of registered (by the Polish Financial Supervision Authority – UKNF) brokers as of December 31, 2022, was 1,478, of which 1,420 entities conducted insurance activities and only 58 conducted reinsurance activities (UKNF, 2024). Employment in the insurance brokerage market 2022 amounted to 6,985 people, including 4,307 people performing brokerage activities and 2,678 employees not involved in brokerage activities (UKNF, 2024). Article 3 point 5) of IDA defines an insurance broker as a natural person or a legal person with a permit issued by a supervisory body (already mentioned by the Financial Supervision Commission) to perform brokerage activities in the insurance field entered in the brokers register. An insurance broker performs activities in insurance distribution on behalf of or for the client's benefit (referred to in IDA as "insurance brokerage activities").

Insurance broker – as any other insurance distributor – has an obligation (before concluding an insurance contract or an insurance guarantee contract) to determine, based on information obtained from the client, its demands and needs and provide objective information about the insurance product in an understandable form to enable the client to make an informed decision (art. 8 par. 1 of IDA). Additionally, insurance brokers – according to Art. 32 par 1 point 4 of IDA - provides advice based on reliable analysis of the insurance products available on the market in a number sufficient to develop a recommendation for the most appropriate contract and explains the grounds on which the recommendation is based, taking into account the complexity of the insurance contract or insurance guarantee contract and the type of client, unless the client submits a declaration of withdrawal from the provision of advice in documentary form (so-called insurance broker's recommendation – Malinowska, 2018; Ziemiak, 2019). A broker recommendation should be provided before concluding an insurance contract and, as a rule, in each case, also when dealing with compulsory insurance or renewal of insurance on the existing terms and conditions (Urbańczyk, 2024). As a result, according to IDA the insurance broker is burdened with the most extensive and comprehensive obligation of advising the client.

It must be noted that Polish legislation does not include any specific provisions on cooperation among insurance brokers. Fundamental to the operations of insurance brokers, IDA not even once mentions the terms "cooperation" or "collaboration" in the said scope. Hence, the forms and the legal framework of such cooperation were shaped by market practice and - to some extent - by jurisprudence (especially regarding the division of brokers' remuneration between cooperating parties). It is safe to say that every form of such cooperation must conform to regulations on entrepreneurs' corporations that are common to every business entity performing economic activity in Poland. Those include in particular:

- 1993 The Suppression of Unfair Competition Act;
- 2007 Competition and Consumer Protection Act.

Additionally, regardless of the type, each manifestation of cooperation between insurance brokers should first consider the general principle arising from art. 17.1 of IDD is to act honestly, fairly and professionally in accordance with customers' best interests. Finally – as stated in recital 16 of IDD – member states should promote a level playing field and competition on equal terms between intermediaries, whether or not they are tied to an insurance undertaking. According to IDD, there is a benefit to consumers if insurance products are distributed through different channels and through intermediaries with different forms of cooperation with insurance undertakings, provided that they are required to apply similar rules on consumer protection.

The analysis of the Polish market shows that insurance brokers' cooperation is usually based on the legal figure of the consortium or cooperation agreements (also those concluded *ad hoc*).

2 Consortium of Insurance Brokers

The contract of the consortium is not directly regulated by provisions of Polish law. Only a few acts mention consortiums as a means of possible business cooperation. The term "consortium" does not define a legal entity but a group of independent entities - parties to the consortium agreement, which forms an obligatory relationship, not an organizational one. Therefore, the consortium has no legal personality, is not a separate business entity conducting independent business, and cannot be the subject of rights and obligations (judgment of the Provincial Administrative Court in Opole of October 27, 2011, II SA/Op 296/2011). For example, art. 73 of the 1997 Banking Law states that to grant a loan jointly, banks may agree to establish a banking consortium. The conditions for granting the loan and its security and designate the bank authorized to conclude the loan agreement must be established in the agreement. Banks bear the risk related to the loan granted in proportion to the financial resources contributed to the jointly granted loan. The Supreme Court acknowledged that the purpose of a bank loan agreement is to place funds at the borrower's disposal, and by doing so, the bank, in exchange for the interest and commission profit specified in the agreement, also agrees to bear a specific risk. The same assumption lies in the purpose of the banking consortium agreement, in which the participating banks aim to share (and consequently reduce) the economic risk associated with the loan agreement. The claim that one of the consortium members sought to guarantee the other not to bear credit risk must be perceived as contrary to the essence and, therefore, the nature (nature) of the consortium agreement (judgment of the Supreme Court of December 15, 2005, V CK 425/05). Similar solutions can be found in the 2004 Act on Healthcare Care Services, financed from public funds. Article 132a gives the possibility of setting up a consortium of healthcare providers. Healthcare providers may jointly apply for the conclusion and performance of a contract to provide health care services, the subject of which is the provision of health care services. In such cases, healthcare providers appoint a representative to represent them in the proceedings for the provision of healthcare services and the conclusion of an agreement. Healthcare providers are jointly and severally liable for the performance of the contract to provide healthcare services. **The above examples were not given without a particular purpose, as they reflect Polish jurisprudence on consortium agreements**. In the judgment of March 6, 2015 (III CZP 113/14) as well as of July 6, 2018 (II CSK 562/17), the Supreme Court explained that "joint venture" agreements cover various forms of economic cooperation. The consortium belongs to those organizations of entrepreneurs, shaped in the practice of trade, which are established to achieve a common economic goal, but do not constitute separate legal entities and do not have legal personality, the basis for their establishment is a joint operation agreement (so-called consortium), when concluding it, the parties, to a wide extent, taking into account individual needs and the nature of the project, exercise contractual freedom and are not bound by the requirement to maintain a uniform organizational and legal form (article 3531 of the Civil Code). Hence, consortiums generally have a temporary existence because they are established to implement one or several tasks based on the principle of common benefits and risks. One of the divisions of these organizations, developed in the doctrine but useful in practice, distinguishes external consortiums, including those that are open to third parties (basically, everyone acts in a common name and under common responsibility, but it is possible to grant a power of attorney to one of the members, and the leading participant of the consortium may act as a leader) or secret (members are connected only by an internal bond, one entity acts externally on its own behalf and as an indirect deputy), or internal, whose function is limited to coordinating the activities of individual participants acting independently. In this decision, the Supreme Court emphasized that the diversity of factual and legal situations prevents a uniform legal classification of the consortium. In other judgments (judgments of November 20, 2014, V CSK 177/14 or of July 9, 2015, I CSK 353/14), the Supreme Court emphasized that the cooperation of contractors seeking to be awarded a public contract and jointly, this order is usually not strict enough to take the form of a civil partnership, Recognizing a specific consortium agreement as a civil partnership agreement is only possible if all the structural features of a civil partnership agreement can be seen in it. Consequently, the appropriate application of the provisions on a civil partnership to a specific consortium agreement requires taking into account the essence of the legal relationship under this agreement and possible differences between the essential elements of this relationship and the elements of the code-type civil partnership agreement. Accordingly, also other courts consider a consortium as an unnamed agreement that creates an obligatory relationship in which each of its members (consortium members) undertakes to participate in a specific manner in the consortium and to act in a specific manner for it, and thus for the benefit of the other consortium members, to achieve the purpose for which the agreement was concluded (judgment of Court of Appeal in Warsaw od July 18, 2019, V ACa 535/18 or of June 7, 2018, V ACa 1439/17).

The consortium agreement was not regulated in the Civil Code or comprehensively included in any other normative act. Still, it was shaped by practice as a response to the demand of economic transactions for the existence of an agreement with specific properties. The basis for establishing a consortium is an agreement on joint action of independently and autonomously acting partners. When concluding it, the parties, to a wide extent, taking into account individual needs and the nature of the project, enjoy contractual freedom and are not bound by the requirement to maintain a uniform organizational and legal form. Neither the doctrine nor the jurisprudence has developed a uniform legal description of the consortium agreement, nor has there been a precise assessment of the effects of its conclusion. It is assumed that a consortium is a contractual legal relationship aimed at cooperation to implement a specific economic project, and its structure is most similar to a civil partnership agreement. As a rule, the cooperation is temporary, the nature of the representation is different, and there is no extensive bond organizational structure or joint property. Since there are neither specific rules nor legal patterns designed specifically for insurance brokers' consortium agreements, it is clear that all remarks on the general concept of consortium agreement under Polish law also apply to two business cooperation models of Polish insurance brokers.

As a result of analyzing consortium agreements concluded by insurance brokers on the Polish market, we can point out the following features of insurance brokers consortium agreements:

- **determining the form of concluding a consortium agreement remains at the discretion of the parties concluding it (judgment of the Supreme Court of October 10, 2015, II CSK 630/14)** - the written form is preferable, primarily if the consortium is based on civil partnership as art. 860 § 2 of the Civil Code states that civil partnership agreement should be confirmed in writing. Although this is a written requirement for evidentiary purposes (*ad probationem form*), it is nevertheless associated with evidentiary limitations resulting from, among others, 74 § 1 of the Civil Code, according to which the reservation of the written, documentary or electronic form without the pain of invalidity has the effect that if the reserved form is not observed, evidence from the testimony of witnesses or from the hearing of the parties as to the fact that the action was performed is not admissible in the dispute (judgment of the Supreme Court of November 25, 1998, II CKN 55/98);

- **consortiums of insurance brokers are generally temporary, as they are established to perform one or several tasks based on the principle of joint benefits and risks** – it is, however, also possible to give examples of "long-lasting" consortiums aimed at constant and joint cooperation, which allows reducing costs of everyday operations, e.g.;
- **The aim of the consortium is typically described as an obligation to jointly provide professional brokerage services to clients acquired by the partners in the field of life and/or non-life insurance** – yet the purpose of the consortium may be established *ab initio*, mainly when partners conclude consortium agreement to obtain and receive a public order for insurance services for a public finance sector entity. Contractors may apply for the award of a public contract independently or in accordance with art. 58 section 1 of the 2019 Public Procurement Law – jointly. It must be however noted that the Polish Supreme Court has numerously expressed its view on this form of cooperation - there are no grounds for automatically qualifying all cooperation agreements (or similarly named agreements), including those concluded in proceedings aimed at awarding and performing a public procurement contract, as civil partnership agreements. Recognizing a specific consortium agreement as a civil partnership agreement is possible when all the structural features of a civil partnership agreement can be seen in it (decision of the Supreme Court of June 6, 2015, III CZP 113/14 or judgment of the Supreme Court of April 3, 2018, II CSK 452/17). Consequently, the Polish market has two major types of insurance brokers' consortium agreements. In the first type, a consortium is established to pursue general cooperation, which is aimed at expanding the portfolio of clients and ensuring proper management of concluded insurance contracts. In the second type, the purpose of the consortium is to conclude a contract on cooperation with a particular client and to set the contractual framework for performing services for that client;
- **all consortium partners, in principle, act in a common name and under joint responsibility; however, it is possible to grant a power of attorney to one of the partners, or a given consortium partner may act as the consortium leader (responsible for contacts with clients, insurers, etc. and thus representing the consortium outside)** - there are also contracts in which the leader's role is not fixed and depends on the type of insurance contract that is to be concluded for the client. This situation occurs in particular when the consortium is formed by brokers specializing in concluding various insurance contracts (e.g. when one of the partners specializes in life insurance and the other in non-life insurance – in such cases an additional purpose of the consortium agreement is to obtain support in areas usually not covered by the practice of a particular broker), for example: broker "A" specializes in non-life insurance, however its client is interested in concluding life insurance contracts for the benefit of its employees. In order not to lose such client, broker "A" concludes a consortium agreement with broker "B", that has experience and expertise in the scope of life insurance

contracts. As a result cooperation between those two brokers may focus not on obtaining new clients but on sustaining current operations of one broker with the support of another. The consortium leader is primarily responsible for the coordination of tasks between partners; coordination (on behalf of the consortium) contacts with insurers regarding brokerage commission (provision) agreements and brokerage settlements, as well as concluding such agreements and finally concluding agreements with clients. Even though in most cases such cooperation scheme is considered (and named in contracts) as consortium it resembles a mediation chain between brokers where commission is split as an incentive for cooperation.

- **the scope of obligations of a particular partner differs depending on the cooperation model – mainly, consortium agreements specify parties' obligations**. It may include obligations to jointly develop insurance offers for clients, to inform each other about activities undertaken for or in the name of the consortium and to observe the principles of loyalty to each other. If partners undertake e.g. to acquire clients and perform further insurance brokerage services for such clients, they typically agree that if any of them acquires a client, then partner "A" will be responsible for performing tasks in the field of life insurance and partner "B" will be responsible to for performing tasks in the field of non-life insurance (or any other type of insurance). Additionally, partners undertake to perform neither actual nor legal actions, resulting in a complete takeover of a particular client by only one partner. What is interesting, though, is that some consortium agreements include a clause under which if the acquired client is interested only in the services of only one of the partners, this Partner may perform insurance brokerage services to such client independently, which will not constitute a violation of the provisions of this agreement.
- **Contract termination clauses may include specific provisions on former partners providing professional insurance broker services to the consortium's clients - solutions in this scope may consist of a clear division of clients between former partners or the possibility of one partner taking over the whole portfolio (or a part of it)**.

3 Cooperation Contracts

Regarding cooperation contracts other than a consortium, their nature and scope vary depending on the extent of agreed cooperation. First, to said contracts, provisions on mandate shall apply respectively (art. 750 of the Civil Code). The provisions relating to contracts for the provision of services to which the provisions on mandate apply accordingly - broadly speaking - indicate that the subject of these contracts is the performance or execution of activities for another person (persons) and in his (their) interest, which consists in an obligation to act diligently - which is associated with the lack of agreement on the obligation to achieve a precisely defined, future, spontaneous material or materially embodied result, considered as a criterion for the proper fulfilment of the main performance by the service provider (hence, it is an agreement of diligent action, not a result) - and also on the personal performance of the service by the contractor (service recipient; contractor), and - as a rule - the contract is based on special trust in the service provider (judgment of the Supreme Administrative Court of August 17, 2023, II GSK 852/20). Additionally, as cooperation contracts often contain elements of intermediation in acquiring clients, the provisions on the agency contract also apply here. Second, it is possible to point out fundamental reasons for the conclusion of ad hoc cooperation agreements, which preferably are:

- **the necessity to obtain professional assistance in providing brokerage services to certain clients** (due to lack of experience, lack of infrastructure and lack of human resources of one of the cooperating parties);
- **the possibility of obtaining a new channel of distribution of insurance brokerage services by the parties to the contract**;

However, it must be noted that at least to some extent, *ad hoc* corporation agreements are also used on the Polish market as a "substitute" of employment contracts, especially in situations where one party is a natural person (and an insurance broker entered into the registry of insurance intermediators kept by Polish Financial Supervision Commission) and the other one is a company. Even though it encompasses the above-mentioned aims, insurance brokers often choose this specific type of contract to optimize tax and social security burdens. Nevertheless, the provision of said services between insurance brokers may be the subject of mandate contracts and employment contracts. This does not mean the employer is free to choose the employment basis. Such a choice is not arbitrary, as it cannot ignore the systemic and generic differences between the mandate and employment contracts. An employment contract and a mandate contract differ significantly. We cannot limit ourselves to the interpretation that a mandate contract may contain features of management and subordination, although not the same as those inherent in the employment relationship (Article 22 § 1 and § 11 of the Labor Code and Art. 750 of the Civil Code). Of decisive importance in the process of distinguishing the nature of the legal relationship between the parties (the employing entity and the employed entity) is the manner of performing the contract, and in particular, the implementation by the contractors - even contrary to the contractual provisions - of the features that characterize an employment contract. This also reflects the fundamental difference between an employment relationship and a mandate contract. It results directly from the Labor Code and art. 750 of the Civil Code. The employment relationship is part of a broader concept of employment, but the subordination of the employee to the employer's management and the performance of work in the place and at the time designated by the employer (agreed with the employer) is the distinguishing feature of employee employment (employment relationship) - art. 22 of the Labour Code. The subject of the mandate contract is a service that is not regulated by other provisions (art. 750 of the Civil Code). Employment in conditions of subordination to the employer's management is based on an employment relationship, regardless of the name of the contract concluded by the parties (judgment of the Supreme Court of October 4, 2022, I PSKP 71/21). Consequently, in such contracts, one party may be regarded as de facto a subcontractor, primarily when the scope of the contract encompasses not only intermediation but also providing brokerage services to the other party's clients (which is of great importance in terms of liability towards such clients). Third, cooperation contracts may be concluded *ad hoc* (for a pre-defined period) to manage a single project or for longer periods. Additionally, such brokerage chains can be organized not only between brokers at the same level as in a consortium, but also in a hierarchical relationship in the sense of a "wholesaler with many retailers". There is no doubt that the entrepreneurial independence of the "retailer" brokers is untouched. They mainly work at the point of advice or sale, but use the access to insurance products and other shared services via the "wholesaler" (which resembles as a broker pool scheme).

4 Remuneration, Compliance with IDD/IDA Requirements and Liability

The issues of consortium partner's remuneration, meeting IDD standards, as well as liability towards clients require special attention as we can point out at least a few different solutions, depending on the type of contract bidding insurance brokers.

In consortium and cooperation contracts, the remuneration of parties is predominantly based on the division of brokerage commission (provision) received from insurers. Such remuneration may be paid to one of the parties (e.g. consortium leader) and redistributed to other parties. In cooperation contracts, it is, in fact, a common rule that one of the contracting parties is granted payment in the form of a fixed percentage of brokerage commission (provision) collected by the other one. In consortium contracts, the mentioned commission is often calculated in the following manner. Each consortium member is entitled to, e.g. ½, the remuneration paid by insurers. The remuneration is paid directly to each member based on invoices issued by each member covering the part of the remuneration due to that member. Such clause may be expanded with stipulation, aimed at preventing possible obstacles in commission collection e.g. that in the event when an insurer is unable to pay the brokerage commission directly to one of the consortium members, other member (members) shall have as the right and shall be entitled to collect the commission of behalf of the first one. It is worth adding that due to the lack of statutory (as described above) or contractual regulations (between the consortium members and between them and the insurer), the consortium leader cannot demand the agreed total remuneration for the brokerage services from the insurer (judgment of the Court of Appeal in Warsaw of 18 February 2009, VI ACa 1152/2008, generally regarding consortium contracts). Finally, if a dispute arises between the insurance brokers consortium and an insurer, the consortium does not have legal personality and, therefore, does not have judicial capacity. In a procedural sense, a party is all entities that are part of the consortium (Supreme Court decision of 27 March 2010, III CZP 25/10).

Moving on to IDD and IDA requirements. It was rightly recognized in Polish insurance law doctrine that "a necessary condition for recognizing that a given broker performs activities for a specific client is that the client grants him an order (which may include a power of attorney to perform legal acts on behalf of the client). If the client uses more than one broker when seeking insurance coverage in a given area, he should precisely and separately divide the scope of the order and power of attorney between the brokers. This does not apply to cases where the brokers involved in servicing a given client have concluded an agreement defining the principles of their cooperation (insurance brokers consortium). In such a case, both a joint order or authorization granted to all brokers participating in the consortium to perform all distribution activities, as well as the division of activities by the client between the consortium members, are permissible" (Orlicki, 2019). Hence, to fulfil IDD and IDA requirements, it is necessary to establish clear rules on the performance of distribution obligations towards clients. Solutions in this scope may vary depending on the nature of cooperation. In consortium contracts, either all or some members may be liable for the performance of said obligations. In cooperation contracts, usually, one party performs all of the mentioned obligations, with certain participation of the other. Regardless of the model chosen in a given contract, the overriding goal should be to act in the best interests of the client, as well as to ensure that the client is provided with the information required by IDD and IDA regulations, in particular:

- to inform the client about the details of conducting insurance brokerage activities (such as the address of the registered office, the number of the entry in the register of brokers, the address of the website on which the register is available, and how to check the entry in the register);
- to execute demands-and-needs test and – as a result of such – to pass objective information to the client about the insurance product in a comprehensible form (in order to allow that client to make an informed decision), with a particular emphasis on assessment of suitability and appropriateness as regards insurance-based investment products;
- to ensure that all necessary steps were made in order to act transparently and to eliminate the risk of possible conflict of interests;
- to ensure the confidentiality of information obtained concerning the performance of insurance brokerage activities.

Finally, the issue of liability. In consortium contracts, which are based on civil partnership, art. 864 of the Civil Code shall apply. According to said provision, partners are jointly and severally liable for the company's obligations. This provision is absolutely binding (peremptory norm). It specifies the liability of partners for the obligations of a civil partnership (or consortium), i.e. the obligations of partners that are not their obligations but result from the activities of the civil partnership. This liability is joint and several, which means that the creditor may demand all or part of the performance from all partners jointly, from several of them or from each of them individually, and the satisfaction of the creditor by any of the partners releases the others - art. 366 § 1 of the Civil Code (Judgment of the Supreme Administrative Court of 11 January 2022, II GSK 2461/21). To determine the circle of entities liable for the obligations of a civil partnership (consortium) - in a situation where the source of the obligation is a contract - it is essential to determine whether a given entity was a partner of the company at the time the obligation arose, or whether it joined the company after the obligation arose (judgment of the Court of Appeal in Białystok of 21 November 2019, I AGa 81/19). The problem occurs when the features of a consortium agreement differ from those of a civil partnership, i.e., when the partners do not include a stipulation on their joint and several liabilities in the contract. It is because of a rule embedded in art. 369 of Civil Code that an obligation is joint and several if it results from a statute or a legal act (e.g. contract). In the scope of establishing the rules of liability of consortium members for the incurred obligation, the appropriate application of the provisions on civil partnership cannot exclude the principle of inadmissibility of the presumption of joint and several liabilities of debtors, because its existence or lack is determined by the act or the will of the parties expressed in the contract, and not the characteristics of the obligation. An independent regulation in this scope is included only in the public procurement law – art. 445 par. 1 of Public Procurement Act states that the contractors referred to in article 58 par. 1 (consortium members) shall be jointly and severally liable for the execution of the contract and for providing security for the proper performance of the contract. Hence the consortium members are not jointly and severally liable towards the ordering party under article 864 of the Civil Code, but under Article 445 of the Public Procurement Act, and this is joint and several liability only towards the ordering party, while the liability under Article 864 of the Civil Code is broader (judgment of the Court of Appeal in Kraków of December 16, 2022, I AGa 22/21). To speak of joint and several liability in the case in question, first of all, a rule on the possibility of assuming obligations with effect for the others should be derived from a contract or a statute and then on the possibility of their representation. Since there is no presumption of joint and several liability, such a rule could not by itself determine the joint and several liability of the consortium members, but only direct representation at most. Such situation occurs e.g. when the person accepting the order performs the act on behalf of the principal, i.e. the relevant rights or obligations are acquired directly by the principal (the person accepting the order acts as an attorney, but granting a power of attorney is not necessary, because in accordance with article 734 § 2 of the Civil Code, in the absence of a relevant agreement, the order includes authorization to perform a legal act on behalf of the principal). Finally, in cooperation contracts, the issue of liability towards clients may be based on the following patterns:

- joint and several liability (if stipulated in the contract);
- direct representation (as art. 734 § 2 of the Civil Code applies to such contracts by virtue of already mentioned art. 750);
- according to article 474 of the Civil Code - the debtor is liable, as for his act or omission, for the acts and omissions of persons with whose assistance he

performs the obligation, as well as persons to whom he entrusts the performance of the obligation (it also applies if the legal representative of the debtor conducts the obligation). It must be noted that the provision of article 474 of the Civil Code does not constitute an independent basis for the debtor's liability and does not prevent the debtor from being released from liability for the actions of persons with the assistance of whom he performs the obligation by demonstrating circumstances that release him from liability towards the creditor (decision of the Supreme Court of 23 April 2021, IV CSK 609/20).

In the last of the indicated options, the debtor is liable for assistants and executors regardless of whether these persons knew that they were acting in the interests of someone other than the debtor and whether they were acting for a fee or free of charge. The legal relationship that the person providing services to the creditor had with the debtor is also irrelevant, mainly whether there was an element of subordination. The debtor is also liable for the actions or omissions of a legal representative whose authorization to perform the obligation may result from an authorized body's act or decision (judgment of the Court of Appeal in Łódź of October 2, 2020, I ACa 140/20).

5 Disputes Settlement

Obviously, with every form of cooperation comes the risk of a dispute between partners. Regarding the Polish insurance brokers market, such disputes typically concern the division or the right to brokerage commission (provision). Neither IDA nor any other act of Polish law considers the issue of brokerage remuneration. Hence, finding the legal basis of a particular claim is necessary to settle such a dispute. As mentioned at the beginning of this paper, legal doctrine and jurisprudence were tasked to establish how such disputes should be handled due to the need for more relevant legislation. This brings us to the fundamental question: when and under what circumstances and conditions does an insurance broker gain the right to its commission (provision)? As B. Kucharski aptly points out, "Polish scholarship, following the example of German law, has formulated the following four conditions for the acquisition of a broker's claim for brokerage (accepted by case law): 1) the broker's intermediary activity in concluding an insurance contract must result from an order given by the insured; 2) the insurance contract must be effectively concluded; 3) there must be a causal relationship between the broker's activity and the conclusion of the insurance contract; and 4) the premium must be paid by the insured in whole or in part" (Kucharski, 2021) and judgment of the Court of Appeal in Warsaw of 3 June 2016, I ACa 1188/15). However, previous remarks consider only commission. Yet it must be noted that in countries like Germany or UK brokers are increasingly being financed through fees that the client has to pay directly. Same scenarios may appear in Poland. In most contracts with clients brokers reserve the right to charge additional fees for e.g. hiring consultants or experts to solve a particular issue regarding insurance. In such case the right to charge a client with a fee by cooperating brokers should be determined by the cooperation contract.

The central axis of most disputes between cooperating insurance brokers is the right to brokerage (commission) when the cooperation is terminated. First of all, the parties to a consortium or cooperation agreement should provide a mechanism for settling brokerage (commission) in the event of termination of cooperation in the content of such agreements. Going further, due to the lack of detailed agreements, the customs accepted in practice in this area should be applied. Following market practice, brokerage commission - i.e. remuneration paid by the insurer, is due and paid to the insurance broker only for concluding or bringing about the conclusion of an insurance contract, regardless of any subsequent changes in the scope of servicing a given contract. Achieving such a specific goal depends not only on the diligence of the insurance broker but also on the actions taken by the potential insured, whose passive behavior may thwart the actions carried out by the broker. Nevertheless, Considering that the broker is responsible for exercising due diligence, the broker's contribution to concluding the insurance contract and its influence on its final shape is important. The broker whose efforts and greatest contribution led to the conclusion of the contract is rewarded, not necessarily the one who finalized its conclusion (judgment of the Court of Appeal in Warsaw of 3 June 2016, I ACa 1188/15). The participation of the intermediary in the activities that led to the conclusion of a given contract is therefore of fundamental importance, even if the contract is concluded through another intermediary or if another contract that pursues the same economic purpose is concluded instead of the contract to be concluded (Fenichel, 1931). **Hence, it is imperative to establish the actual role of each broker in the conclusion of a particular insurance contract**. E. Kowalewski points out in this scope that if the broker who made efforts to conclude the agreement was subsequently replaced by another broker who concluded the agreement, the brokerage is due to the first broker if the conclusion of the insurance agreement was made on the basis created by him. The signing itself is formal in nature, and the influence of the specific broker on the form of the concluded insurance agreement is decisive (Kowalewski & Serwach, 2008). However, this may prove problematic when each cooperating insurance broker is authorized to represent the client. If only one of the insurance brokers was authorized to represent the client in relation to the insurer (and the other was responsible for other activities and did not directly participate in the process of concluding the insurance contract), the creditor of the claim for brokerage will be the broker authorized to represent. In turn, the claim of the second broker for "participation" in the brokerage will be based on the provisions of the contract, or on article 471 of the Civil Code. In the doctrine of insurance law, it is accepted that more than one insurance broker may act simultaneously on behalf of the insured to conclude an insurance contract. A power of attorney may be granted to several persons with different or even the same scope of authorization. From the point of view of brokerage practice, the admissibility of appointing several proxies with the same scope of activity is of primary importance. In such a case, each of them may act independently on behalf of the principal, which results from art. 107 of the Civil Code, according to which, if the principal has appointed several proxies with the same scope of authorization, they may act independently unless the content of the power of attorney states otherwise. If such a situation occurs, we may point out two possible scenarios – either only one of the brokers shall be awarded the right to a brokerage (commission) or said commission should be split to all parties claiming the right to it. The doctrine does not exclude the possibility that several brokers may be entitled to commission-based remuneration, in which case legal solutions are sought in the principles of divisibility of benefits regulated in the Civil Code (Fras, 2009) – as it is stated in article 379 § 1 and 2 of the Civil Code:

- If there are several debtors or several creditors and the performance is divisible, both the debt and the creditors' receivable debt shall be divided into as many mutually independent parts as many debtors or creditors there are. Those parts shall be equal if nothing else follows from the circumstances.
- A performance shall be divisible if it can be made in parts without an essential change of its object or value.

Moreover, the already mentioned B. Kucharski postulates that Civil Code provisions on the agency contract may be applicable *per analogiam*, at least to the extent (Kucharski, 2021). The same Author concludes his remarks on disputes between insurance brokers that "The issue of the right to brokerage in the event of a change of broker should be resolved taking into account the contribution of a specific broker in shaping the concluded agreement and based on analogously applied provisions on agency, which in a certain way privilege the previous agent. The proposed principle does not exclude the division of brokerage in some situations, as well as the awarding of brokerage to a new broker, depending on the significance of the changes in relation to the agreement proposed by the first broker. The adoption of the above-mentioned principles reduces the attractiveness of attempts to take over the client in situations where the selection of a new broker would be of a non-meritorious nature, i.e. unjustified by the low quality of the services of the previous broker".

Against this background, the literature highlights the possible conflict of interest between the insurer and the broker. When negotiating an insurance contract, the broker should be guided primarily by the interests of the insured, not the insurer or his own, by striving to maximize the commission at the insured's expense (Pokrzywniak, 2005). In turn, the insurer is not entitled to interfere in the terms of service agreed between the broker and their client or in the client's choice of broker. Nevertheless, even taking into account the fact that the broker represents the client and acts as an intermediary between the person seeking insurance coverage and the insurer, leading to the conclusion of the insurance contract, they also provide a service for the insurer, for which they usually receive remuneration from the latter. This specific three-party relationship is exposed to the occurrence of a conflict of interest. The broker is obliged to act solely in the interests of their client, the client is obliged to behave loyally towards the broker, and the insurer is obliged to refrain from any interference in the relationship between the client and the broker. On the other hand, it has no influence on which broker representing a given client receives the brokerage paid by him, the above depends primarily on the broker's involvement in striving to conclude the contract and its final shape. In addition, a conflict of economic interests should be noted; the insured is usually interested in obtaining the most financially advantageous insurance option, and the broker should represent such an interest of the client; on the other hand, the amount of his brokerage is often a derivative of the amount of the premium; the higher the premium, the higher the brokerage, which also fulfils the insurer's interest. To sum up, the doctrine indicates that the described conflict of interests occurs because the interest of the insured (i.e. the person whose interests the broker should protect) is not identical to the interest of the insurer (the entity that *de facto* pays for concluding the insurance contract). Because insurance brokers cooperate with various insurers, they are responsible for securing the interests of policyholders, in particular, for selecting an offer that best meets their needs and demands. The above considerations lead to the conclusion that if the client employs more than one broker. Such authorization should not raise any doubts, and even if the client independently, regardless of the broker's involvement, negotiates the contract with the insurer, which is also possible because by granting a power of attorney, the principal does not give up any subjective rights, the broker's remuneration is mainly dependent on how he performs the service entrusted to him, in particular whether he performs it properly in the context of the aspects mentioned above of the tripartite relationship between the insured, the broker and the insurer. However, it should be mentioned that these statements only refer to the remuneration in the form of a commission but not to the fee case.

6 Evidence of Co-Opetition

Co-opetition within the insurance market is exemplified mainly by insurance companies. More evidence is needed on the scale and motivation of co-opetition among other entities, like insurance intermediaries. There is qualitative research on tied insurance agents (Krymarys, 2016) but nothing about insurance brokers, where potential competition is much stronger. The Fair Play survey is an infrequent occasion to examine insurance brokers' co-opetition. It takes place before the Annual Congress of Insurance Brokers in Poland. The survey, in the form of CAWI, aims to choose the best insurance companies based on brokers' opinions. However, other issues linked to insurance brokers' activity are also tackled within the questionnaire. Data from the surveys are available under the permission of the Association of Polish Insurance and Reinsurance Brokers (https://www.spbuir.pl).

An Insurance Broker Congress annually gathers 400–500 brokers, one of the most significant market events. Not all insurance brokers participate in the Congress, and not all participating brokers fill out the questionnaire, so the survey's outcome cannot be considered representative. Moreover, brokers taking part in the annual Congress are, on average, more interested in networking and able to cover costs. Nevertheless, the Fair Play survey has an exploratory potential.

6.1 Quantitative Analysis

In the Fair Play surveys of 2023 and 2024, questions concerning collaboration among insurance brokers appeared. However, some brokers (N=254) took part in both surveys, and the difference between 2023 and 2024 for this group is statistically significant (Wilcoxon test, Z=2.653, p=0.008). It was the reason why the authors did not merge the answers of surveys 2003 and 2004, and excluded all answers from 2023. Table 7.1 presents the leading indicators of respondents (N=398).

There is no publicly available data on the characteristics of insurance brokers in Poland. The age and experience structure shows that most respondents are 34–54. At the same time, professional experience is spread more evenly across periods. This means that new brokers also enter the job in later years. The cross-analysis identified two big groups, the first of those aged 35–44 and experienced 11–15 (N=60), and those aged 45–54 and experienced 21–25 (N=48). Most brokers work within broker companies as employees (76.9%). Some brokers cooperate constantly with broker companies (7.8%), and finally, some solo brokers do not work with broker companies or cooperate constantly (11.6%).

Collaboration among insurance brokers is characteristic as it happens within extreme competition, for example, a situation when more than one broker represents a client. Hence, the use of the co-opetition concept is fully justified. Nevertheless, the scale of collaboration is very significant. More than 70% of brokers

Table 7.1 Characteristics of Fair Play survey 2024

	2024	
	N	**%**
gender		
female	178	44.7%
male	212	53.3%
no data	8	2.0%
	age in years	
25–34 [recoded as 1]	48	12.1%
35–44 [recoded as 1]	126	31.7%
45–54 [recoded as 2]	145	36.4%
55–64 [recoded as 2]	58	14.6%
65+ [recoded as 2]	21	5.3%
	professional experience as an insurance broker in years	
-5 [recoded as 1]	59	14.8%
6–10 [recoded as 1]	62	15.6%
11–15 [recoded as 1]	95	23.9%
16–20 [recoded as 2]	56	14.1%
21–25 [recoded as 2]	62	15.6%
26–30 [recoded as 2]	45	11.3%
31+ [recoded as 2]	6	1.5%

Source: own calculations based on Fair Play survey 2024

(respondents) cooperate with other brokers somehow (Table 7.2). In the latter analysis, the answers were recoded into two (binary) options: no collaboration – 0 and collaboration – 1.

Initial analysis identified a group of significant predictors of collaboration among respondents: business model (level of specialization, Table 7.3), the value of professional third-party liability insurance (Table 7.4), and experience. All answers were presented and recoded as cardinal values. Professional experience was recoded into three clusters (0–10 years, 11–20 years, and 21+).

According to the Chi-square test, five variables (Tables 7.1, 7.2, 7.3, 7.4, and 7.5) were significant in the analysis (Table 7.6) and were chosen for further consideration: experience {1,2}, the value of professional liability insurance {1,2},

Table 7.2 The scale of co-opetition

	2024	
	N	%
Yes, often [recoded as 1]	87	21,9%
Yes, occasionally [recoded as 1]	201	50,5%
No [recoded as 0]	110	27,6%

Source: own calculations based on Fair Play survey 2024

Table 7.3 Level of specialization

In which direction would you like to develop your brokerage business?	**2024**	
	N	%
Narrow specialization [recoded as 3]	61	15.3%
Maximum versatility [recoded as 1]	60	15.1%
Intermediate model with outlined specializations [recoded as 2]	241	60.6%
I don't know/I haven't thought about it [recoded as 1]	36	9.0%

Source: own calculations based on Fair Play survey 2024

Table 7.4 Professional liability insurance

Liability insurance for brokerage activities is mandatory and has a minimum amount of warranty. We want to ask you about the guarantee amount. Please choose one answer from the following:	**2024**	
	N	%
I have the minimum guarantee sum. and I have not thought about changing it [recoded as 1]	60	15.1%
I have the minimum guarantee amount. but I was thinking about increasing it [recoded as 1]	59	14.8%
I have an increased guarantee sum. and I have not thought about changing it [recoded as 2]	124	31.2%
I have an increased guarantee sum. but I was thinking about increasing it [recoded as 2]	74	18.6%
I don't know [recoded as 1]	81	20.4%

Source: own calculations based on Fair Play survey 2024

institutional independence {1,2,3}, age {1,2}and the preferred level of specialization {1,2,3}. There are several methods for identifying variables that could predict willingness to collaborate among respondents, such as classification and binary logistic regression. The authors opted for binary logistic regression using recoded variables (as already presented in the above tables). The analysis aims to model the relationships between variables within the available sample (not generalize the results to the entire population of Polish brokers), and logistic regression can effectively identify these relationships and estimate the strength of their influence.

A binary logistic regression was carried out to assess the effect of experience, the value of professional liability, institutional independence, age and the preferred level of specialization on the likelihood of a broker's cooperation with other insurance brokers. The overall model (Table 7.7) used 93.5% of cases and was statistically significant when compared to the null model, (X^2 (7) = 70.575, $p < 0.01$), explained 24.7% of the variation of cooperation (Nagelkerke R^2) and correctly predicted 74.2%, and the Hosmer and Lemeshow Test (X^2 (8) = 0.191) shows that the data fit the model well. Experience ($p = 0.027$), the value of professional liability ($p < 0.001$), and institutional independence ($p = 0.024$) were significant but the age ($p = 0.493$) and the preferred level of specialization ($p = 0.110$) were not. The model provides insight into the importance of particular variables for brokers' cooperation:

- more experienced brokers are 1.967 times the odds of cooperating with other brokers (95% CI 1.080; 3.580);

Table 7.5 The level of independence

		N	%
I am a broker working for a brokerage firm.		306	76.9%
I am an independent broker, but I work with brokerage firms.		31	7.8%
I am an independent broker.		46	11.6%
Missing	System	15	3.8%

Source: own calculations based on Fair Play survey 2024

Table 7.6 List of significant predictors: Chi-square test

			Independent variable	**Asymptotic Significance (2-sided)**	**df**	**Value**
Significant	Yes	1	value of professional liability insurance	.000	1	25.949
		2	institutional independence	.000	2	25.540
		3	experience	.001	1	10.547
		4	age	.025	1	5.014
		5	preferred level of specialization	.038	2	6.523

Source: own calculations based on Fair Play survey 2024

- brokers with higher than the minimal value of professional liability insurance are 3.100 times the odds of cooperating with other brokers (95% CI 1.832; 5.248);
- independent brokers are 0.347 times the odds of cooperating with other brokers compared to brokers employed within brokerage firms (95% CI 0.163; 0.741).
- independent brokers working with brokerage firms are 14.980 times the odds of cooperating with other brokers compared to brokers employed within brokerage firms (95% CI 1.993; 112.573);

Comparison of independent brokers working with brokerage firms with other occupations is problematic as all independent brokers working with brokerage firms cooperate with other brokers. Experience, together with higher than the minimal value of professional liability insurance, increases the chances of brokers' cooperation. There are significant differences in the brokerage model. The least likely to cooperate are solo brokers without fixed cooperation with brokerage firms.

6.2 *Qualitative Analysis*

The qualitative research followed the quantitative and was based on open questions about the reasoning for collaboration and the causes for its lack. Depending on a

Table 7.7 Variables in the equation

		B	S.E.	Wald	df	Sig.	Exp(B)	95% C.I.for EXP(B)	
								Lower	Upper
Step 1[a]	experience(1–2)(1)	.208	.304	.471	1	.493	1.232	.679	2.234
	professional_ liability(1–2)(1)	1.131	.269	17.757	1	<.001	3.100	1.832	5.248
	independence(1–3)			7.485	2	.024			
	independence(1–3) (1)	20.285	7283.296	.000	1	.998	645191109.128	.000	.
	independence(1–3) (2)	-1.057	.386	7.485	1	.006	.347	.163	.741
	specialization(1–3)			4.413	2	.110			
	specialization(1–3) (1)	-.186	.313	.353	1	.552	.830	.450	1.533
	specialization(1–3) (2)	-.778	.387	4.043	1	.044	.459	.215	.980
	age(1–2)(1)	.676	.306	4.894	1	.027	1.967	1.080	3.580
	Constant	.319	.312	1.048	1	.306	1.376		

[a] Variable(s) entered on step 1: experience(1–2), professional_liability(1–2), independence(1–3), specialization(1–3), age(1–2).
Source: own calculations based on Fair Play survey 2024

declaration of collaboration respondents could provide reasoning, as to why they cooperate or why they do not cooperate (N=264). The answers were coded according to content analysis to clarify the outcome. Coding categories were derived directly and inductively from the raw data, using a constant comparative method (Glaser & Strauss, 1967). As there is no previous research co-opetition in Poland this analysis is mostly explorative. The quantitative part provides a potential characteristic of cooperating brokers but is not clear enough to pose any hypothesis concerning the reasoning of cooperation.

Answers concerning reasons for cooperation are much more extended and diversified, compared to lack of cooperation. Not all respondents answered open questions. There is a great variety of expressed opinions, from single words to full descriptions of motives. One category, 'client', is subcodded to achieve higher accuracy. The authors use the word clouding (frequency of overall occurrence) and co-occurrence model. In case of lack of collaboration, authors use a tree of codes.

The overall picture presents the word cloud for the codes (Fig. 7.1). The most frequent codes are the client (oriented approach), synergy effect, specialization, but also knowledge and experience.

The code co-occurrence model allows for identifying a network structure of codes. Below is the map of codes using code occurrence mode, which counts how many documents contain simultaneously two codes, regardless of the position in the document.

The code map below shows code occurrence in brackets and links to other codes, straight lines, and the width of lines depends on frequency. Figure 7.2 shows two

Fig. 7.1 The word cloud of reasoning collaboration [2024]. Source: Own calculations based on Fair Play survey 2024

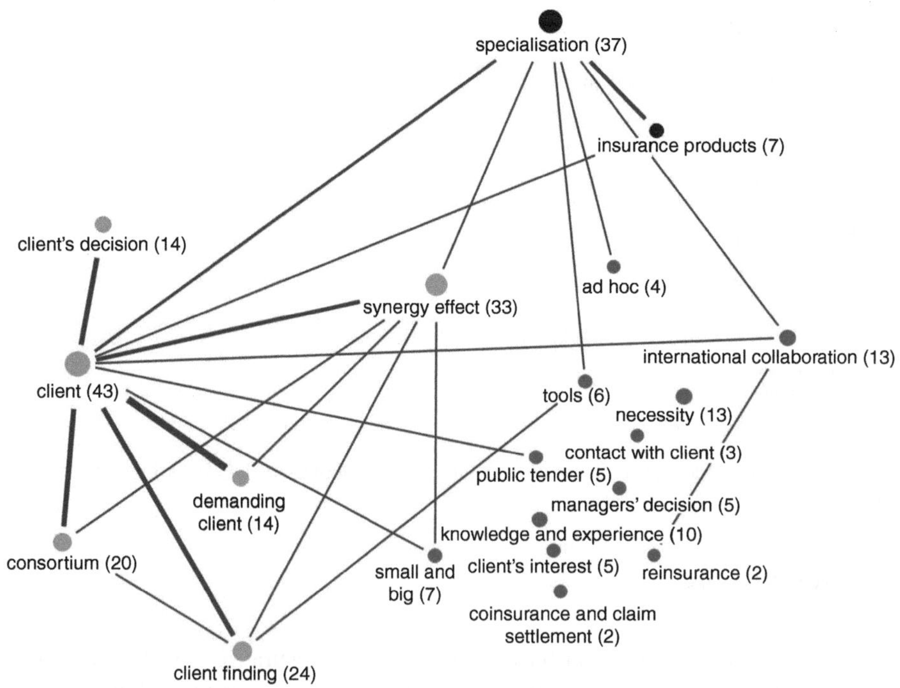

Fig. 7.2 The code co-occurrence model. Source: Own calculations based on Fair Play survey 2024

patterns in reasoning collaboration with other brokers. The first is linked generally to a client (oriented approach) in different contexts, such as the synergy effect, creating a consortium, finding a client (thanks to a broader offer), seeing the need for a unique solution due to clients' complexity or clearing clients' demand for collaboration with other brokers. The second leading pattern is linked to the synergy effect thanks to specialization. It allows the sharing of knowledge and experience and gives access to particular insurance products. The rest of the codes are diverse reasons, like a necessity, international collaboration linked to reinsurance, ad hoc, client's interest, managers' decision, tools, and public tender conditions. Interesting is a pattern *client-synergy effect-small and big*, that suggests the existence of such models of co-opetition in Poland.

According to responses from insurance brokers, a lack of collaboration could stem from a perceived "no need" (Fig. 7.3). Many brokers noted that such cooperation is beyond their decision-making authority. Interestingly, the third response identifies a lack of willingness. Only 5% referred to competition. While a lack of trust or (legal) security was also mentioned, it is not considered the main issue. Overall, the results suggest that the primary reasoning is associated with a specific business model and aligns with the findings from the quantitative analysis.

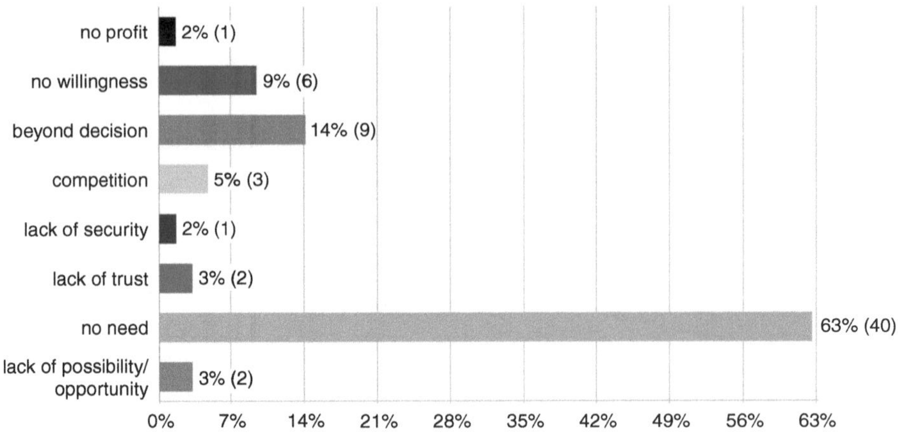

Fig. 7.3 Tree of codes: no collaboration. Source: own calculations based on Fair Play survey 2024

7 Conclusions

Co-opetition is a pretty popular business model in the insurance industry. European law primarily deals with co-opetition among insurance companies; however, the Insurance Block Exemption Regulation expired on 31 March 2017. This regulation allowed relatively broad collaboration, typically considered an anti-competition practice: joint creation and distribution of compilations, tables, and studies within research and development agreements. However, insurance companies still cooperate with coinsurance or insurance fraud detection co-opetition of intermediaries has much smaller recognition.

Although it is not regulated in Polish law, the consortium of insurance brokers seems to be a popular form of collaboration and has a specific legal understanding of local jurisprudence. Consortia are generally temporary, based on the principle of joint benefits and risks from providing professional brokerage services. Generally, partners act under a common name and are under joint responsibility but specify parties' obligations simultaneously.

Cooperation contracts are agreements of diligent action, not results, based on trust in the service provider. They have general roots in the Civic Code. There are various approaches; however, most are temporal due to needing professional assistance or within the public tender. Regardless of the legal form, remuneration and liability are important issues. That is why dispute settlement is significant in both cases.

The empirical analysis of brokers' co-opetition in Poland, based on surveys taken before the annual Congress of Insurance Brokers, is not representative. Hence, the outcome cannot be generalized. Nevertheless, it proves the existence of co-opetition and provides examples of reasoning for and against collaboration among respondents. Quantitative analysis showed that cooperation depends on the level of mandatory professional liability insurance; the higher the level, the stronger the collaboration for the respondents. Collaboration takes place not only within insurance broker companies that requires specialization within a team available only with high turnover. It happens also between individual brokers and insurance broker companies for various reasons, revealed in the qualitative part.

The qualitative part shows the reasoning behind both collaboration and lack of collaboration. Motives for collaboration are much more diversified. The narration focuses on the client (a client-oriented approach). Frequently, the need for cooperation is the client's decision or the outcome of risks' complexity. Collaboration assures synergy effects due to specialization and knowledge /experience sharing. An interesting and frequent motive is international cooperation. Surprisingly, within the respondents' answers, lack of collaboration results from "no need" rather than lack of trust. "No need" can be identified with small risks or an insurance broker company with broad specialization.

Although the samples are not representative, they give an interesting insight into the co-opetition of insurance brokers. The statistically significant difference between the surveys of 2023 and 2024 of the same respondents regarding cooperation suggests this phenomenon changes dynamically, and data comparison should be conducted very carefully. The further research could focus on the required legal framework to make co-opetition more effective. The empirical analysis could show scale but also prove motives and issues linked to co-opetition.

The legal framework for insurance broker cooperation is obsolete, and competition is solid; nevertheless, co-opetition is quite alive, at least for the respondents. The research suggests that cooperation is a natural state in a market where players mostly focus on an intermediate business model with outlined specializations but no deep specialization.

References

Bengtsson, M., & Kock, S. (1999). Cooperation and competition in relationships between competitors in business networks. *Journal of Business & Industrial Marketing*, *14*(3), 178–194. https://doi.org/10.1108/08858629910272184

Brandenburger, A. M., & Nalebuff, B. J. (1996). *Co-Opetition* (First Edition). Doubleday Business.

Czakon, W. (2018), Network coopetition, in Fernandez A-S., Chiambaretto P., Le Roy F., Czakon W. (eds), The Routledge Companion to Coopetition Strategies, Routledge, Abingdon. https://doi.org/10.4324/9781315185644-5

Fenichel, Z. (1931). Umowa o pośrednictwo (Agency contract). *Głos Prawa*, *1*, 16–30.

Fras, M. (2009). Prawne aspekty konkurencji na rynku pośrednictwa ubezpieczeniowego (Legal aspects of competition in the insurance brokerage market). *Rozprawy Ubezpieczeniowe*, *nr 2(7)*, 155–172.

Glaser, B. G., & Strauss, A. L. (1967). *The Discovery of Grounded Theory: Strategies for Qualitative Research*. Aldine.

Gnyawali, D. R., He, J., & Madhavan, R. ("Ravi"). (2006). Impact of Co-Opetition on Firm Competitive Behavior: An Empirical Examination. *Journal of Management*, *32*(4), 507–530. https://doi.org/10.1177/0149206305284550

Gnyawali, D. R., & Park, B.-J. (Robert). (2011). Co-opetition between giants: Collaboration with competitors for technological innovation. *Research Policy*, *40*(5), 650–663. https://doi.org/10.1016/j.respol.2011.01.009

Hora, W., Gast, J., Kailer, N., Rey-Martí, A. & Mas-Tur, A. (2018). David and Goliath: causes and effects of coopetition between start-ups and corporates. *Review of Managerial Science*, 12, 411–439. https://doi.org/10.1007/s11846-017-0273-9

Koszarna, S. (2022). Rozwój definicji koopetycji (Developing the definition of coopetition). *Studia i Prace Kolegium Zarządzania i Finansów*, 187, 27–55. https://doi.org/10.33119/SIP.2022.187.2

Kowalewski, E. (2008). Wynagrodzenie brokera ubezpieczeniowego (Insurance broker remuneration). *Prawo Asekuracyjne*, 2, 3–15.

Krymarys, I. (2016). Kooperencja agentów ubezpieczeniowych (Insurance agents cooperation). *Wiadomości Ubezpieczeniowe*, 2, 135–144.

Kucharski, B. (2021). Prawo do kurtażu w razie zmiany brokera ubezpieczeniowego (Right to brokerage in the event of a change of insurance broker). Wiadomości Ubezpieczeniowe, 1(2021/1), 15–28. https://doi.org/10.33995/wu2021.1.2

Luo, Y. (2007). A coopetition perspective of global competition. *Journal of World Business*, *42*(2), 129–144. https://doi.org/10.1016/j.jwb.2006.08.007

Malinowska, K. (2018). Notion of "Large Risks" – Legal Considerations in the Context of Polish and European Law. *Prawo Asekuracyjne*, *4*(*97*), 18–30.

Orlicki, M. (2019). Rozkład obowiązków pomiędzy dystrybutorówww procesie zawierania umowy ubezpieczenia. Dokumentowanie realizacji obowiązkówustawowych związanych z dystrybucją ubezpieczeń (Distribution of duties between distributors in the process of concluding an insurance contract. Documentation of the implementation of statutory duties related to the distribution of insurance). *Wiadomości Ubezpieczeniowe*, *2*(2019/2), 3–13. https://doi.org/10.33995/wu2019.2.1

Pattinson, S., Nicholson, J., & Lindgreen, A. (2018). Emergent coopetition from a sensemaking perspective: A multi-level analysis. *Industrial Marketing Management*, *68*, 25–35. https://doi.org/10.1016/j.indmarman.2017.09.005

Pokrzywniak, J. (2005). *Broker ubezpieczeniowy - ubezpieczający - ubezpieczyciel: Stosunki zobowiązaniowe (Insurance broker - insured - insurer: contractual relations)*. Branta.

UKNF. (2024). *Raport o Stanie Rynku Brokerskiego w 2023 roku (UKNF Report on the State of the Brokerage Market in 2023)*. the Polish Financial Supervision Authority – UKNF.

Urbańczyk, A. (2024). *Obowiązki informacyjne dystrybutorów ubezpieczeń (Information obligations of insurance distributors). W Nowe zasady dystrybucji ubezpieczeń. Zagadnienia prawne*. Wolters Kluwer Polska.

Wiener, M., & Saunders, C. (2014). Forced coopetition in IT multi-sourcing. *The Journal of Strategic Information Systems*, *23*(3), 210–225. https://doi.org/10.1016/j.jsis.2014.08.001

Ziemiak, M. P. (2019). Pre-contractual Information Duties of Insurers. A German and Polish Approach. *Prawo Asekuracyjne*, *2*(99), 152–164. https://doi.org/10.5604/01.3001.0013.5837

The Importance of EU Soft Law in Insurance Distribution: The Case of Poland

Monika Szaraniec

1 Introduction

Soft law, and thus also the open method of coordination, is an expression of new governance in the European Union. Non-binding acts represent a departure from the traditional form of governance based on the classic community method. For these reasons, a model of lawmaking has emerged in which formally non-binding resolutions, guidelines, positions, opinions or books have forced a systemic approach to the issue and then led to its standardization.

This represents a departure from the traditional perception of soft law as an instrument set aside for the EU to carry out activities of a purely supportive, coordinating or complementary nature to the actions of member states. In terms of the functioning of the EU single financial market, the legislator has equipped supervisory authorities (national and EU) with the power to issue soft law, which not only interprets the provisions contained in directives and regulations, but also supplements and clarifies their provisions.

The author indicates that there is a trend away from binding, binding norms of insurance market law toward issuing rules and soft law. Although soft law is not legally binding it can often pave the way for legally binding standards (it can lead to the initiation of legally binding standards). The actual effectiveness of soft law becomes important especially in those areas where there is a lack of legal regulation or there are loopholes, most recently in the field of new technologies.

Opinions, resolutions, recommendations, list of warnings of supervisory authorities (national and EU) do not have legal binding force (binding), but they have

This article presents the results of the Project No. 033/EPC/2023/POT, financed from the subsidy granted to the Krakow University of Economics.

M. Szaraniec
College of Law, Krakow University of Economics, Krakow, Poland
e-mail: monika.szaraniec@uek.krakow.pl
ORCID: 0000-0002-3721-3179

P. Marano (ed.), *Emerging Legal Frontiers in Insurance*,
AIDA Europe Research Series on Insurance Law and Regulation,
https://doi.org/10.1007/978-3-032-09716-3_8

certain effects in the sphere of law and as also enforce their application on participants of the insurance market (insurance distributors, customers).

This article is largely concerned with the new instrument of supervision of the insurance market, which are recommendations issued by EIOPA and the Insurance Supervisory Commissions (in Poland). In particular, the location of recommendations within the legal system, the procedure for issuing them, as well as the assessment of the impact of recommendations on the proper and safe functioning of insurance distribution will be considered. In addition, the article attempts to assess whether the past actions of the supervisory authorities are appropriate and whether soft law is an appropriate and effective supervisory instrument in terms of eliminating regulatory gaps.

2 *Soft Law* in Micro-Prudential Supervision and Its Role in EU

The tasks of EBA, ESMA i EIOPA (hereinafter referred to as the Authorities or ESA) have been specified in Regulations (EU) 1093/2010,[1] 1094/2010[2] and 1095/2010,[3] and they are similar, with certain differences following from the characteristic features of the specific market segments (banking, investment, insurance) in which the Authorities operate.

Micro-prudential oversight is a type of external supervision of individual nature, exercised by administrative authorities. It is a manifestation of state intervention in the functioning of the financial market and economic activities of an entrepreneur (financial institution and financial intermediary). This supervision is exercised so as to ensure proper functioning of the internal financial market of the European Union. In a broad sense, the oversight implements the licensing function (by granting authorizations for the establishment of an entrepreneur and initiation of business, permits for appointing particular persons as members of the management board), the regulatory and administrative review functions, current (prudential) supervision,[4]

[1] Regulation (EU) No 1093/2010 of the European Parliament and of the Council of 24 November 2010 establishing a European Supervisory Authority (European Banking Authority), amending Decision No 716/2009/EC and repealing Commission Decision 2009/78/EC (OJ L 331, 15.12.2010, p. 12 as amended).

[2] Regulation (EU) No 1094/2010 of the European Parliament and of the Council of 24 November 2010 establishing a European Supervisory Authority (European Insurance and Occupational Pensions Authority), amending Decision No 716/2009/EC and repealing Commission Decision 2009/79/EC (OJ L 331, 15.12.2010, p. 48, as amended), hereinafter referred to as the Regulation.

[3] Regulation (EU) No 1095/2010 of the European Parliament and of the Council of 24 November 2010 establishing a European Supervisory Authority (European Securities and Markets Authority), amending Decision No 716/2009/EC and repealing Commission Decision 2009/77/EC (OJ L 331 of 15.12.2010, p. 84 as amended).

[4] Consisting in the control, exercised by the supervisory authority, of compliance by financial institutions with prudential standards. Prudential standards mean special legal norms setting out the requirements imposed for the purpose of limiting the assumption of excessive risk by financial institutions and increasing the security level of the financial system, and, in consequence, ensuring an appropriate level of protecting the interests of persons entrusting their financial means to such institutions. So: R. Mroczkowski, *Nadzór nad funduszami inwestycyjnymi*, Warszawa 2011, p. 45.

consolidated supervision[5] and supplementary supervision.[6] In a narrower sense – it covers the activities of defining, applying and enforcing prudential standards. Prudential standards define specific operative models intended to ensure the security and stability of operations of supervised institutions. Their application allows to cut down the risk to an appropriate level, which translates into the security of the entire financial system. One of the instruments of intervention of EBA, ESMA and EIOPA in the internal financial market of the EU is the delivery of guidelines and recommendations addressed to appropriate national supervisory authorities or financial market operators (financial institutions). Although the guidelines have no binding force, in certain cases, once the conditions of the EIOPA regulation are met, the national supervisor may be bound by the actions and decisions of the ESAs, which have so far had soft functions such as signalling, warning and coordination.[7]

2.1 Guidelines and Recommendations: Meaning and Legal Character

For recommendations, the TFEU provides several grounds for their issuance by the basic EU institutions such as the Commission, the Council and the European Central Bank. This catalog is not exhaustive, as recommendations, in accordance with the CJEU ruling in the Grimaldi case, are issued by the institutions when they do not have the competence to issue legally binding acts or when the issuance of such an act is not considered necessary by the institution concerned. It should be stressed that guidelines are not mentioned in Article 288 TFEU as a source of EU law, the TFEU in Articles 5(2), 26(3), 120, 121 indicates the obligation to issue this type of legal act. It follows from the cited provisions of the CJEU that guidelines

[5] Consolidated supervision is an element of security of the Union financial system. It was introduced in a situation when individual supervision over financial institutions forming a part of holding structures was insufficient. Although the law does not define this supervision type, its essence is to monitor financial institutions forming a part of holdings – for the purpose of assessing the operative risk relating to the fact of shareholding links with other entities. This supervision is exercised on the basis of consolidated financial statements, covering the parent entity and its subsidiaries. The exercise of consolidated supervision does not exclude individual supervision.

[6] Supplementary (additional) supervision is exercised over entities forming a part of a financial conglomerate. A financial conglomerate may be considered a group formed by entrepreneurs conducting their activities in at least two sectors of the financial, banking, insurance or investment market. A financial supervision authority, already existing in the structure of supervisory authorities in the financial market, acquires an additional function of coordinator, together with additional powers necessary to exercise supplementary supervision over financial conglomerates.

[7] M. Fedorowicz, A. Michór, (2011), p.24.

are intended to be of a general nature and to indicate how Member States should behave.[8]

Recommendations, on the other hand, should be distinguished from guidelines, which are also EU soft law. They usually specify how a legally binding norm is to be implemented and their purpose is not to create new law, but to clarify existing legal norms.[9]

L. Senden qualified recommendations as steering instruments and guidelines as interpretative instruments.[10] She states that both recommendations and guidelines are legal instruments, that they refer to the law, that their purpose is to guide or direct the actions of another in a certain way, and that they are legally non-binding. What distinguishes them, according to Senden, is that the purpose of a recommendation is to cause a certain action by those to whom it is addressed. By contrast, the purpose of guidelines is to clarify how a given provision should be understood or applied.[11]

In my view, such distinctions would sort out the distinction between guidelines and recommendations and de lege ferenda the EU legislator should recognize and sort this out in the EBA, ESMA and EIOPA regulations.[12]

2.2 Procedure for Reviewing Guidelines and Recommendations

Guidelines and recommendations have no binding force, however, EIOPA has disciplinary measures to persuade the addressee to comply with the instruments. The EIOPA Regulations lay down a review procedure, requiring that, within two months from the delivery of a guideline or recommendation, each appropriate national supervisory authority or supervised entity (financial institution) should confirm whether or not the national supervisory authority or supervised entity intends to comply with the adopted instruments. If the national supervisory authority or financial institution does not intend to comply with a guideline or recommendation, it is obliged to notify that to EIOPA and specify reasons for the above. A disciplinary measure to be imposed on the national supervisory authority or financial institution is publication by the Authority of the information (and, possibly, also the reasons given) about non-compliance with a particular guideline or recommendation. In addition, EIOPA may decide, on a case-by-case basis, to publish the justification

[8] R. Grzeszczak, M. Słok-Wódkowska, (2015), pp. 90 and 92.

[9] Ibid, pp. 90 and 92.

[10] L. Senden, (2004), p. 156.

[11] R. Grzeszczak, M. Słok-Wódkowska, (2015), p. 90 and 92.

[12] Article 16 of the EIOPA Regulation lists these two supervisory instruments (guidelines and recommendations) without making any distinction between them or indicating when they should be used.

provided by the national supervisory authority for not complying with a particular guideline or recommendation. The national supervisory authority shall be informed in advance of such publication. Such publication shall serve as a signal. This supervisory measure is expected to warn the customer of the financial service against the financial institution that fails to comply, in its activities, with the EU guidelines and recommendations adopted by EIOPA within the framework of the internal financial market of the European Union. Such measure is not meaningless bearing in mind high sensitivity of financial markets to any negative information.[13]

2.3 *Relationship Between EIOPA and KNF*

The Polish Financial Supervision Authority (hereinafter referred to as KNF) is one of the authorities forming a part of the European System of Financial Supervision (KNF representatives take part in the works of ESA). A potential area for cooperation between KNF and EIOPA is the power to express opinions and positions by national supervisors in relation to the adoption by EIOPA of supervisory measures in the form of *soft law*.[14] In respective situations, EIOPA conducts open public consultations with regard to guidelines and recommendations, and analyzes potential costs and benefits correlated to the guidelines and recommendations. Such consultations and analyzes must be proportionate to the scope, nature and impact of the guidelines and recommendations.[15] In addition, it must be pointed out that the national supervisory authority is obliged to confirm (within two months from the delivery of a guideline or recommendation) if the authority complies or intends to comply with the particular guideline or recommendation. However, if the national supervisory authority does not comply with the instrument or does not intend to do so, the authority is obliged to notify that to EIOPA and give relevant reasons. In the light of the above, *soft law* instruments adopted by EIOPA are not legally binding on national supervisory authorities, however, the authorities are obliged to reply to the guidelines and recommendations received from EIOPA. This is because EIOPA is obliged to publish information that a given national supervisory authority does not comply or does not intend to comply with a given guideline or recommendation. EIOPA may also, on a case-by-case basis, decide to publish the reasons for non-compliance with a particular guideline or recommendation, as given by the appropriate national supervisory authority. The national supervisory authority is notified about such publication in advance.[16]

---

[13] So: A. Michór, (2011), p. 312.

[14] EIOPA may adopt guidelines and recommendations that are addressed to national supervisors and financial institutions.

[15] Art. 16 (3) of Regulation (UE) No. 1094/2010.

[16] See: Art. 16 (3) of Regulation (UE) No. 1094/2010. Moreover, if this is required under a guideline or recommendation, a financial institution must, in a clear and detailed way, notify if the financial institution complies with the guideline or recommendation.

Non-binding legal acts cannot have direct effect, and therefore a national supervisory authority or financial institution cannot derive its powers directly from recommendations or guidelines. However, according to the TSUE ruling in the *Grimaldi* case study,[17] recommendations will have indirect effect. The same should apparently apply to guidelines. National supervisory authorities are therefore obliged to take into account the guidelines and recommendations issued by EU institutions when issuing their own regulations

In Poland, micro-prudential oversight is exercised by the Polish Financial Supervision Authority (KNF).[18]

3 The Substance and Legal Bases of Delivering Recommendations by KNF in the Polish Insurance Market

The question of legal status of recommendations adopted by KNF has been given much attention in Polish literature.[19] KNF recommendations are an instrument of influence on the financial (banking, insurance and investment) market operators and, therefore, according to the principle of legality and in the interest of legal transactions, the basis for their adoption should be clearly stipulated in the provisions of law. The principle of legality has been expressed in Art. 7 of the Constitution of the Republic of Poland, and it consists in the requirement imposed on public authorities to act under and within legal provisions.[20]

According to Art. 365 of the Act of 11 September 2015 on insurance and reinsurance activities,[21] KNF was given the right to issue recommendations addressed to insurance and reinsurance undertakings[22] to an extent necessary to implement guidelines and recommendations adopted by EIOPA in accordance with Art. 16 of Regulation (EU) 1094/2010.[23] EIOPA may deliver guidelines and recommendations addressed to appropriate authorities supervising the insurance market which operate in the Member States. Accordingly, so as to enable KNF to legally introduce in

[17] *In Case C-322/88.*

[18] For more on this subject, see: M. Szaraniec, (2017), p. 277 ad 284–288.

[19] As far as recommendations in the insurance market are concerned, see.: A. Tarasiuk-Flodrowska, (2011), p. 218–227; B. Mrozowska, (2012), p. 30–47; E. Kowalewski, M. Ziemiak, (2014), p. 15–30.

[20] The above principle has been repeatedly analyzed in case-law. E.g., see: the decision of the Supreme Court of 18 January 2005, WK 22/04, OSNKW 2005, nr 3, poz. 29, Biuletyn SN 2005, nr 3, poz. 23, and the judgment of the Constitutional Tribunal of 23 March 2006, K4/06, OTK-A 2006, nr 3, poz. 32, or the judgment of the Constitutional Tribunal of 16 March 2011, K 35/8, OTK-A 2011, nr 2, poz.11.

[21] Dz. U. 2024, poz. 838, hereinafter referred to as u.d.u.r.

[22] Art. 365 (1) and (2) u.d.u.r.

[23] For more on that subject, see: M. Szaraniec, (2016), http://sic.pravo.upjs.sk

the Polish insurance market EIOPA's guidelines and recommendations addressed to national insurance and reinsurance undertakings, it was necessary to vest such an instrument of impact in the supervisory authority. It must be emphasized that the Act on insurance and reinsurance activities confers on KNF the power to adopt guidelines to an extent necessary to implement EIOPA guidelines and recommendations delivered under Art. 16 of Regulation (EU) 1094/2010. Moreover, the legislator, under Art. 365 (1) item 2 u.d.u.r., confers on KNF also the power to adopt guidelines for the following purposes:

1. to ensure compliance of the activities of insurance and reinsurance undertakings with the provisions of law,
2. to prevent infringements of the interests of policyholders, insured persons, beneficiaries or persons entitled under insurance contracts,
3. to reduce the risk inherent in the activities of an insurance or reinsurance undertaking,
4. to ensure permanent capacity of an insurance undertaking to fulfil its obligations.[24]

In the light of the above, the Act on insurance and reinsurance activities provides for extensive powers of KNF to deliver guidelines whenever the supervisory authority ascertains a violation to legal provisions or infringement of interests of policyholders, insured persons, beneficiaries, or threats to the fulfilment of obligations (implementation of EIOPA guidelines and recommendations probably fits also into the purposes specified under Art. 363 (1) item 2 u.d.u.r.). In the explanatory memorandum of the draft u.d.u.r., it was argued that adoption of such guidelines would allow for quick reaction (communication) of the supervisory authority when the authority identified a risk of unlawful behavior of insurance or reinsurance undertakings without a need to initiate individual proceedings. At the same time, this would also guarantee to supervised entities access to knowledge about the position of the supervisory authority in respect of proper operation of the insurance market.

Another important novelty introduced in Art. 365 u.d.u.r. is the possibility left to an insurance or reinsurance undertaking to declare that the undertaking does not intend to comply with the recommendation.[25] This refers to situations in which an insurance undertaking does not comply with the recommendations of the supervisory authority delivered in implementation of EIOPA guidelines and recommendations. In such situation, the insurance undertaking is obliged to notify that to KNF, and the latter is obliged to publicize (disclose) the information.

[24] Art. 363 (1) item 2 u.d.u.r.

[25] See: Art. 363 (4) u.d.u.r.

Such legal solution confirms previous opinions expressed in literature of the subject that recommendations are standards of conduct recommended by KNF, whose observance cannot be enforced by the supervisory authority through imposing sanctions. Recommendations should be approached as instructions for conduct, making an instrument of preventive impact on insurance practice. Nevertheless, this legal solution can be treated as an additional element reinforcing the protection of the customer of an insurance service through information in the form of public warning about non-compliance of insurance undertakings with recommendations adopted by KNF. Such obligation is prescribed under statutory law, which obligates KNF to make available to the public information on the insurance undertakings that decided not to follow the recommendations of the supervisory authority. Such publicized information can be an obstacle for insurance undertakings to acquire new customers, and for the existing customers – and inspiration to change the insurer in the future. In situations when recommendations are adopted by KNF for the purposes laid down in Art. 365 (1) item 2 u.d.u.r., the legislator also leaves an option to an insurance undertaking to not to comply with the instrument delivered. However, in such event, the legislator imposes on the insurance undertaking a requirement to indicate the methods according to which the undertaking is going to achieve the purposes of conduct laid down in the guidelines. Information about the scope of non-compliance with the provisions of the recommendation and information about the methods of achieving the purposes laid down in the recommendation must be provided by the insurance undertaking to the supervisory authority, and the authority makes the information publicly available. It should be emphasized that provision of such information is an obligation of insurance undertakings. As a consequence of the above, when it comes to recommendations delivered by KNF to insurance undertakings as a part of implementing the purposes laid down in Art. 365 (1) item 2 u.d.u.r., an insurance undertaking has no real possibility to opt out of implementing the recommendation, however, the undertaking is free to choose the methods according to which it is going to achieve the purposes laid down in the instrument (there is no leeway when it comes to the implementation of purposes, however, the addressee is in a position to achieve the purposes through means chosen at the addressee's discretion). An analysis of the discussed provision leads to a conclusion that the insurance undertaking must implement the recommendation, possibly, using methods other than the ones indicated by KNF.

As a result, it should be concluded that, in the applicable provision of Art. 365 u.d.u.r., the legislator points to instruments adopted in implementation of EIOPA recommendations – and they are non-binding on insurance undertakings both when it comes to the means and purposes.[26] On the other hand, other recommendations

[26] This refers to recommendations issued under Art. 365 (1) item 1 u.d.u.r. For more on this subject, see: M. Szaraniec, (2017), p.284–288.

are binding on insurance undertakings when it comes to implementing the purposes, and non-binding when it comes to the means of such implementation.[27]

Therefore, a question arises what happens if the insurance undertaking does not comply with the recommendation adopted by KNF under Art. 365 (1) item 2 u.d.u.r., which is identified in the course of ex-post supervision. By their very nature, recommendations do not belong to the category of legally binding legislative acts, and KNF may not enforce their observance by the insurance undertaking through supervisory measures. As a result, *de lege ferenda,* it would be legitimate to introduce a legal provision under which, in case of an omission to provide information about the lack of intention to follow an adopted recommendation by an insurance undertaking, the supervisory authority would be empowered to publish such information *ex officio*. Such public information, announced as a warning, would reinforce protection of the customer of an insurance service. In practice, it can be imagined that an insurance undertaking does not comply with the obligation to provide KNF with information about non-following the recommendation.

The Act also contains a provision on the statutory obligation to conduct consultations of a draft recommendation with interested parties and institutions and to assess predictable social and economic consequences (in terms of costs and benefits) of the instrument before preparing the draft guidelines.[28]

Therefore, it seems legitimate to say that recommendations are standards of conduct recommended by KNF whose observance, however, cannot be enforced through state coercion.[29] These are general and abstract norms, being a reaction of the supervisory authority to identified threats to the operation of insurance undertakings. They should be approached as instructions (principles) of recommended conduct. Therefore, the opinion expressed in literature seems legitimate that recollection of such principles is not legislating but fulfilling the mission of market supervisor who must make sure that supervised entities operate according to the applicable law.[30] For the above reasons – as opposed to other instruments prepared under statutory authorization – KNF recommendations may not impose on their addressees any obligations but only recommend specific actions.[31]

In addition, it must be emphasized that KNF recommendations do not fit into the category of generally applicable legislation since they have not been referred to in Art. 87 of the Constitution of the Republic of Poland.[32] For the above reasons, KNF recommendations cannot serve as basis for the delivery of an administrative decision in the light of their non-imperative status (no sanctions imposed by KNF),

[27] This refers to recommendations issued under Art. 365 (1) item 2 u.d.u.r.

[28] Art. 365 (2) and (3) u.d.u.r. For more on the subject, see: M. Śliwa-Wajda, P. Wajda, (2023), p. 3–25.

[29] So: For more on this subject, see: M. Szaraniec, (2017), p. 277 ad 284–288.

[30] M. Orlicki, (2015),p. 26.

[31] So: R. Kaszubski, (2006), p. 78.

[32] S. Wronkowska, (2005), p. 26.

and cannot be subject to the review of administrative courts.[33] In case of delivery by KNF of an administrative decision based on a recommendation, a possibility is postulated to declare its invalidity on account of missing legal basis for its adoption, under Art. 156 (1) item 2 of the Polish Code of Administrative Procedure.[34] On the other hand, the legal basis for decisions and judgments may be the provisions of generally applicable law interpreted according to the recommendations.[35] In consequence, recommendations cannot be considered the sources of generally applicable norms. In literature, it has been pointed out that they also cannot be treated as sources of internal law (internal management acts) because, in the light of Art. 93 of the Constitution of the Republic of Poland, insurance undertakings (including banks) are not organizationally subordinated to KNF.[36]

Guidelines and recommendations are supervisory measures of corrective status and fit into preventive supervision. KNF is responsible for proper operation of the insurance market and, thanks to guidelines and recommendations, it can prevent unfavorable phenomena in that market by influencing the operations of supervised entities.

As a result, it should be concluded that the national legislator adjusted u.d.u.r. to the requirements of Union law in respect to the adoption of recommendations and guidelines for insurance undertakings also when it comes to the use of insurance agents' services.[37]

Such provisions are missing in the currently applicable Polish Act of 15 December 2017 on insurance distribution[38] (implementing the Insurance Distribution Directive[39]). Therefore, *de lege ferenda*, it should be postulated that in the future u.p.u. the legislator includes legal provisions analogous to the ones adopted in u.d.u.r. when it comes to the delivery by KNF of guidelines and recommendations

[33] A. Skoczylas, (2002), p. 58.

[34] T. Nieborak (2011), p. 78.

[35] So: T. Nieborak, (2008), p. 26.

[36] However, in literature, different opinions can be found on that matter. E.g., see: T. Czech, (2009), p. 70–71, where the author discussed positions presented in literature in this regard. No less convincing is the judgment of the Constitutional Tribunal of 28 June 2000, K 25/99, OTK 2000, nr 5, poz. 141, in which the requirements were formulated whose fulfilment allows to adopt acts of internal legislation addressed to entities functionally subordinate to the state authority. The Constitutional Tribunal explained that an authority entitled to the above may only be a constitutional authority, and the acts of internal legislation themselves may only relate to constitutionally defined public tasks. These considerations are decisive for the conclusion that KNF is not authorized to adopt acts of internal legislation addressed to insurance undertakings (banks), because KNF is not a constitutional authority and it does not perform constitutional public tasks. For more on that subject, see: R. Tupin, (2001), z. 1, p. 87.

[37] So far, KNF has adopted: Recommendations for insurance undertakings on the adequacy of products of 22 March 2016, Recommendations for insurance undertakings on the product management system of 22 March 2016, and Guidelines for insurance undertakings on insurance distribution of 24 June 2014.

[38] The Act of 15 December 2017 on insurance distribution (Dz. U. 2023, poz. 1111, 1723).

[39] Directive (EU) 2016/97 of the European Parliament and of the Council of 20 January 2016 on insurance distribution (recast) (OJ L 26, 02.02.2016, p. 19) – IDD.

in relation to insurance brokers since – as highlighted above – KNF exercises direct supervision over their activities. In addition, KNF must have a legal basis to introduce, in the Polish insurance market, EIOPA's guidelines and recommendations in relation to insurance brokers and other insurance distributors.[40]

4 The Role of Soft Law in Introducing New Technologies to the Insurance Market

The above considerations allow to assume that the micro-prudential supervisory authorities (on the national and EU level), to a large extent, eliminate gaps in the legislative framework by adopting guidelines and recommendations addressed to financial institutions. The lack of legislation on the Union level forces the national supervisory authorities to search for appropriate and effective supervisory instruments in the legal solutions adopted in other countries across the world and in Europe for the development of InsurTech and their cooperation with the traditional insurance distributor. An adequate example may be the activities undertaken in the context of creating Innovation Hubs and Regulatory Sandboxes.[41]

In literature of the subject an opinion was expressed that oversight over financial innovations is connected with the concept referred to as policy trilemma. Under this concept, supervisory authorities should aim to: 1. provide clear rules, 2. maintain market integrity, and 3. encourage financial innovation.[42] According to academic authors, the main burden of monitoring the market in this regard will be on supervisory authorities. They will use the so called mechanisms of market self-regulation by issuing guidelines or creating *Innovation Hubs* or *Regulatory Sandboxes.* Such activities should be based on rules simplicity but, at the same time, enhance transparency, reduce bureaucratic burdens so as to ensure certainty, predictability, stability and coherence of financial provisions, as well as increased competition. Rules simplicity can, by extension, help promote capital formation, hedging, and other financial services by lowering costs to consumers and thereby encouraging a larger and more diverse group to enter the market.[43] In this context, there are new opportunities for innovation and growth and new challenges, particularly for regulation and regulators. Lately, the particular challenge for regulators has been the need to encourage and support disruptive innovation in order to enhance financial inclusion and support economic growth.[44] Extensive interaction between regulators and market participants provides the necessary background for cautious experimentation with, and regulation of *Innovation Hub*, that is an institutional solution as a part of which *FinTech* entities, both regulated and non-regulated (e.g. enterprises which fail to obtain

[40] For more on that subject, see: M. Szaraniec, (2017), p. 326–331.

[41] So: M. Szaraniec, (2020), p. 34.

[42] B. Chris, Y. Yadav, (2019), p. 242.

[43] Ibid., p. 243–248.

[44] So: D. A. Zetzsche; R. P. Buckley; J. N. Barberis; D. W. Arner, (2017): p. 38.

license), establish a relation with the regulatory authority to discuss matters relating to their activities (sharing information, opinions, etc.) and to obtain clarification relating to the legality of their business models (regarding the models of cooperation, among others, between innovative insurance companies (*InsurTech*) and traditional insurance distributors) without the option to test innovative solutions on customers. As a part of an *Innovation Hub* program, an operator in the *InsurTech* industry may obtain assistance in identifying appropriate legal provisions, rules or supervisory positions applicable to the given operator, business model, offered product or financial service and, on top of that, the operator may obtain information on the terms of the exercised supervision, procedures of licensing a given type of activity or documents and guidelines available on the website of the supervisory authority. The purpose of such *Innovation Hubs* is to promote certainty among *InsurTech* companies and encourage development by such companies of the research previously carried out. On this occasion, supervisory authorities play the role of a consultant, and their position is not binding, which means that it does not guarantee that the suggested solution is the right one. Such opinions may not be relied on before state authorities or courts, because they do not constitute legal opinions or interpretations of law. Undoubtedly, however, *Innovation Hubs* imply a completely new role and a completely new approach of supervisory authorities in relation to *InsurTech*.[45]

So, a significant step activities undertaken by supervisory authorities in the world (apart from Innovation Hub) was launching virtual *Regulatory Sandboxes*,[46] which offer controlled space to innovative enterprises in which such enterprises may test innovative *FinTech* solutions for a limited period with the support of national supervisory

[45] See: M. Fras, M. Szaraniec, (2019), p. 90–109. The following countries were forerunners in this regard: 1. Australia: The innovation hub launched in 2015 assists FinTech start-ups in navigating the Australian regulatory system: "[E]ligible businesses can request informal guidance from ASIC"; 2. China: Regular outreach with the FinTech sector "is aided by the National Internet Finance Association (NIFA), which guides and supervises the implementation of national policies on the licensing process and key regulatory issues."; 3. Luxembourg: CSSF has a special department for financial innovation, established in early 2015, which functions as CSSF's innovation hub; 4. Germany: Bundesanstalt fir Finanzdienstleistungsaufischt (BaFin) offers close contact and advice to FinTech start-ups; 5. Japan: The Japanese Financial Services Agency launched a FinTech Support Desk in December 2015; 6. Singapore: The Monetary Authority of Singapore (MAS) established a financial technology and innovation group with an innovation lab known as "Looking Glass @ MAS" as well as a FinTech Office; 7. South Korea: The Government established a FinTech Centre in 2015; 8. Taiwan: The Financial Supervisory Commission established a FinTech office in 2015 and implemented a FinTech Pilot Program; 8. Thailand: Bank of Thailand has set up a FinTech clinic; 9. Sweden: Established a National Innovation Council "to provide support and advice to established and startup businesses alike on issues such as regulatory and permit requirements."; 10. United Kingdom: Project Innovate included the establishment of an innovation hub in 2015. So after: D. A. Zetzsche; R. P. Buckley; J. N. Barberis; D. W. Arner, (2017), p. 40–43.

[46] The first regulatory sandboxes were created in 2016 in: United Kingdom (04/2016), Hong Kong (09/2016), Indonesia (09/2016), Malaysia (10/2016), Singapore (11/2016), Abu Dhabi (11/2016) and in Australia (12/2016). So after: D. A. Zetzsche; R. P. Buckley; J. N. Barberis; D. W. Arner, (2017), p. 64–66.Then, further development of regulatory sandboxes took place, covering also Central and Eastern Europe. See, for example, the solutions in Lithuania: https://www.oecd.org/finance/insurance/Lithuania-review-of-the-insurance-system-2018.pdf The entities to be accepted

authorities (the authority may intervene at any stage of product testing) before they meet all the requirements in the licensing process or succeed in that regard to a limited extent. Innovative enterprises are obliged to file an application (they undergo a simplified authorization process adjusted to their needs) to join the program, and the mere acceptance of their application by the respective supervisory authority is to increase their credibility both among customers and investors. *Regulatory sandboxes* in different countries differ from one another, however, the scope of this article does not allow to discuss such questions in more detail. Still, the policy of regulatory sandboxes reduces the risk of court proceedings for violation by *InsurTech* companies of their obligations to regulatory authorities, and helps the supervisory authorities monitor the market, by enabling them to weigh advantages and disadvantages for the sake of preserving appropriate competition on the market. *Sandboxes* expressly seek to encourage innovation. They offer regulators a means to acquire insight into the development process for innovations, give input into their design, and better understand how emerging products and services might operate in the real world. Particularly for early-stage innovations, sandboxes can be helpful in reducing the pervasive information uncertainties attaching to the growth of algorithms and Al, as well as to the viability of new data. Although sandboxes come in different guises, with *Innovation Hub* and jurisdictions varying in what terms they offer, the guiding idea is simple enough: rather than be subject to restrictive or complex rules that elevate regulatory risk and potentially stifle innovation, the sandbox offers a means of testing new ideas in a simplified, interactive regulatory environment.[47]

5 Examples of EIOPA and FSA Guidelines and Recommendations on New Technologies and Other Matters – Mentioned

For example, the lack of legal regulations resulted in the fact that the decisive importance in terms of the possibility to apply cloud solutions on the Polish financial market should be attributed to the Communiqué of the Polish Financial Supervision

will negotiate with the Bank of Lithuania mitigation of certain requirements for the duration of testing a business model or products. In October 2018, the Polish Financial Supervision Authority (KNF) took steps to launch a regulatory sandbox in Poland and started to recruit operators, that is enterprises willing to test innovative *FinTech* solutions. The sandbox was to operate as a decentralized model. An operator could be an insurance undertaking, but also a startup accelerator. The testing environment was to be both virtual, i.e. in the form of a computer system simulating market behaviors, and operate with the involvement of actual customers, although without the option of investing any real financial means. The entire process was to be monitored and substantially supported by the supervisory authority. Unexpectedly, in March 2019, KNF suspended the launch of the regulatory sandbox because of non-finalized operator contracts, rules or the KNF's own procedures. For more on that subject, see: M. Fras, M. Szaraniec, (2019), p. 90–109.

[47] D. W Arner, D. A. Zetzsche, R. P Buckley, J. N. Barberis, (2017), p.291–292. For more on that subject, see: M. Szaraniec, (2020), p. 35.

Authority of 23.01.2020. (hereinafter: the Cloud Communiqué)[48] At the same time, it was emphasized at the outset that any guidelines, recommendations or other documents presenting the position of European supervisory authorities, including EIOPA, on the identical subject do not apply to supervised entities.[49] This provision may be seen as problematic in the case of projects within international capital groups involving Polish supervised entities. Nevertheless, according to the Cloud Communiqué referred to here, the European guidelines do not apply to Polish financial entities supervised by the ESA:

1. EBA outsourcing guidelines of 25 February 2019. (EBA/GL/2019/02),[50]
2. EIOPA Guidelines for Outsourcing to Cloud Service Providers (EIOPA-BoS-20-002),[51] – EIOPA repealed such guidelines in December 2024,[52]
3. Financial Stability Board (FSB) Guidance - Third party dependencies in cloud services,[53]
4. ESMA Guidelines - Guidance on outsourcing to cloud service providers (ESMA50-157-2403).[54]

[48] The Office of the Financial Supervision Authority has published (16.01.2025) that, as of 17 January 2025, the communication of 23 January 2020 regarding the processing of information by supervised entities in public or hybrid cloud computing (the so-called Cloud Communication) is revoked. This document has so far systematized the requirements and expectations placed on supervised entities when implementing cloud services in the financial sector. The FSA informs that the repeal of the above regulation and the cancellation of the Cloud Communiqué is dictated by the convergence of the scope of the DORA Regulation and the implementing acts issued in connection therewith with the revoked guidelines and the Cloud Communiqué. In the opinion of the FSA, leaving the aforementioned acts in force would create a risk of interpretation doubts that could arise in view of the regulation of the same aspects by these acts and by the provisions of the DORA Regulation.

[49] Communiqué of the Office of the FSC of 23 January 2020 on the processing of information by supervised entities in a public or hybrid computing cloud (https://www.knf.gov.pl/knf/pl/komponenty/img/Komunikat_UKNF_Chmura_Obliczeniowa_68669.pdf) (accessed 30.09.2024), together with questions and answers (Q&A) issued to this Communiqué with regard to the application of the Communiqué of the FSC of 23 January 2020, as well as extensive studies created on its basis by industry organisations: PolishCloud - Standard for Information Processing Implementations in Cloud Computing (https://zbp.pl/getmedia/3b776dc0-654d-4da4-a764-4b89ec366ad8/PolishCloud) (accessed 30.09.2024); Polish Insurance Association - Standard for Information Processing Implementations in Cloud Computing. A study for the insurance sector (https://piu.org.pl/wp-content/uploads/2021/06/standard-chmura-obliczeniowa-1.pdf) (accessed 30.09.2024).

[50] https://www.eba.europa.eu/sites/default/documents/files/documents/10180/2761380/7551b1c5-534d-44aa-b524-61eb8929154d/EBA%20revised%20Guidelines%20on%20outsourcing_PL.pdf?retry=1 (accessed: 30.09.2024)

[51] https://www.eiopa.europa.eu/sites/default/files/publications/eiopa_guidelines/guidelines_on_outsourcing_to_cloud_service_providers_cor_pl_0.pdf (accessed 30.09.2024).

[52] https://www.eiopa.europa.eu/eiopa-revokes-previous-guidelines-avoid-duplications-and-overlaps-dora-2024-12-19_en (accessed 10.01.2025).

[53] https://www.fsb.org/wp-content/uploads/P091219-2.pdf (accessed 30.09.2024).

[54] (accessed 30.09.2024).

The version of the EIOPA Guidelines on Cloud Insurance Outsourcing in force until the end of 2024 was addressed to national supervisors and informed insurance market participants on how outsourcing regulations should be applied to cloud service providers. Insurance intermediaries (agents, insurance brokers) are not part of this circle, which seems to distinguish the EIOPA Guidelines from the KNF Communication. Thus, however, according to the position taken by the KNF, the ESA Guidelines were not at all applicable to domestic entities to the extent that they overlap with the FSC Communication.[55]

Such a solution may raise some doubts - but it seems clearer for supervised entities than a situation where two different documents regulating the same issues in practice would be in place. Undoubtedly, however, the relationship between the EIOPA Guidelines and the KNF Communication, as well as the potential differences between these positions, are of particular interest in the context of the requirement for national supervisors and financial institutions to make every effort to apply the EIOPA Guidelines under Article 16(3) of Regulation 1094/2010. However, this provision provides for the possibility not to comply with the EIOPA Guidelines and Recommendations, which the FSC has used by presenting a national approach.[56] Such an approach by a national supervisor may, however, raise concerns, as the EBA and EIOPA aim to harmonize at the EU level the regulatory requirements for outsourcing and, in particular, cloud outsourcing,[57] which, in practice, will be the case, e.g. when a foreign branch of an insurance company operating in Poland will apply the KNF's Communication and a major insurance company from an EU Member State will apply the EIOPA Guidelines.[58]

The KNF's position in the Communication in question took the form of a practical map for the regulated sector in the process of migration to cloud computing. The Communication, on the one hand, met the expectations of direct support for supervised entities and, on the other hand, set itself the goal of eliminating interpretation doubts. The KNF concretized many concepts, creating new definitions and clarifying existing requirements, while addressing most of the demands raised in industry discussions.[59]

Another problem in the Polish insurance market is the performance of an analysis of the customer's needs and requirements by the insurance distributor. According to the Polish Insurance Distribution Act (implementing the IDD) - before concluding an insurance contract, the insurance distributor determines, on the basis of information obtained from the customer, the customer's requirements and needs and provides objective information about the insurance product in an understandable form, in order to enable the customer to make an informed decision.

---

[55] J. Byrski, H. Hoser, (2020), p.61.

[56] Ibid, p. 61.

[57] D. Karwala, M. Szwarczyńska, (2019), No. 4870.

[58] J. Byrski, H. Hoser, (2020), p.62.

[59] W. Wojturska, (2022), p. 42.

So much for the recipe, but in practice it is unclear exactly what this APK should look like. On the Polish market, one encounters a rather different approach to this process, ranging from a rather cursory questioning of the customer very generally about their needs, through the implementation of various tables and forms to streamline the process, to the implementation of a needs and requirements analysis into sales systems.

All of these solutions have their advantages and disadvantages, but we also see in the course of the audits carried out by the FSC that the expectations of the national authority regarding the analysis of needs and requirements are quite clear. It certainly cannot be a process done in a shoddy manner and definitely needs to be properly documented.

However, apart from the guidance from the audit, the Commission has not yet generated any concrete position on what an analysis of customer needs and requirements should actually look like by 2023. There are also no such recommendations and guidelines at EIOPA level. This is probably related to the different distribution models in the member states and the fact that the IDD has a minimum scope of implementation.

Due to a problem in the Polish insurance market with regard to the preparation and documentation of the customer needs analysis by insurance distributors, the FSA has taken action in 2023. 26 June 2023. The KNF Authority unanimously adopted a new *Recommendation U on good bancassurance practices*.[60] The aim of *Recommendation U* is to improve the standards of bancassurance activities and to define the conditions for stable development of the bancassurance market. A key element of the new *Recommendation U* is to ensure that insurance products offered through bancassurance provide adequate value for the customer.[61]

The new version of *Recommendation U* provides some valuable insights into how needs and requirements analysis should look in bancassurance, which is also probably worth transferring to other distribution channels.

A distributor, which is an insurance intermediary, should have procedures in place to prevent the offering of insurance products that are not adapted to customers' requirements and needs. The procedures should include both rules for the identification of customer requirements and needs and how to assess whether the insurance product is in line with the customer's requirements and needs. What is important is that such procedures should relate not only to the identification of the customer's requirements and needs itself, but should also describe how the distributor came to the conclusion that this and not another product is best for the customer in question. One could say that this is the most difficult part of such a procedure.

The KNF has also proposed a very interesting construction when it comes to third-party insurance. Namely, a policyholder (a party to an insurance contract)

---

[60] https://www.knf.gov.pl/komunikacja/komunikaty?articleId=82885&p_id=18

[61] https://www.knf.gov.pl/dla_rynku/regulacje_i_praktyka/rekomendacje_i_wytyczne/sektor_ubezpieczeniowy/Rekomendacje_U

intending to conclude such an insurance contract should have procedures in place allowing it, as a policyholder, to obtain information on the requirements and needs of potential clients so as to enable the insurance distributor to offer an insurance contract meeting the requirements and needs of such clients. Thus, we are faced with a rather interesting construction, where the duties related to the analysis of needs and requirements are in practice shifted to the policyholder (party to the insurance contract for a third-party account). After all, the Act on distribution clearly states that it is the distributor's task to obtain information from the customer in the process of needs and requirements analysis, and in the light of TSUE case law the policyholder (in a contract for a third-party account) is the distributor.[62]

Thus, in the process of analyzing needs and requirements, the customer should be asked, among other things, about the risks it wants to insure, which in total is quite obvious and already implemented in practice today. At the same time, the KNF also expects the customer to be shown the limitations and exclusions of the insurance company's liability.

As another example of the analysis of customer needs and requirements in the Polish insurance market, the KNF has submitted for consultation a draft of new recommendations for insurance companies regarding insurance distribution.[63] Their overriding aim is to ensure that companies offer products that have an appropriate value for customers. Through the recommendations, the KNF also wants to increase the level of protection of customers' interests by ensuring that insurers apply the law on insurance distribution in a uniform and consistent manner, and to eliminate irregularities it has identified in this process.

With regard to the obligations of the insurance company vis-à-vis customers in insurance distribution, the draft primarily regulates the analysis of customer needs and requirements. In addition to the obligation to clearly separate the needs and requirements analysis from the other distribution stages, to keep the questions simple, to provide the customer with adequate time to read and respond, the KNF obliges insurance companies to ensure that the needs and requirements analysis of the customer shows, in particular:

- for what circumstances the customer would like to be covered and what the customer's insurance requirements are, including what sum insured or sum assured is consistent with the customer's requirements and needs,
- what are the specific characteristics or situation of the customer, in order to assess whether the exclusions or limitations of liability do not conflict with the requirements and needs of the customer.

The national supervisory authority also emphasized that the use for the needs and requirements analysis of information provided by the customer at earlier stages of the cooperation (e.g. when concluding other insurance contracts) is only permissible

[62] *Mariusz Fras, Oskar Zgonina,* (2022), p. 97–113.

[63] https://www.knf.gov.pl/dla_rynku/regulacje_i_praktyka/Publiczne_konsultacje

with the express consent of the interested party and provided that the scope and source of the information is specifically indicated to the customer and that confirmation of its correctness and validity is obtained from the customer. The client's refusal to provide the information necessary to identify his or her requirements and needs does not allow the company to make an offer. The exception is compulsory insurance, but then the insurer ensures that it can prove that the customer refused to provide additional information for the assessment of its requirements and needs prior to the conclusion of the insurance contract.

The manner in which the needs and requirements analysis is documented should ensure that the undertaking is able to prove that the information and data it has used for that purpose were obtained from the customer and that the customer has confirmed their accuracy. In turn, the documentation should be retained until the insurance contract's statute of limitations has run.

In this area, the KNF also recommended that the insurance company should only make contract proposals to the customer that are in line with the customer's requirements and needs, and familiarize the customer with the provisions of the contract template and other information and documents required by law and supervisory recommendations.

In my view, the draft recommendation should be extended to include insurance intermediaries (in Poland, insurance agents and brokers), as over 90% of insurance contracts are concluded in Poland through insurance intermediation.

It should be noted that there is a lack of guidance related to the analysis of needs and requirements by *robo-advisers* (via online platforms or mobile applications), which use algorithms to automatically create a customer profile of an insurance product. The insurance product data is assessed by an algorithm and the *robo-advisor* matches the financial product to the customer and risk profile and generates the required insurance service. Identifying the legal framework for robo-advisers and their responsibility for performing the analysis of customer needs and requirements is a challenge for the EU legislator, as well as for supervisors.

6 Final Conclusions

The lack of EU regulations forces national supervisory authorities to look for appropriate and effective supervisory instruments in the adopted solutions of other countries in the world and in Europe for the development of InsurTech and their cooperation with the traditional insurance distributor. The activities undertaken related to the creation of *Innovation Hubs* and *Regulatory Sandboxes* seem to be the right way out in this situation. In the absence of consistent and unambiguous guidelines at EIOPA level, *Innovation Hubs* and *Regulatory Sandboxes* are not homogeneous institutions, as each country decides on their subject matter. In view of the freedoms and rules of the EU single insurance market in terms of cross-border business, *de lege ferenda* more activity and concrete solutions should be requested from EIOPA on this and other topics. Legal solutions in this respect in the insurance market are far from the banking and investment market. Certain issues in the insurance market are treated selectively, which adds to the lack of legal certainty and inconsistency, thus hindering the development of new technologies in the insurance market.

New technologies pose new challenges for supervisors, the greatest after the 2008 global financial crisis. The lack of regulation is forcing national supervisors to step up and assign them new roles. They have to take into account new risk models and new business models, and thus innovative technologies in the insurance market will have to be supported by supervisors. As far as action is concerned, it is related to the creation of expert working groups and forums, the publication of communications, guidelines and recommendations, which are proposals for new policies for the insurance market to benefit from new technologies while being prepared for the resulting potential risks. Their new role is that, in the absence of regulation, they actually have to find on their own (using models from other countries) a way to prevent disruptive distortions of competition or customer safety, while encouraging and supporting innovation.[64]

Finally, it is difficult not to see that the introduction of new technologies in the insurance market is mainly based on market self-regulation through '*soft law*' (guidelines and recommendations). An analysis of the current construction of guidelines and recommendations in the current legislation allows the thesis that the legislator has 'reinforced' the implementation of these guidelines and recommendations by their addressees. They are binding on the addressees as regards the realization of their objectives, but not as regards the means of their realization. The disciplinary tool in this construction is the possibility for the supervisory authority to disclose (publish) the information it has received regarding the refusal of the supervised entity to comply with the issued guidelines and recommendations. All these solutions mean that the introduction of new technologies in the insurance market can take place through the issuance of guidelines and recommendations, but solutions in this regard developed at EU level are necessary.[65] The design of the EU single

[64] So: M. Szaraniec, (2020), p. 36.

[65] On 2 August 2024, Regulation (EU) 2024/1689 of the European Parliament and of the Council of 13 June 2024 laying down harmonised rules on artificial intelligence and amending Regulations (EC) No 300/2008, (EU) No 167/2013, (EU) No 168/2013, (EU) 2018/858, (EU) 2018/1139 and (EU) 2019/2144 and Directives 2014/90/EU, (EU) 2016/797 and (EU) 2020/1828 (Artificial Intelligence Act) (Text with EEA relevance) entered into force - https://eur-lex.europa.eu/legal-content/EN/TXT/?uri=CELEX%3A32024R1689 - which is the world's first comprehensive regulation on artificial intelligence. The Artificial Intelligence Act aims to ensure that artificial intelligence developed and used in the EU is reliable, with safeguards to protect citizens' fundamental rights. The regulation aims to establish a harmonised internal market for artificial intelligence in the EU, encourage the use of this technology and create an environment conducive to innovation and investment. Member States have until 2 August 2025 to designate competent national authorities to oversee the application of the rules on artificial intelligence systems and carry out market surveillance activities. The Commission's Office for Artificial Intelligence will be the key implementing authority for the Artificial Intelligence Act at EU level, as well as the enforcement authority for general-purpose artificial intelligence models. Most of the provisions of the Artificial Intelligence Act will become effective on 2 August 2026. However, the bans on artificial intelligence

insurance market means that action on this issue should be mandatory, harmonized and consistent for the entire market and individual Member States.

References

Byrski, J., & Hoser, H. (2020). *Wpływ Komunikatu Urzędu Komisji Nadzoru Finansowego z dnia 23.01.2020 roku dotyczący chmury obliczeniowej na rynek ubezpieczeń w Polsce, Prawo Asekuracyjne* nr 3/2020.

Chris, B., & Yadav, Y. (2019). "*Fintech and the Innovation Trilemma*." *Georgetown Law Journal*, vol. 107, no. 2.

Czech, T. (2009). *Charakter prawny rekomendacji KNF, Przegląd Prawa Publicznego* nr 11.

Fedorowicz, M., & Michór, A. (2011). *On the legal nature of the decisions of the new European Union financial market supervisory authorities, European Judicial Review*, 2011/11.

Fras, M. & Szaraniec, M. (2019).*Nowe technologie w dystrybucji ubezpieczeń - bariery i ułatwienia w prawie polskim i unijnym. Wybrane zagadnienia prawne, Prawo Asekuracyjne* nr 2/2019.

Fras, M., & Zgonina, O. (2022). *ECJ– Group organizer as a distributor by the terms of IDD Commentary Judgement of the Court (First Chamber) of 29 September 2022 in case C-633/20, Bundesverband der Verbraucherzentralen und Verbraucherverbände – Verbraucherzentrale Bundesverband eV v. TC Medical air ambulance agency GmbH*, Wiadomości Ubezpieczeniowe 2022/4.

Grzeszczak, R., & Słok-Wódkowska, M. (2015). The European financial supervision system and the EU mandate of national supervisors - selected aspects, *Insurance News*, 2015/1.

Karwala, D. & Szwarczyńska, M. (2019). *Nowy Komunikat KNF w sprawie outsourcingu chmury obliczeniowej, Dziennik Ubezpieczeniowy* 2019, nr 4870.

Kaszubski, R. (2006). *Funkcjonowanie źródeł prawa bankowego publicznego*, Zakamycze.

Kowalewski, E., & Ziemiak, M. (2014). *W sprawie legalności wytycznych Komisji Nadzoru Finansowego, Wiadomości Ubezpieczeniowe*, nr 3.

Michór, A. (2011). *Administracyjnoprawne formy ingerencji europejskich organów nadzoru na rynku finansowym Unii Europejskiej, Ekonomia i Prawo*.

Mroczkowski, R. (2011). *Nadzór nad funduszami inwestycyjnymi*, Warszawa.

Mrozowska, B. (2012). *Bancassurance – regulacje prawne i samoregulacja rynku, Prawo Asekuracyjne*, nr 3.

Nieborak, T. (2008). Aspekty prawne funkcjonowania rynku finansowego Unii Europejskiej, Warszawa.

Nieborak, T. (2011). [in:] *Ustawa o nadzorze nad rynkiem kapitałowym. Komentarz*, (eds.) T. Nieborak, T. Sójka, Warszawa.

Orlicki, M. (2015). „Rekomendacje i wytyczne KNF – dialog nadzorowany, czyli «miękkie prawo» z twardym skutkiem", Prawo Asekuracyjne nr 2, s. 3–14.

Orlicki, M., & Rekomendacja, U. (2015). wytyczne dystrybucyjne, projekt ustawy o działalności ubezpieczeniowej i reasekuracyjnej – szansa na zmianę praktyki zawierania i wykonywania ubezpieczeń grupowych, *Prawo Asekuracyjne*, nr 1.

Senden, L. (2004). *Soft Law in European Community Law*, Hart Publishing, p. 156.

Skoczylas, A. (2002). *Środki ochrony banku w postępowaniu przed Komisją Nadzoru Bankowego (wybrane zagadnienia), Prawo Bankowe*, nr 2.

Szaraniec, M. (2016). *The role of recommendations and guideline of the financial supervision commision (KNF) In combating the irregularities on the banking and insurance market in*

---

systems deemed to pose unacceptable risks will apply after just six months, while the provisions on so-called general-purpose artificial intelligence models will apply after 12 months. To complete the transition period before full implementation, the Commission has launched the AI Pact (https://digital-strategy.ec.europa.eu/en/policies/ai-pact). Under this initiative, AI developers are encouraged to voluntarily adopt key AI Act obligations before the legal deadlines.

Poland, Studia Iuridica Cassoviensia, nr 1, published by Pavol Jozef Safarik, University in Kosice, Faculty of Law, http://sic.pravo.upjs.sk.
Szaraniec, M. (2017). *Działalność gospodarcza pośredników ubezpieczeniowych. Studium publicznoprawne*, Warszawa.
Szaraniec, M. (2020). *Regulatory gaps concerning the introduction of new technologies in insurance distribution - the new role and activities of supervisory authorities. Outline of the problem, Prawo Asekuracyjne* 2/2020.
Szaraniec, M. (2022). *Insurance Outsourcing: a Legal Analysis.* [W:] *Marano P., Noussia K. (red.), The Governance of Insurance Undertakings: Corporate Law and Insurance Regulation (AIDA Europe Research Series on Insurance Law and Regulation;* vol. 6), Cham: Springer, p. 71–93.
Śliwa-Wajda, M. & Wajda, P. (2023). *Konsultacje projektów rekomendacji prowadzone przez Komisje Nadzoru finansowego – aspekty prawno-unijne*, Wiadomości Ubezpieczeniowe nr 2/2023.
Tarasiuk-Flodrowska, A. (2011). *Wybrane problemy prawne bancassurance w świetle rekomendacji dobrych praktyk*, Zeszyty Naukowe Uniwersytetu Ekonomicznego w Poznaniu.
Tupin, R. (2001). *Glosa do wyroku TK z dnia 28 czerwca 2000 roku (sygn. Akt K 5/99), Przegląd Sądowy*, z. 1.
Wojturska, W. (2022). *Outsourcing chmurowy a reżim działalności nadzorowanej zakładów ubezpieczeń, Przegląd Ustawodawstwa Gospodarczego*, nr 4/2022.
Wojturska, W. (2022). *Outsourcing w technologii cloud computing w działalności krajowych zakładów ubezpieczeń*, Warszawa.
Wronkowska, S. (2005). *Podstawowe pojęcia prawa i prawoznawstwa*, Poznań.
Zetzsche, D. A., Buckley, R. P., Barberis, J. N., & Arner, D. W. (2017). "*Regulating a Revolution: From Regulatory Sandboxes to Smart Regulation*," *Fordham Journal of Corporate and Financial Law* 23, no. 1.

MIX
Papier aus verantwortungsvollen Quellen
Paper from responsible sources
FSC® C105338

If you have any concerns about our products,
you can contact us on
ProductSafety@springernature.com

In case Publisher is established outside the EU,
the EU authorized representative is:
Springer Nature Customer Service Center GmbH
Europaplatz 3, 69115 Heidelberg, Germany

Printed by Libri Plureos GmbH
in Hamburg, Germany